I0815404

Willie Nelson

All the Albums

Willie Nelson

All the Albums

GEOFFREY
HIMES

THE STORIES BEHIND THE MUSIC

Contents

6. *Spirit*

FOLLOWING HIS MUSE, 1991–2000 136

7. *You Don't Know Me*

THE DECLINE & ALL THAT JAZZ, 2001–2011 162

8. *Last Man Standing*

THE COMEBACK, 2012–2025 186

Introduction

People love to swap stories about Willie Nelson—his live shows, his offstage escapades, his home life. And as those anecdotes get retold, they get altered and embellished—often by Nelson himself—and become more legend than history.

What never changes, however, is the music he recorded. When he performed "Funny How Time Slips Away" at the RCA Victor Studio on April 8, 1965, for example, it was preserved on tape and it sounds the same now as it did that day in Nashville. This is one instance where time doesn't slip away, doesn't change with passing years. What happened that day happens again every time we drop the needle on the record or click "play" on Spotify.

Not only does the recording take us back to the past; it takes us directly to the reason we care about Nelson in the first place: the music he made. Yes, many of us are drawn to him for his charismatic persona: the dope-smoking Zen master who shrugs off industry formulas and legal troubles with equanimity. But you can find guys like that in bars and racetracks all over America. What makes us single out Nelson for attention is the music.

That's why this book takes a different approach to telling Nelson's story. My friend Joe Nick Patoski wrote the definitive biography of Nelson's life: 2008's *Willie Nelson: An Epic Life*. Nelson himself co-wrote two full-length autobiographies: *Willie: An Autobiography* with Bud Shrake in 1988 and *It's a Long Story: My Life* with David Ritz in 2015. Those books do a splendid job with the life—childhood, arrests, marriages, record labels, movies, close calls, and success.

Now I want to write the definitive biography of his music. I want to illuminate how the songs changed as Nelson moved through all his *Phases and Stages*. I want to explore how the recordings cast their spells upon us, the listeners, at each stop along the way.

Of course, I will provide enough information about his personal life and career progress to provide some context for the recordings, just as Joe Nick discussed the recordings to shed light on the life and the career. But I will reverse the emphasis, using the life to illuminate the recordings, not the other way around.

Many people will argue that what matters about music is what it tells us about the singer. An artist's offstage life might be interesting; it might provide some helpful background, but that's not what's important about popular song. The reason we devote so much time, money, and energy to music is not what the songs tell us about some celebrity we'll never meet but what those songs tell us about ourselves.

We don't have to live Elvis Presley's life or Beyoncé's life, but we do have to live our lives. And that's not an easy thing to do. We have to negotiate inevitable loss and unexpected love, short-lived triumphs and enduring injustice, betrayal by those closest to us and the kindness of strangers. We have to understand not only our own lives but also the lives around us. What do they really mean when they say this or do that? Nothing clarifies those situations quite like a sparkling rendition of a great song.

Sure, psychologists and sociologists, politicians and philosophers, can analyze these problems in greater depth and at greater length. But they are handicapped by trafficking only in ideas about observable, external behavior. But songs, which employ both words and music, can reveal external circumstances and internal reactions, can examine both ideas and feelings. Because our greatest challenges in life involve both thoughts and emotions, the best aid for those trials must include both as well.

What first bonds each of us to Nelson is the way a specific song reverberates with our own situation. That resonance may shed light on a particular problem of ours or a problem that someone close to us has or merely comfort us by proving that someone else has felt the same thing. Sometimes it's helpful to just gain some perspective on the situation by hearing it in someone else's mouth and not our own.

Willie, touring behind *Red Headed Stranger*, in November 1975.

Peaches

Take "Funny How Time Slips Away," for example. It doesn't matter who the woman was who inspired the lyric—or even if there was one particular woman who fit the story; maybe she was an invented or composite character. What matters is that we've all had that experience of running into an ex-lover or former best friend unexpectedly—or we've observed it happen to others, or we've imagined it happening to us later.

It's a confusing situation. Here's someone who inspired love and happiness when they entered our lives—and pain and bitterness when they left. You never know how much of each emotion lives on inside you until time has gone slipping away and you encounter that person again. Only when it happens will you know how much lingering affection and how much lasting anger remain. How will you handle it?

We can only hope that we will be as cool, calm, and collected as Nelson is in this song. "Well, hello there," his narrator sings, as casually as if he'd seen her the day before. How's he doing? He's doing fine. How's her new love? Did she tell him that she'd love him till the end of time?

And this is where the narrator reveals he's not as forgiving as he seems. Here he slips in the knife: Yeah, well, that's the same thing you said to me. He recovers and goes back to small talk: He's gotta go; he'll see you around. But before he departs, there's one more stab of the knife: "Remember what I tell you: In time, you're going to pay."

It's an astonishingly efficient mini-drama, evoking the whole history of a relationship in three stanzas, a 130-word monologue. And the meaning of the title is ambiguous—for "funny" can mean "humorous," but it can also mean "peculiar." Both meanings are applicable here. Yes, it's a bit comical when two people who were so intense once upon a time can seem so nonchalant now. But it's also a bit strange how much feeling hides behind that façade.

Willie in the publicity photo for the 2004 album, *It Always Will Be*.

Bloody Mary Morning

But these lyrics wouldn't be as effective as they are without this particular music. Even before the singing starts, the relaxed triplets through the seven-chord relax the listener into the offhanded start unaware of the surprising shift to come.

And when the vocal enters, lagging behind the beat, it lets us know that it's in no hurry to get to the point; this is just friendly conversation between two old friends who have bumped into each other: "My, it's been a long, long time." Nonetheless, there's a tension in the air, the way the sixth note in the scale begins the melody over the four-chord, the way the vengeful lines end on an unexpected minor-two-chord, and the way the title line begins high on the seventh note of the scale over the five-chord before it slips and slides its way back down to the root.

These are small, nuanced touches, barely noticed by the nonmusician listener. But every listener will subconsciously sense that something's a little off-kilter, that a grudge is burning beneath the friendly banter. This would be Nelson's approach for the rest of his career: seasoning his songs with just enough jazz and blues harmonies to keep the listener off-balance, but not too much to spoil the song's essential character as easily accessible country music.

Reinforcing this tension between the familiar and unfamiliar was his vocal phrasing. His syllables came out relaxed and plummy, but an anxiety-producing space often opened between their expected arrival and their actual late entrance.

The vast majority of Nelson's songs deal with similar subject matter: troubled relationships—love that has either fallen apart, is falling apart, or was thwarted before it had a chance to begin. In most cases, the response is the same: The pain and frustration is unflinchingly acknowledged, but the singer never loses his dignity nor his will to keep moving forward.

This may seem like a narrow range of human experience to focus on, but the way Nelson copes with these losses can be applied to almost any kind of defeat: career reversals, economic hard times, health problems, bad government, death in the family, departure of old friends. Whatever the challenge, it doesn't help to deny reality—but neither does it help to get hysterical or fall apart. Nelson's songs provide an example for all of us in these situations.

A lot of things can change while time slips away. A singer's style can change from year to year, decade to decade. With Nelson, who recorded his favorite compositions again and again, we can trace that evolution through a single song: "Funny How Time Slips Away."

The original demo was recorded for Pamper Music, the music publishing company run by Nelson's employer Ray Price and Price's business partner, Hal Smith. These are surprisingly elaborate arrangements for recordings that are designed not to be released to the public but to entice other artists to record the songs. Often, such demos are little more than a voice and a guitar or piano—just enough to document the bare bones of the song and leave the rest to the artist's creativity. Then again, many artists lack the imagination to hear the possibilities of a song unless you spell it out for them, and so Pamper preferred fleshed-out demos.

As a result, this demo for "Funny How Time Slips Away" begins not with Nelson's voice but with cooing female harmonies. There's so much echo on the lead vocal that it sounds like Nelson is singing inside an airplane hangar. Despite these distractions, the essential chemistry of the song is in place: the casual, offhanded tone, the less-than-convincing shrug of indifference, the vocal's deliberate lag behind the beat, the unexpected chord changes to throw the listener off-balance, and the twist of the knife at the end. Long before anyone knew who he was, Nelson was already a master of songwriting and singing.

The first released version was a single from Nelson's friend Billy Walker, released in June 1961. The two men had known each other in Dallas in the late '50s, when both were trying to get a foothold in the music business. Walker succeeded first, scoring two Top 15 country singles by 1959. That was the year Nelson landed in Nashville after trying his luck in Oregon, Washington State, San Diego, Missouri, and Houston without much success.

Nelson stayed with Billy Walker and his wife, Betty, for three months. At one point, Nelson was so desperate for cash that he offered to sell "Funny How Time Slips Away" and five other songs to Walker for five hundred dollars. "Just hang on to them a while longer," Walker told him, "Something's bound to click." Walker had recorded Nelson's "The Storm Within My Heart" in 1959 without much reaction and tried again with "Funny How Time Slips Away."

That single peaked at #23, but it remained Walker's best-known song because it was so different from everything else in country music at the time. Walker had a handsome voice, and he settled into the ballad structure with a sweet vocal reinforced by a chiming piano. His fans requested it at almost every show.

Nelson had released a handful of singles for small Texas labels, but he got his first real break when New York City's Liberty Records (riding high on hits by Jan & Dean, Bobby Vee, and Del Shannon) decided to open a country division in 1961 to be headed by Texas songwriter Joe Allison. On a recommendation from Harlan Howard, Allison promptly signed Nelson.

On June 14, 1962, Nelson went into the Columbia Recording Studio on Nashville's Music Row to work on songs for his first-ever, full-length album: *. . . And Then I Wrote*. As the title implies, the record emphasized the only thing Nelson was known for at that point: the songs he had written for other artists. With Allison producing, Nelson was joined by the town's A-Team pickers, including guitarist Harold Bradley, steel guitarist Weldon Myrick, drummer Buddy Harman, and pianist Hargus "Pig" Robbins. One of the songs they cut that day was "Funny How Time Slips Away."

It didn't stray too far from Walker's hit version—the tinkling piano and cooing female vocals are still there. As was standard practice in those days, there were no solos, and Nelson wasn't allowed to add his distinctive guitar playing to the arrangement. Instead, he was told to focus on his vocal, and that's the most interesting aspect of the track.

He sings in a lower key than Walker and with a hint of resentment that Walker's wistful nostalgia lacks. Nelson is already pushing and pulling at the vocal phrasing—holding out key words and rushing other words to keep up with the band. Some Nashvillians thought this was incompetence, but it was actually the first hint of his singing genius. It made him sound more conversational on the small-talk sections and more biting on the little digs at his ex.

When Liberty closed down its country division in 1964, Nelson quickly signed with Monument Records but left in a huff after one single. On the rebound, he signed with RCA and had a single with them by Thanksgiving, beginning an eight-year association with the label.

On April 8, 1965, he went into the studio with producer Chet Atkins and A-Teamers such as guitarist Jerry Reed, steel guitarist Pete Drake, and bassist Henry Strzelecki to finish up Nelson's first RCA album, *Country Willie: His Own Songs*. Once again, a new label wanted him to showcase the songs he'd written for others, and so again he tackled "Funny How Time Slips Away."

It's a step backward from the Liberty version. The tempo is slightly brisker, and the picking is pretty, but you can tell Nelson is trying to stay on the beat more to satisfy the RCA honchos. You can also sense how awkward he feels trying to betray his own instincts. He's not as rhythmically disciplined as Walker, but neither is he as inventive and expressive as he was for Liberty. He sounds stiff and disengaged—a sign of his future battles with RCA.

In 1972, when he was finally free from RCA, he signed with Atlantic Records, which was launching a new country music division. Jerry Wexler, the producer who had worked with Ray Charles and Aretha Franklin, handled Nelson's next two studio albums, masterpieces both. The third and fourth albums were supposed to be a studio gospel collection and a live recording from the Texas Opry House in Austin on June 29, 1974. But before they could be released, Atlantic closed up shop in Nashville and Wexler went back to New York.

When the orphaned live album was finally released as part of the 1993 box set, *Willie Nelson: A Classic & Unreleased Collection*, it was revealed as one of the highlights of the singer's career. He had already assembled one of the greatest live bands in country music history: steel guitarist Jimmy Day, fiddler Johnny Gimble, harmonica player Mickey Raphael, pianist Bobbie Nelson, bassist Bee Spears, and drummer Paul English. A highlight of the show was a medley of "Funny How Time Slips Away," "Crazy," and "Listen to the Blues" (aka "Night Life").

Here was Nelson unleashed. He was leading the way with his acoustic guitar "Trigger," and his vocal phrasing is more adventurous than ever. When he asks about his ex's new love and adds, "I hope he's doing fine," he buries the comment in a rush of low notes to convey that he doesn't hope any such thing. And when he reminds her that she made the same promises to him, he belts out the phrase, "Gee, ain't it funny," and then snaps it off to underline the irony.

That's followed by a gorgeous fiddle solo from Gimble, the best proof of how much musicians love to dig into Nelson's jazz-inflected changes. The improvisatory freedom of the performance that the jazz/blues feeling was now as much a part of the playing as the writing.

After Atlantic left town at the end of 1974, Nelson signed with Columbia and released the 1975 album, *Red Headed Stranger*, that finally made him a star. In December of that year, he went into the Autumn Sound Studio in Garland, Texas, to cut the follow-up album, *The Sound in Your Mind*. Once again, a new label wanted its own versions of Nelson's best-known songs, so he recorded a new version of the eight-and-a-half-minute medley—"Funny How Time Slips Away," "Crazy," and "Night Life"—that had become a staple of the live shows. Day and Gimble were gone, replaced by rhythm guitarist Jody Payne; but the rest of his road band was on hand to translate their stage sound to the studio.

This isn't as bold as the Texas Opry version, which found Nelson taking his push-and-pull phrasing to an extreme and the pickers cutting loose. The Garland version is more controlled, more unified, as if every member of the band were tuned into the same wavelength as the singer. Trigger was out front as never before, answering every vocal line with an acoustic guitar fill as if a duet partner. Mickey Raphael's harmonica and Bobbie Nelson's piano took turns serving this same call-and-response function. Everything was understated with relaxed confidence that they can convey both the equanimity and the tartness of the story. It doesn't get much better than this.

That confidence reinforces the song's story about remaining optimistic despite the damage done. If we listen to it as a reflection on our own romantic disasters, we can borrow that poise and apply it to our own lives. Not for nothing is the album called *The Sound in Your Mind*, for it's not enough for a singer-songwriter to make a sound in their own mind about their own lives—it's necessary to make that sound echo in our minds and help us with our lives.

Three years later the same band—bolstered by a second bassist and a second drummer—recorded *Willie and Family Live* at Harrah's Casino in Lake Tahoe, Nevada, in April 1978. If *Red Headed Stranger* had defied contemporary-country standards with its stripped-down minimalism, this live show defied it with rock-influenced maximalism. The beefed-up rhythm section gave the beat a wallop, and the soloists went wherever the moment took them.

Here was further proof that this was one of the greatest live bands in country music history. The "Funny How Time Slips Away" medley was still in the setlist, and this is a strong version. It gives the players a chance to stretch out on their instruments, even if it lacks the concentrated focus of the Garland version.

As the 1970s turned into the 1980s, Nelson used his newfound, hard-won celebrity to pay back the people who befriended and helped when he was first starting out by recording either tribute albums to them or duet albums with them. It wasn't uncommon for those guests to ask if they could sing "Funny How Time Slips Away" with Nelson, and he was always glad to oblige.

Ray Price, for example, had once been successful enough to help out Nelson by hiring him as a songwriter for Price's publishing company, Pamper Music, as a bandmember and later as a bassist, even turning Nelson's composition "Night Life" into a Top 30 country hit. By 1980, though, Price hadn't had a Top 10 country single in five years, and Nelson reminded everyone what a splendid singer Price was on the duet album, *San Antonio Rose*.

Their version of "Funny How Time Slips Away" is the slowest of all versions Nelson has released, but that languorous pace over an ultra-relaxed rhythm

Kevin Smith, Willie, and Mickey Raphael perform in front of the Texas state flag at the Schottenstein Arena in Columbus, Ohio, on May 14, 2014.

section serves to showcase the sheer elegance of the two singers. They use very different timbres—Nelson's tenor is a bit nasal and twangy, while Price's baritone is smooth and satiny—but they roll each vowel around in their mouths as if savoring it. And they share such a sure grasp of rhythm that they can anticipate the beat or delay it without ever losing track of it.

Nelson sings the first and third stanzas, Price the second, and they share the tag. You can hear them finessing each syllable, finding just the right place to let it drop. And the instrumentalists—Nelson, Raphael, guitarist Grady Martin, steel guitarist Buddy Emmons, and vibraphonist Moses Calderon—display a similar approach.

Faron Young had made Nelson a lot of money when the latter needed it the most by recording the Nelson composition "Hello Walls" in 1961. It stayed at #1 on the country charts for nine weeks and even rose to #12 on the pop charts. It was a debt Nelson was glad to repay in 1985, when Young hadn't had a Top 10 single in nine years. Their album of duets, *Funny How Time Slips Away*, included both "Hello Walls" and the title song.

This is less successful than the Price duet. Young always had a tendency to sing aggressively, and on a lot of songs that worked to his benefit. But "Funny How Times Slips Away" is too subtle for that approach, and he seems more intent on proving his vocal chops are intact than in serving the song's story. It's exciting, yes, but at a cost.

The collaboration with Young took place after Nelson's lungs collapsed in 1981 while swimming in Hawaii. As he recovered, he devoted more time to songwriting, with rejuvenating results. But when he performed live, his setlist remained pretty much the same, and the "Funny How Time Slips Away" medley was always a centerpiece of the show.

And it didn't matter that they did mostly the same songs every night, because they never played a song exactly the same way twice. Often they drifted quite far from the shore, as Hank Williams' old gospel hymn put it. This bothered fans who wanted to hear the songs sound the same way they did on the radio, but it delighted those who were willing to return again and again because there was always new music to hear—even if not new songs.

The core of Nelson's band—Mickey Raphael, Bobbie Nelson, Jody Payne, Bee Spears, and Paul English—were improvisers who would add a new lick here and hold out a phrase longer there. Eventually Nelson hit on a compromise: He would sing

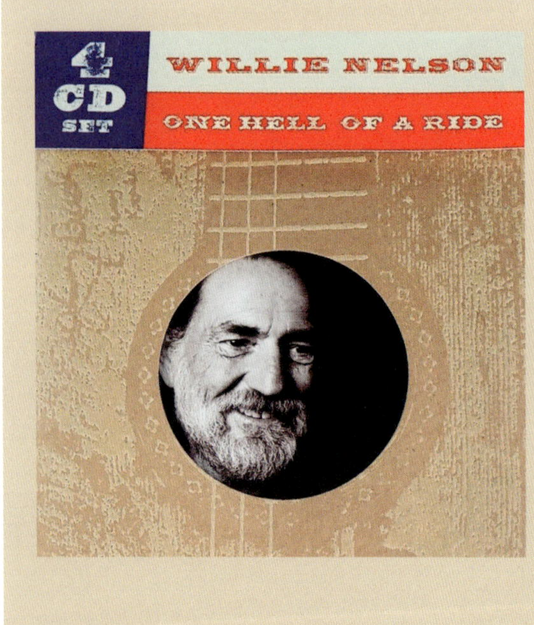

Willie Nelson
***One Hell of a Ride* (Columbia/Legacy)**
Recorded: 1954–2007
Released: April 1, 2008
Willie Compositions: 49/100
Top 40 Singles: "Johnny One Time" (Country #36), "Bring Me Sunshine" (Country #13)
Album Chart: Country #46

This four-CD box set has the advantage of inclusiveness. The one hundred songs crammed onto the four CDs are pulled from all eras and all labels, beginning with the rare 1954–55 demo, "When I've Sang My Last Hillbilly Song," continuing through three pre-Liberty singles, the RCA years, the Columbia hits and duets to the Island and Lost Highway years. The emphasis is almost exclusively on singles rather than album cuts, but if you want a collection of the basics in one place, this is the one to get. The ninety-eight-page booklet is lavishly illustrated and includes a strong essay by Nelson biographer Joe Nick Patoski. **Grade: A-**

the choruses so they sounded familiar and the verses every which way but the same. Thus, he satisfied both groups of fans. You can hear this when he plays "Funny How Time Slips Away" again on the live albums *Live from Austin TX* (recorded 1990, released 2006) and *Live at Billy Bob's Texas* (recorded 2003, released 2004).

After serving as Nelson's label for eighteen years, from multiplatinum smashes to quirky projects selling tens of thousands, Columbia Records finally cut the umbilical cord in 1994, dropping Nelson from its roster. As if to prove them wrong, Nelson made some of his most interesting records for labels as big as Capitol and Island and as tiny as Justice, Step One, Transatlantic, Finer Arts, Free Falls, and Luck. (We'll sort out this underrated era in Chapter Six, "Spirit: Following His Muse, 1991–2000.")

As one millennium turned into another, Nelson seemed to lose his way. He wasn't writing much, his health problems seemed to sap his energy, and his album concepts lacked originality and/or follow-through. There were a few gems among the disappointments, but not enough. He was still a reliable draw on the road, but even the shows lacked their old sparkle. Then, just when his old creativity seemed exhausted, just when it seemed he might be consigned to oldies hell, he turned everything around. He formed a partnership with producer/songwriter Buddy Cannon that sparked a songwriting reawakening and a series of albums that made the most of that material, surrounding it with smartly chosen cover tunes.

One Hell of a Ride

We'll cover all these phases and stages in the chapters ahead. Along the way, we'll provide a brief box for most of Nelson's albums—all the studio recordings, and as many of the live, duet, soundtrack, guest-appearance, and reissue titles as seem important. For each album, we'll list recording dates, release date, chart information, the number of Nelson compositions/co-writes out of the total tracks, a thumbnail album review, and a letter grade for the music's quality. At left is a sample box for a box set, one of the best introductions to his whole career.

Nelson has enjoyed an unusually long career of music-making, but it hasn't been a straight line. It has twisted and turned, and we'll be as honest about the downs as the ups, and about the failures as the triumphs. But for all the changes, certain qualities have always shone through. Nelson could always sing about heartache in a way that recognized the pain but maintained dignity and determination in the face of it. And he reinforced the words with compatible music, music grounded in Texas dance halls but flavored with the rhythmic elasticity and harmonic surprises of jazz and blues.

The more Nelson changed, the more he kept coming back to a core identity. "Funny How Time Slips Away" exemplified that in the beginning, and the song reconfirms that truth almost every night he takes the stage. It's a song so flexible that it could be a Top 10 R&B single for Joe Hinton in 1964 and again for Dorothy Moore in 1976, while Narvel Felts had a #12 country hit with the song in 1975. It was an album track on *Elvis Country*, a key part of Presley's 1968–72 comeback phase. Al Green and Lyle Lovett won a Grammy Award for their duet version of the song in 1994, and Glen Campbell and Nelson did the same in 2017.

But the song has always belonged to Nelson. No one understood the song's inner tensions—both verbal and musical—better than the song's author. Beneath his easygoing delivery, he revealed the persistent pain of an old breakup as well as the resolve to not let it show. In doing so, he shed valuable light on the experience or expectation of every listener who ever heard the song in any of its many iterations.

Ain't it funny how time slips away.

CHAPTER 1

...And Then I Wrote

SIDEMAN & SONGWRITER, 1933–1964

It's an uncomfortable but undeniable fact that the realms of literary fiction and poetry have been dominated by white males from wealthy or upper-middle-class backgrounds, especially before World War II. There are two possible conclusions one can draw from this. One can conclude that genetic talent is concentrated in this demographic group, or one can conclude that talent is evenly distributed across all populations but has a better chance of being developed and expressed in by those who can afford a college education and a period of working on the craft without needing a full-time job.

If you were born into a world where literature and education were readily accessible, as were Missouri's Tommy Eliot, New Jersey's Billy Williams, and Connecticut's Wally Stevens, you might grow up to be T. S. Eliot, William Carlos Williams, or Wallace Stevens and write some of the twentieth century's best poetry. But what if you were a Texan like Hugh Nelson, Cindy Leigh Walker, or Sam Hopkins and were too poor, too female, and/or too dark-skinned to enjoy such access? What would you do with your innate gift for (and delight in) putting words together? You might direct that aptitude toward the most obvious vehicle for writing verse in your environment: popular song. You might grow up to be Willie Nelson, Cindy Walker, or Lightnin' Hopkins and write some of the most enduring country and blues songs ever penned. Your social and economic status would have no effect on your likelihood of having verbal talent, but it would have a tremendous impact on if and how that gift is expressed.

Willie Hugh Nelson was born on April 29, 1933, in Abbott, Texas, a town of less than 700 people between Waco and Dallas. There weren't poetry readings and book clubs in Abbott, but there was music everywhere—in the cotton fields, in church, in the movie theaters, and via a new arrival to the Nelson home: a radio that broadcast the way words were being put together by Texans such as Ernest Tubb and Bob Wills and by such

Willie's late-'60s publicity photo.

East Coasters as Irving Berlin and Hoagy Carmichael. Here were some role models for a grade-school wordsmith to emulate.

Nelson started writing poems when he was four, and when he got his first guitar at the age of six, he started putting his poems to music. By age eight, he was getting paid to play guitar in Johnny Rejcek's polka band. By age eleven, he decided to make his own songbook like the ones published by his heroes.

Nelson handwrote each copy of *Songs by Willie Nelson*, an extremely limited first edition, carefully drawing the lariat rope that spelled out the words, "Waco, Texas," the biggest city near Abbott. What was most striking about the volume was the songs' adult subject matter: love affairs gone bust, leaving the singer lonely and penitent. It seemed these songs were merely a reflection of the country and blues songs he heard on the radio, an impersonation of the heartbreak he was too young to have experienced firsthand at eleven—even if he had had a series of elementary-school girlfriends.

But his sister, Bobbie, knew better. When she was two and her brother was six months old, their parents split up. Mother Myrle went off to Washington State, and two years later Ira moved to Fort Worth. The two children were left with Ira's parents, known as Mama Nelson and Daddy Nelson, though they were, in fact, the siblings' grandparents. Myrle and Ira would return to visit semi-regularly, and Bobbie would talk in later years about standing on the curb, holding hands with Willie, as they bawled their eyes out watching the car of one parent or the other drive away.

So, Willie knew deep, inconsolable heartbreak at an early age. His grandmother, widowed when Daddy Nelson died of a stroke in 1939, was by all accounts a wonderful substitute parent, raising the kids on a school cafeteria worker's wages and a diet of religious music. But the repeating cycle of his birth parents appearing and disappearing, a cycle Willie was powerless to break, was devastating. He had to go on, but how could he go on? This was the dilemma that fueled his earliest songs—and most of his songs for the rest of his life.

The final entry in *Songs by Willie Nelson* was a lyric called "Starting Tonight," which has this chorus: "Starting tonight/I'm gonna quit running round/ Your Daddy's coming home to you." On one level, this sounds like a classic country song: A faithless

An eleven-year-old Willie hand-lettered this songbook in 1944.

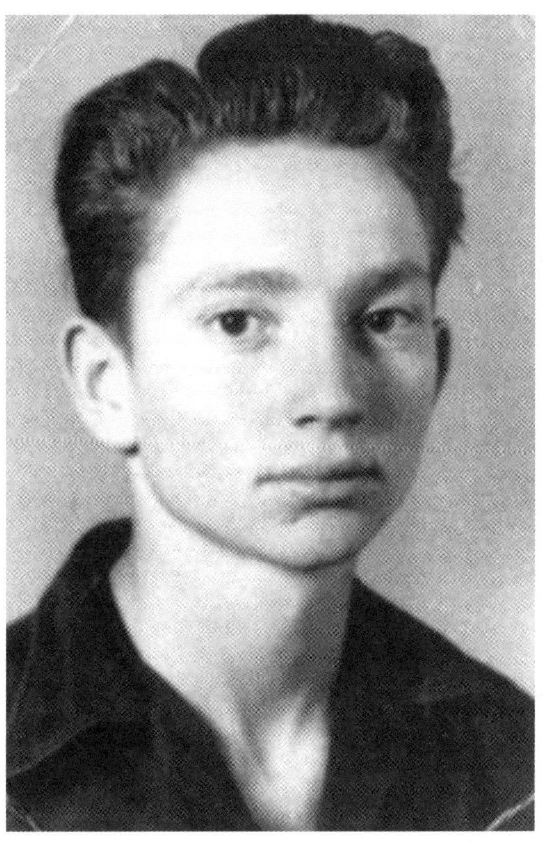

Willie as a junior at Abbott High School in 1949.

the money he brought home and she could tell he would not be dissuaded.

His desire to escape manual labor could not be understated, he often said. He hated picking cotton, but he went away from those fields with valuable raw materials for a music career. "I picked cotton with all different kinds of people," he told *Gallery* magazine in 2001. "A lot of black cotton pickers, Mexicans, Czechoslovakians, Bohemians, Germans, and me. Everybody was whistling and singing different things. It was a great opera. I learned a lot about music and singing right there in the cotton fields."

He also learned a lot from the Best Movie Theater in the nearby town of West, Texas. Like most of his friends, he wanted to be like the cowboys on the screen—hard-edged, terse men who could wrestle a steer to the ground or hurl a bad man through a barroom window. While most boys wanted to be the gun-shooting, lasso-tossing, big-hatted guy on a stallion, Willie also wanted to be the tough dude who would soften when he picked up a guitar to sing. Here, he believed, was proof that a man could be both.

These movie-screen heroes were more than guys in white hats who shot straight and caught the bad guys, he wrote in *It's a Long Story: My Life*. "They were men who cradled guitars in their arms and sang

husband promises his wife he'll do better, maybe not this morning, maybe not this afternoon, but surely tonight. It's the prototype for dozens of songs Nelson would later write on the same theme. But on another level, given Nelson's family situation, it could be the song of a father, "your daddy," telling his son he's coming home to stay.

Already Nelson is marrying two paradoxical elements in a song: an admission that wrong has been done and pain has been suffered and an assurance that you have to keep moving forward with a sense of dignity and hope. He would express it more artfully in the decades to come, but the template for his life's work was already there.

Willie loved country music—especially the Western swing of Bob Wills—but he was intellectually curious at a young age, and he would spin the radio dial in search of other sounds: big-band swing, blues, gospel, even polka. He hated picking cotton, so he talked his way into jobs at local polka halls, honky-tonks, and shoeshine stands. His grandmother didn't like him playing music in beer joints, but she needed

Willie in the US Air Force, 1950.

Willie as a football player at Abbott High School.

the stars down from the heavens. Even though they were macho men who feared no rustler, they sang sweetly, effortlessly, and proudly."

He learned a lot from his sister, Bobbie. He would sit beside her at the piano and absorb the way a song moved from chord to chord. So, even before he got a guitar, he knew the architecture of the music. And his grandmother gave him voice lessons, emphasizing the importance of drawing breath from deep in one's abdomen and strengthening one's lungs and vocal cords with that uprush of air.

"I started out doing that real early," he told *Goldmine* in 1995. "I'd heard Frank Sinatra sing, so I knew he had strong lungs. I really don't know if he practiced voice control as I did, but he must have had that sort of instruction somewhere along the way. . . . Early on, I did do a lot of phrasing. Of course, a lot of it was 'If you can't do it this way, do it another.' Maybe I couldn't do it exactly the way Ernest Tubb or Frank Sinatra did it, so I would do it the way that made it easy for me."

From the time he started high school to the time he signed a record contract with Liberty Records, Nelson had to work odd jobs to pay the bills—and some of them were pretty odd. He worked as a pawn-shop clerk, tree trimmer, dishwasher, saddle maker, and door-to-door salesman for Bibles, vacuum cleaners, and encyclopedias. He tried the US Air Force and Baylor University but didn't last long at either. His priority was always his songs, and if that conflicted with the day job, well, there was always another gig around the corner. There are probably dozens of folks you've never heard of who had as much talent but not nearly as much determination.

For a while, Nelson thought he'd become a preacher. He liked the idea of performing from a pulpit, charming the congregation into paying attention and then explaining how they could overcome pain and loss with a faith in the future. It was not so different from the profession he ultimately chose, but he was better at singing than talking, so he decided to work with a guitar rather than a Bible. Besides, he loved the women and the drinking too much.

"I had considered being a preacher earlier in life," he told *Musician* magazine in 1982. "I decided it was too hard a work and not enough money. So, I figured the next best thing was to write songs with a message. Maybe they don't all have a message, but I don't want to waste three minutes of somebody's time. There must be something in there.

"A song has a better chance of being heard by people who truly need a message more than a sermon preached at some obscure church at the edge of town. The guy who really needs to hear that sermon is probably drunk in a bar several miles away. Now that guy needs to hear an encouraging word, just as much as, if not more than, those people who have dressed up and gone to church to show off their new clothes."

"I've found out there's no difference between a beer joint and a church," he told *Vanity Fair* in 1991. "Both sets of people I saw in both places were having a good time. It's just that, in one of them, the lights were a little darker."

Eventually he started getting jobs in his chosen field. He picked up jobs as a guitarist and bassist in honky-tonk bands. His sister, Bobbie, older by two years, was a pianist/organist who got her kid brother a job with the Texans, a band led by her husband, Bud Fletcher. Willie sold songs to other singers. He put out his own singles. He became a disc jockey in towns all over Texas—and even one in Washington State.

The radio jobs suited him. He got to play the songs he loved—even if he played them on a turntable, not a guitar. He was not shy about promoting his own singles and upcoming live shows. And he got to use his flair for language in a DJ's tongue-twisting patter. Every time he came on the air, he introduced himself as "This is your old cotton-picking, snuff-dipping, tobacco-chewing, stump-jumping, gravy-sopping, coffee-pot-dodging, dumpling-eating, frog-gigging hillbilly from Hill County, Willie Nelson."

Willie Nelson: A Classic & Unreleased Collection

Willie Nelson
Willie Nelson: A Classic & Unreleased Collection
(Rhino)
Recorded: 1957–1987
Released: 1993
Willie Compositions: 33/64
Top 40 Singles: NA
Album Charts: NA

This box set, originally sold only on the QVC shopping channel with Nelson himself as pitchman, is a superb compilation of rarities both unreleased and out of print. Historically, the most important are both sides of the 1957 "No Place for Me"/"Lumberjack" single and thirteen of the more obscure Pamper Demos. Musically, the most important are the outtakes and alternate takes from his two Atlantic albums, *Shotgun Willie* and *Phases and Stages*, as well as a terrific 1974 live album, *Live at the Texas Opry House, 1974*, slated to be Nelson's fourth Atlantic LP before the label shuttered its country division. Almost as interesting are some mid-'80s recordings with Bob Wills, fiddler Johnny Gimble, Ray Price, steel guitarist Jimmy Day, and Merle Haggard's Strangers. Hard to find, but well worth it. **Grade: A+**

His first recording was a two-song tape he made at KBOP-AM in Pleasanton, Texas, sometime in the winter of 1954–55. As a disc jockey at the station, it was easy for Nelson to use its equipment after hours to record two of the songs he'd been performing live. He'd just recently recorded a batch of songs in Houston as the guitarist in Dave Isbell & the Music City Playboys, several of which were released by Sarg Records in Luling. Nelson figured if Charlie Fitch, the owner of Sarg, would release songs as ordinary as Isbell's, he might release Nelson's.

One song was Nelson's original, "When I've Sang My Last Hillbilly Song" (*sic*). It was only a minute and a half long, but even so, it contained just six different lines of lyric, repeated ad nauseum over a bouncy melody clearly indebted to Lefty Frizzell. The flipside was "The Storm Has Just Begun," one of the lyrics in *Songs by Willie Nelson*. This was much more striking, with vivid descriptions of an impending thunderstorm—the gathering clouds and lighting flashes—and the way in which weather parallels a looming fight with a lover. But this vocal was as stiff as the other. Fitch never replied to the pitch.

It was two more years before a Nelson recording was actually released. He had moved from Fort Worth to Denton to Eugene to San Diego to Portland, Oregon, to reunite with his absconded mother. Nelson landed another DJ job at KVAN in Vancouver, Washington, just across the Columbia River, and started playing in local clubs. He needed a record to promote the live gigs on the radio and to sell at the shows. Once again, he used his station's equipment to record two songs: his own "No Place for Me" and Leon Payne's "Lumberjack."

This was a step forward. Ringer Buddy Fite's steel guitar gave the music some atmosphere, and Nelson himself sounded more confident over the original's honky-tonk beat. The lyrics anticipated a long career of songs about the coming crack-up of a romance and his aching but stoic coping with that fact. "Lumberjack" was a kind of novelty folk song, not unlike Pete Seeger's "Erie Canal" or Merle Travis's "Sixteen Tons"—and Nelson talked some lines and sang others like an expert storyteller. It was an aspect of his music he never repeated.

He sent the tape off to Starday Records in Houston, and they agreed to press it, but only if Nelson paid up front for the copies. He offered it with an 8×10 photo over the air for one buck and reportedly sold three thousand copies in the Portland/Vancouver region, but it never got out of the area.

Nite Life: Greatest Hits & Rare Tracks (1959–1971) / Things to Remember: The Pamper Demos / Face of a Fighter / Crazy: The Demo Sessions / The Early Years

Nelson had eloped with Martha Matthews when he was eighteen and she was sixteen, the same age that sister Bobbie got married. Martha had even more Cherokee blood than Nelson himself, and by all accounts—including Nelson's—it was a tempestuous marriage of violent altercations and passionate reconciliations. As Willie pursued his musical dreams with low and inconsistent income, Martha supported the growing family—Lana, Susie, and Billy were born in 1953, 1956, and 1958, respectively—with waitressing jobs. Both waitresses and musicians attract customers in ways that can create jealousy in a spouse—and neither of the newlyweds handled it that well.

But things slowly started turning around. Mae Axton, co-writer of Elvis Presley's "Heartbreak Hotel," heard Nelson's songs in Vancouver and encouraged him. So did DJ Uncle Hank Craig, who volunteered to be Nelson's manager. Jack Rhodes, co-writer of Porter Wagoner's "A Satisfied Mind," bought the publishing rights to a Nelson song. Pappy Daily's D Records, Houston's top indie country label, offered Nelson a recording contract. His first single, "Man with the Blues" backed with "The Storm Has Just Begun," had better players, some female singers, and a lead singer growing with confidence. This sounded like what was on country radio, even if it wasn't sufficiently different to stand out.

Much better was the next single, "What a Way to Live" backed with "Misery Mansion." The latter was a clever rewrite of Axton's "Heartbreak Hotel," a residence for the brokenhearted, even if the music was rather stilted. Much better was the single's A-side, an incongruously joyful, swinging number about a "lonely man" barhopping to forget about the woman who broke his heart. Or maybe that's the point: better these jukeboxes and crowded joints than an unhappy home.

Here are the first hints of Nelson's push-and-pull phrasing and ambiguous self-assurance in the face of heartache. It doesn't hurt that Houston's legendary Gold Star Studio and a backing band featuring guitarist Paul Buskirk and Bob Wills' steel player Herb Remington were far better than anything Nelson had yet worked with. And Nelson was in a stretch where he was sounding markedly better every month than he had the month before.

Nelson had moved to Houston to be closer to his label. The desperate songwriter approached bandleader Larry Butler at the Esquire Ballroom and offered to sell him "Mr. Record Man" and three more songs for ten bucks apiece. Butler refused, saying they were worth a lot more than that. Instead of buying these goldmines at fire-sale prices, Butler loaned Nelson fifty dollars and hired him as a guitarist.

Nelson moved his family to Pasadena, a Houston suburb, and would drive thirty minutes each way to his nightly gig at the Esquire. As he drove, he sang to himself; and one evening the phrase, "The night life ain't a good life, but it's my life," popped out. He wrote the first half of the song on the way to the club, played the show, and finished the song on the way home.

"Why ain't the night life a good life?" he told *Playboy* in 1981. "Well, back then it wasn't. And from a religious standpoint, it's not the good life. The night life is beer joints and the women of the evening and the honest man blowing his hard-earned money in some beer joint on some dance hall floozy. . . . It is a hard life for a musician who works six nights a week, four hours a night, for just a little money. At the time, I think I was getting ten dollars a night."

It may well have been the best week of songwriting Nelson would ever have, for he also wrote "Crazy" and "Funny How Time Slips Away" on his daily commute to the Esquire—a trio of songs that would stay in his live show for half a century. "The easiest place for me to write," he told *Playboy*, "is in a car, moving."

There's a way "Night Life" falls out of a major chord into a minor that suggests the sun going down, the daytime people going home to their families, and the nighttime people crawling out of the woodwork with their whiskey, perfume, and snare drums. These are characters, more interesting than the day people but less trustworthy, too. The night life is alluring, even addictive, but it's a hard life—and the more you get used to it, the harder it is to leave behind.

Buskirk recognized what Nelson was doing in these sophisticated songs lost in the buzz of the night life. He hired the kid from Abbott to teach guitar at Buskirk's music school. It was Buskirk who had first turned Nelson on to the French Gypsy-jazz guitarist Django Reinhardt and continued to expand his younger friend's ears with non-country records.

"I listened to Django's records, especially songs like 'Nuages' that I would play for the rest of my life," Nelson says in *It's a Long Story: My Life*. "I studied his technique. Even more I studied his gentleness. I loved the human sound he gave his acoustic guitar. . . . He wasn't greedy for the spotlight. His delight came in quiet creation. In this way, he influenced me perhaps more profoundly than any single musician."

Buskirk bought the rights to Nelson's "Night Life" and "Family Bible" and resold fractions of both of them to Walt Breeland and Claude Gray, a local DJ who was recording for Daily. Gray's version of "Family Bible" went all the way to #7 on the national country charts in 1960, but Daily refused to release "Night Life," saying it wasn't country enough. It was not the last time a record executive would make that complaint about Nelson's music.

Gray wasn't the first artist to cover a Nelson composition—Billy Walker had recorded "Crying in the Night" in 1959—but Gray was the first to have a hit with one. The songwriting credit on the single's label read "Breeland-Gray-Buskirk," but it soon became common knowledge within the country music community that the song was written by Nelson.

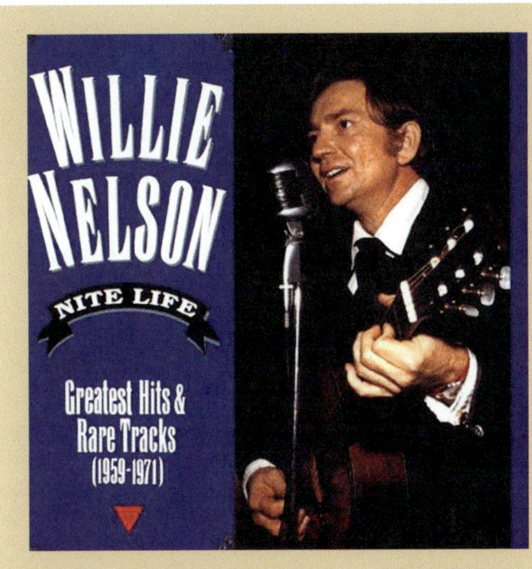

Willie Nelson
Nite Life: Greatest Hits & Rare Tracks (1959-1971)
(Rhino)
Recorded: 1959-1971
Released: 1989
Willie Compositions: 16/18
Top 40 Singles: NA
Album Charts: NA

Nelson's first three singles (plus one B-side) from Houston in 1959 are the highlights on this one-CD compilation of early recordings. The disc is fleshed out with two Pamper Demos, eight Liberty singles and four RCA singles. It comes with thorough if somewhat academic notes. **Grade: B+**

Willie (second from left) performs, circa 1955, in Texas. His sister Bobbie is second from the right.

Buskirk was so angry that Daily refused to release "Night Life" that he organized a session in early 1960 to do the song with Nelson singing lead. He released it as "Nite Life" on his own label Rx Records (motto: "Prescription for Happy Times") and credited the performers as "Paul Buskirk and His Little Men, Featuring Hugh Nelson."

The man born as Willie Hugh Nelson had never sounded this good. He had written one of the best songs he would ever create, building his story around the claim that the night life ain't a good life. But is it really as bad as he claims? He may be nursing a broken heart, but that's eased by this milieu of liquor and other substances lubricating the chance of new romance—or at least some terrific music. Nelson's wonderfully ambiguous vocal isn't tilting the scales in one direction or another as he circles the beat, as if pondering where to land.

And then a bridge appears, launched by Nelson's acoustic guitar figure. The song's weary, fatalistic verses are suddenly countered by a painful cry demanding that we "listen to what the blues are saying." We listen but soon slip back into the noirish verses once again. For all its sophisticated jazz chords, elegantly played by Buskirk, Remington, and tinkling pianist Bob Whitford, this is a blues, simultaneously a diagnosis of heartache and a cure for it, like the honky-tonk demimonde it describes. And what are the blues saying? That maybe this isn't a good life, but it's the only life he's got.

If this version has a flaw, it's that the ensemble gives it too much of a cool-jazz feel, too relaxed for its own good. Maybe Daily was right and this arrangement wasn't country enough. Nelson's greatest recordings would come when he put the country music signifiers in the foreground and the bluesy jazz in background, allowing the tension between the genres to reinforce the tension already in the lyrics.

"I was listening to a lot of people who were jazz influenced a long time before I really knew I was listening to jazz, through western swing," he told

Gallery in 2001. "I found out later that they had been listening to the jazz greats, Django Reinhardt, Stephane Grappelli, and all those guys. So, I had been sort of influenced by blues and jazz earlier, just by listening to people like Bob Wills. Early on, I wrote 'Night Life,' 'Rainy Day Blues' and several songs with a blues flavor."

Nelson clearly loved the pop-jazz of Django Reinhardt and Frank Sinatra as much as he loved the country music of Lefty Frizzell and Floyd Tillman. But he knew that if he wanted to connect to an audience of folks like himself, people from working-class, smalltown Texas, he was going to have to speak to them in the vocabulary of country music. He would be able to slip in jazz flavorings—an unexpected chord here and a quirky phrasing there—as long as country music was at the fore. And except for a handful of jazz side projects, that's how he operated ever after.

Publicity photo for "Wee Willie Nelson," KVAN disc jockey and performer in Vancouver, Washington, 1957.

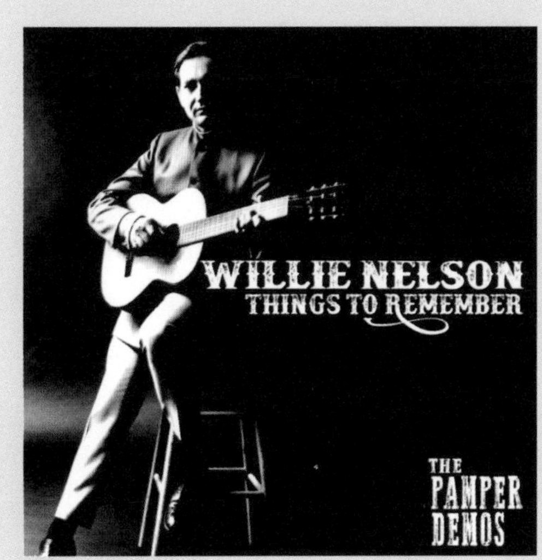

Willie Nelson
Things to Remember: The Pamper Demos
(Real Gone)
Recorded: 1960-1966
Released: July 13, 2018
Willie Compositions: 28/28
Top 40 Singles: NA
Album Charts: NA

This collection offers not only the best quantity of Pamper demos but also some of the best quality, including the only available Pamper versions of "Funny How Time Slips Away," "Night Life," "Hello Walls," "Little Things," and "Within Your Crowd." **Grade: B+**

"Family Bible" kept Nelson going, even if his own singles had made little impact. He had moved his family from Fort Worth to Eugene to San Antonio to San Diego to Portland to Springfield to Fort Worth to Houston, but the gig money never covered the bills. Finally, he decided to heed Mae Axton's advice and move to Nashville, the town where country songs were bought and sold.

"I felt like Nashville was where the store was," he told *Musician* in 1982, "and if I had anything to sell, I'd better take it to the store. Chet Atkins was not in Abbott, Texas, or even Waco. But even when I was living in Nashville and living on my songwriting royalties, I had to go down to Texas and play the circuit, 'cause I wasn't in demand in the rest of the country."

Nelson arrived in Nashville late in 1960, determined to make this songwriting thing work. He stayed with Billy Walker, who had recorded a few of his songs and would soon have a modest hit with "Funny How Time Slips Away." Nelson began hanging out at Tootsie's Orchard Lounge. Songwriters would gather there in hopes of snagging a performer on break from the Grand Ole Opry show at the Ry-

Willie's publicity photo, circa 1965.

He dusted the snow off and went home. He was twenty-seven—old for the music business—but his greatest artistic and commercial successes were all ahead of him.

Cochran had a fifty-dollar-a-week draw from Pamper Music, a publishing company owned by singer Ray Price and businessman Hal Smith. When they offered Cochran a fifty-dollar raise, he insisted they give it to his new friend Nelson instead. The two men became inseparable, and they wrote dozens of songs and recorded them in versions that mimicked the new countrypolitan sound in hopes of getting cuts on actual records for sale. They kept at it from 1960 through 1966.

Pamper Music demos were famous in the music biz, but the general public had no way to hear them except for a few pirate recordings of questionable legality. Industry insiders loved them, for they could enjoy Nelson's idiosyncratic singing, even if it was considered too weird for radio. And they could hear

man Auditorium, right across the alley. Nelson joined a crew that included Roger Miller, Harlan Howard, and Hank Cochran—songwriting legends now but songwriting wannabes then.

"Living in Nashville, there was a competitiveness that you got into," he told *GRAMMY Magazine* in 1994. "The writers hung out together and—'What have you written lately?' And you'd have get-togethers where four or five writers would sit around and pass the guitar around and play their latest songs. This was kind of a motivator for most young writers—go home tonight and write something. And plus the fact that if you did, you could probably get some money and that helped a lot. I wrote a lot more back then, plus I felt like I had a lot more to say back then."

But there was little money coming in, and Nelson felt like he was spinning his wheels once again. His family was living in Dunn's Trailer Court, in the same trailer that Roger Miller once rented. The sign outside the court read, "Trailers for Sale or Rent," inspiring the opening line of Miller's biggest hit, "King of the Road." But it wasn't inspiring Nelson, and by the Christmas season of 1960, he was broke and brokenhearted. He got really drunk at Tootsie's one snowy night and decided to end it all.

"I had a little bit to drink," he remembers in *Country Music: An Illustrated History*, "and I decided I'd go out and lay down on the highway. It was right there on Broadway in Nashville at like two in the morning. I don't know what happened up until then. I just woke up a-laying on the highway. I'm surprised I'm still here."

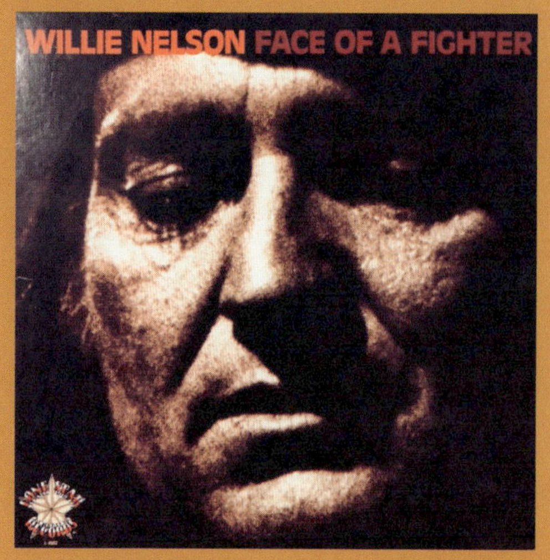

Willie Nelson
***Face of a Fighter* (Lone Star)**
Recorded: 1960–1966
Released: 1978
Willie Compositions: 27/28
Top 40 Singles: NA
Album Charts: NA

This compilation, released by Nelson's own Lone Star label, was first issued as a ten-song LP, then reissued as an eighteen-song CD. It's light on background information, but the CD version does include seven songs unavailable anywhere else. **Grade: B-**

his voice not only on well-known songs but also on gems that never became hits.

"Healing Hands of Time," for example, is an acute observation of how our recovery from loss takes place on two different planes. While our conscious selves are shedding tears and gnashing teeth, our subconscious selves are adjusting to the new reality and preparing us to move on. As Nelson sings, "They're working while I'm missing you/Those healing hands of time/And soon they'll be dismissing you/From this heart of mine." The music moves as patiently as a slow hymn, but the blues chords make it clear how much hell one has to go through to get to heaven.

"Within Your Crowd" is a brilliant analysis of class and culture as the narrator advises his girlfriend to find someone in her own group because she doesn't fit in his. "Country Willie" is a variation on the same theme, warning the upwardly mobile woman who "called me Country Willie the night [she] walked away," that she may regret her decision someday.

"A Moment Isn't Very Long" is a bait-and-switch song. The narrator recounts how for a moment he forgot his ex, how for a moment he found comfort in another's arms, as if he's explaining how he's recovered from his heartache. But then he punctures the balloon with the title line, "But a moment isn't very long."

It's astonishing how many crucial songs Nelson wrote and demoed for Pamper Music: not only the four songs that he often sang as a medley in his live shows—"Funny How Time Slips Away," "Crazy," "Night Life," and "Hello Walls"—but also songs that wound up as the title tracks on such albums as *Country Willie* (1965), *Good Times* (1968), *Pretty Paper* (1979), *Healing Hands of Time* (1994), and *December Day* (2014). That's right—as late as 2014, he was still returning to the Pamper era for songs to record.

Prague Frank's Nelson discography lists seventy-four Pamper demos, and sixty-two of them have been officially released—even though Nelson re-recorded (and often re-recorded again) many of them as album cuts in future years. There are five principal batches of these tracks: eighteen on *Face of a Fighter*; twelve on *A Classic & Unreleased Collection*, mentioned above; fifteen on *Crazy: The Demo Sessions*; fourteen on *Willie Nelson: The Early Years*; and twenty-eight on *Things to Remember: The Pamper Demos*. There's not as much overlap as you'd think—the eighty-seven tracks on the five sets include sixty-two different songs.

As clues to his evolution, these are invaluable. As musical experiences, they are less exciting. The vocals are always interesting, but the arrangements and playing around the vocal often aren't. Nelson already had a vision, but he hadn't yet learned how to find the people and the arrangements to realize the sound in his head.

Price recognized the untapped talent. He offered Nelson a job as a bassist in his band, the Cherokee Cowboys. Price, Hank Williams' roommate for the final year of the latter's life, and the creator of the "Ray Price Shuffle" that revolutionized country music, was a real star. He gave his young Texan bassist a taste of what stardom was like. It tasted good.

Willie Nelson
***Crazy: The Demo Sessions* (Sugar Hill)**
Recorded: 1960–1966
Released: February 11, 2003
Willie Compositions: 15/16
Top 40 Singles: NA
Album Chart: Country #32

It's fascinating to hear the young Nelson trying out early versions of these fifteen songs such as "Crazy," "I Gotta Get Drunk," and "Undo the Right"; but he hadn't yet learned how to make great records. Ten of the songs are unavailable elsewhere. **Grade: B**

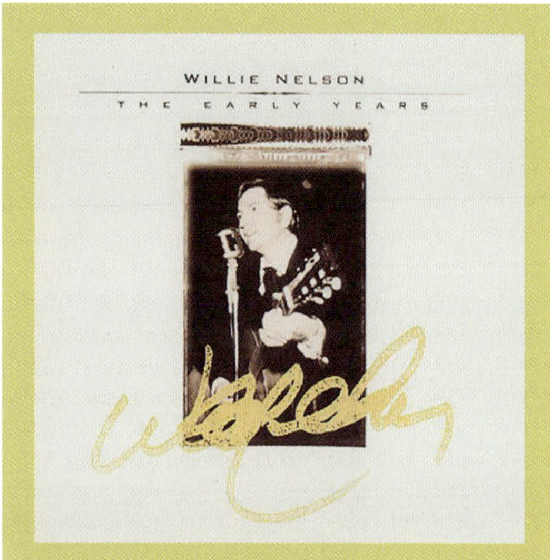

Willie Nelson
The Early Years **(Scotti Bros.)**
Recorded: 1960–1966
Released: July 24, 2020
Willie Compositions: 13/14
Top 40 Singles: NA
Album Charts: NA

These fourteen songs are the leftovers from the Pamper Music demos after everyone else had their pick. Three are unavailable elsewhere. **Grade: C+**

Price plucked "Night Life" from his Pamper catalog and recorded it as the title track for his 1963 album and made it the opening number of his live shows. It's a remarkably tasteful version, the steel guitar moaning like a ghost over drum brushes. Price's creamy crooning justifies his nickname as the "Frank Sinatra of country music." Perhaps it's too elegant for its own good, giving little hint of the full ashtrays and empty bottles the lyrics evoke. But it hit #28 on the country charts and inspired pop versions by Doris Day and Al Hirt in the next eighteen months.

Top 30 hits were nice and all, but it was number-ones that really boosted your reputation and bank account. When Cochran heard Nelson's latest creation, "Hello Walls," he knew it could be a hit. The leisurely melody line suggests a normal conversation, but the listener soon realizes the conversationalist is anything but normal. Not only is he talking to the walls, the window, and the ceiling about his recently departed lover—he thinks the house is talking back to him.

"I started working in a garage at the Pamper office," Nelson remembers in *Willie: An Autobiography*. "There was just a door, a window, a guitar, and the walls. I started talking to the walls, like I had done when I was a child in Abbott reading the pages of the *Star-Telegram* that kept the wind out. Hank walked into the garage, and on a piece of cardboard, I had written 'Hello Walls.'"

Nelson played it for established star Faron Young at Tootsie's one night, and the singer asked if he could cut it. Cochran, sitting nearby, according to Patoski, shouted, "Hell, yeah!" before Nelson could reply. Nelson, who always needed money sooner rather than later, offered to sell Young the rights to the song for five hundred dollars.

Young, realizing how much money the song was about to make, loaned Nelson the money and let him keep the rights. Young's premonition was correct. The song went to #1 on the country charts and remained there for nine weeks. It even rose to #12 on the pop charts. Later, after cashing a fourteen-thousand-dollar royalty check, Nelson French-kissed Young at Tootsie's. Decades later, Nelson paid off his five-hundred-dollar debt to Young with a thirty-eight-thousand-dollar steer.

Buoyed by the success, Cochran made sure another new Nelson song, "Crazy," was on the jukebox at Tootsie's. Patsy Cline's husband Charlie Dick heard it there and dragged Nelson and Cochran back home to play it for his wife. The song combined the sophisticated dreaminess of "Night Life" with the notion from "Hello Walls" of love as a kind of mental illness. "Crazy" is not an easy song to sing, what with its huge melodic intervals and ever-shifting jazz chords. Even a vocalist as gifted as Cline struggled with it when she recorded it in 1961. She finally mastered it when producer Owen Bradley convinced her to stop imitating Nelson's demo and sing it her own way.

"Of all the versions of my songs covered by other artists," Nelson told the authors of *Country Music: An Illustrated History*, "it's my favorite . . . a perfect rendition [sung with] delicacy, soul, and perfect diction. . . . She understood the lyrics on the deepest possible level."

Once Cline got it, she had one of the most compelling country singles ever released. The diving and leaping melody mirrored the narrator's plunging and surging confidence, while the ever-shifting harmonies suggested the uncertainty about why they kept pursuing a maddening lover. It became Cline's biggest pop single at #9, and a #2 country hit as well. Nelson recorded it himself the following year on his first-ever album, *. . . And Then I Wrote*. Even better is his original version, which finally emerged on the 2003 album, *Crazy: The Demo Sessions*. Linda Ronstadt enjoyed a #6 pop hit with the song in 1977.

Suddenly, Nelson was one of the hottest songwriters in Nashville. That had always been one of his ambitions, but it wasn't the only one. He still wanted to sing on records and on stages—and not just a few tunes before Ray Price took the stage. He wanted a recording contract of his own.

... And Then I Wrote

When the successful indie pop label Liberty Records opened a country division in 1961, the company asked Joe Allison, a songwriter for Merle Travis and Faron Young, to head it up. He signed up some of his favorite old-timers—Bob Wills, Floyd Tillman, Warren Smith—but he needed some new blood. When Hank Cochran, seeking a deal of his own, shared some of Nelson's Pamper demos, Allison immediately recognized what a giant talent this nobody was.

Willie holds his debut album before an interview on KPHO TV in Phoenix on December 14, 1962.

Allison quickly signed Nelson and Cochran and brought the former into a Nashville studio. But he immediately ran into the same problem other people had had recording Nelson. Unless his backing musicians had played with him for a while, his accompanists were driven crazy by his tendency to sing behind and ahead of the beat. Allsion reconvened the sessions in Los Angeles with a band featuring three legends—New Orleans drummer Earl Palmer, future Merle Haggard guitarist Roy Nichols, and Johnny Cash guitarist Johnny Western—but the problems persisted. The musicians simply didn't have time to acclimate to the elastic phrasing that made Nelson such a distinctive singer.

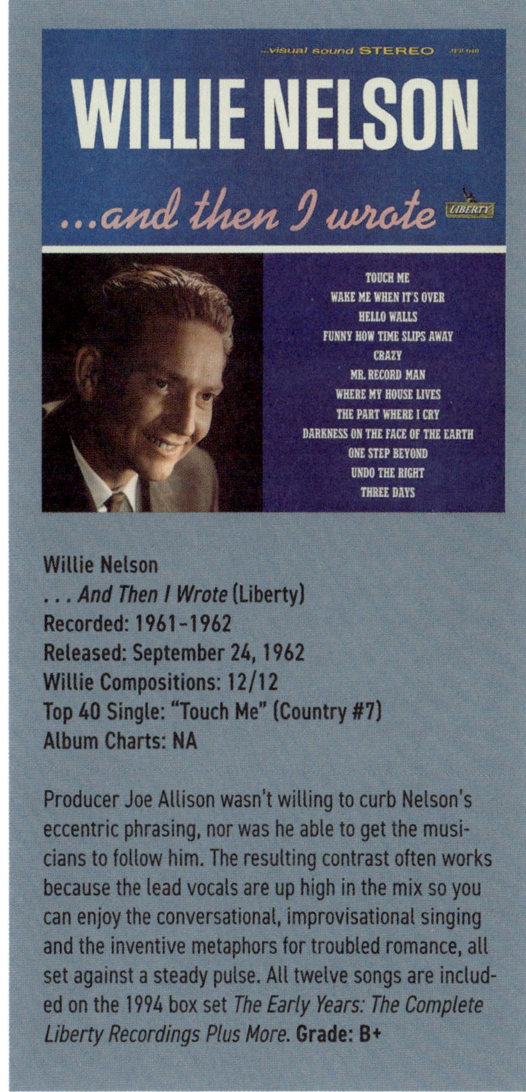

Willie Nelson
. . . *And Then I Wrote* (Liberty)
Recorded: 1961–1962
Released: September 24, 1962
Willie Compositions: 12/12
Top 40 Single: "Touch Me" (Country #7)
Album Charts: NA

Producer Joe Allison wasn't willing to curb Nelson's eccentric phrasing, nor was he able to get the musicians to follow him. The resulting contrast often works because the lead vocals are up high in the mix so you can enjoy the conversational, improvisational singing and the inventive metaphors for troubled romance, all set against a steady pulse. All twelve songs are included on the 1994 box set *The Early Years: The Complete Liberty Recordings Plus More*. **Grade: B+**

Finally, Allison took Nelson's voice out of the musicians' earphones, placed baffles between the band and the singer, and told the instrumentalists to play straight time and let Nelson do whatever the hell he was going to do. Then he added oohing vocalists to smooth over the dichotomy. Allison mixed the tracks so Nelson's vocal is way out front, never eclipsed by the steady rhythms or the backing vocals.

What the listener got were ingenious songs from the Pamper demos, groundbreaking vocals, and minimized accompaniment that didn't so much support the lead singer as add dramatic contrast. This wasn't the optimal approach, but it was the best of Nelson's studio albums in the '60s.

Before the first album, . . . *And Then I Wrote*, was released on September 4, 1962, Liberty paved the way with five singles from the Allison sessions. The first, released just after Thanksgiving Day 1961, was "The Part Where I Cry" backed with "Mr. Record Man." Both were examples of Nelson dreaming up new ways to sing about busted love. The A-side compares a love affair to a stage play, where the actor has to tackle different scenes, most painfully the one where he has to cry. The B-side takes the form of a radio listener phoning the DJ and asking where he can find that recording of "a lonely song about a lonely man like me."

Willie sings with Shirley Collie at the Riverside Park Ballroom in Phoenix on December 13, 1962.

The B-side of the third single was "Where My House Lives," the monologue of a man gazing on his former address and imagining that traces of the love that once flourished there still remain. The B-sides of the fifth and thirteenth singles were architectural sequels: "There's Gonna Be Love in My House" and "Misery Mansion." For anyone who asks, "How many ways can you tell the same old story of heartbreak?" Nelson's answer is, "The possibilities are endless."

The A-side of the third single was "Touch Me." Despite its title, this is not an invitation to a would-be lover on the cusp of succumbing. It's a dare to an observer who can't believe the singer's claims of heartbroken desolation. "Touch me," Nelson sings, as he dances around the steady pulse of the mid-tempo beat, "and you'll know how you'd feel with the blues." The pain he feels is communicated not so much by the words he sings as by the long pauses between them. It was a strange country song, but it was Nelson's second hit, #7 on the Billboard singles chart.

The first was the A-side of the second single, "Willingly," a duet with his soon-to-be-wife Shirley Collie. Nelson was still married to his first wife, Martha, and Shirley to her first husband, DJ Biff Collie. Shirley was an up-and-coming country singer who'd been touring as part of Red Foley's show while scoring two Top 25 singles and duets with Lefty Frizzell and Warren Smith. When Allison paired Nelson and Collie for three duets, the singers connected not only musically but romantically as well.

You can hear that on "Willingly," a #10 hit. This Cochran composition is sung by two strangers who leap into forbidden love voluntarily with no excuses. Collie's high soprano and Nelson's trebly tenor sound a bit thin and giddy when separated but create a sturdy bond when joined. The flip side was "Our Chain of Love," written by Nelson, a lament for the broken links between two lovers. Instead of trading lines, Nelson and Collie sing a close-harmony dual lead, uncannily like an Everly Brothers song. It was the best example of Collie's unusual ability to match Nelson's every quirky delay and rush forward, something the band never got the hang of.

"Shirley sang as close harmony to me as anybody possibly can," Nelson wrote in *Willie: An Autobiography*. "She second-guessed me. Like with my band today, they always guess where I'm going to go with a song. Shirley could sense that, too. Shirley and I were pretty much on the same level of thinking music-wise."

Nelson's fourth Liberty single featured two more Nelson/Collins duets. The A-side, "You Dream About Me," is the highly unusual Nelson composition about a positive, uncomplicated love. The second, "Is

This My Destiny" by June Carter's sister Helen, is a swooning lament where the two voices and a loud steel guitar swoop up and down to ask if sorrow, pain, and woe are their fate.

When Nelson's debut album, . . . *And Then I Wrote*, was finally released on September 4, 1962, none of the four duets were included. Two more duets were recorded in 1963 but never released. Nelson's first and most personal duet partnership never got the chance to fulfill its tantalizing possibilities. As soon as their divorces came through, Nelson and Collie married in 1963, and the two toured together for a few years.

But when Nelson's three children with Martha came to live with him, he demanded that Shirley stay home with them. She would never release an album under her own name, and she would never have the musical career she so richly deserved.

Only five of the ten songs on Nelson's first five singles were included on . . . *And Then I Wrote*, which was filled out by his most famous songs ("Hello Walls," "Funny How Time Slips Away," and "Crazy"), "Three Days" (a #7 hit for Faron Young earlier that year), "Undo the Right" (a Cochran co-write), and two more new ones.

Here's Willie Nelson

Allison soon left Liberty for a better job with Dot Records. Taking over the reins was Tommy Allsup, an Oklahoman who'd played lead guitar with Buddy Holly and Bob Wills. It seemed like a good fit for Nelson, who was just two years younger and a confirmed Wills disciple. But Allsup didn't seem as impressed by Nelson's writing or singing as Allison

Willie performs at the Riverside Park Ballroom in Phoenix on December 13, 1962.

had been. The new producer pressed Nelson to record vintage country classics and new material from Music Row and then buried the vocals under strings, singers, and steel.

The results weren't successful commercially or artistically. Allsup produced four singles for Nelson, and none of them reached the Top 30. He also produced most of Nelson's second album, *Here's Willie Nelson*, which included both sides of the Allison-produced #25 hit "Half a Man." Only three more Nelson compositions were included, as Allsup chose less interesting songs than those left in the can. The two Bob Wills classics are given vigorous, enjoyable workouts, and two ballads are left alone sufficiently for Nelson to work his vocal magic.

Willie Nelson
***Here's Willie Nelson* (Liberty)**
Recorded: July 1962
Released: July 1, 1963
Willie Compositions: 4/12
Top 40 Single: "Half a Man" (Country #25)
Album Charts: NA
This is a disappointing follow-up to the debut album. Producer Tommy Allsup buries songs good and indifferent under heavy-handed strings and backing vocals. Singer and producer can only find common ground on a pair of up-tempo Bob Wills swing numbers and a pair of stripped-down ballads by Hank Cochran and Donny Dill. "Half a Man," the only hit single, was a leftover from the debut album sessions. All twelve songs are included on the 1994 box set: *The Early Years: The Complete Liberty Recordings Plus More.* **Grade: C-**

The Untitled Third Liberty Album/ The Early Years: The Complete Liberty Recordings Plus More

We now know that Nelson recorded a lot more than the twenty-four album tracks and eleven non-album single tracks released by Liberty in 1961–1963. Liberty had scheduled the third Nelson album for November 20, 1963. It wasn't given a title, but Allsup had picked out the eleven songs, closely following the model of the unsuccessful second album.

But before it could be released, Liberty was sold to the electronics corporation Avnet, which shut down the country division. Once again, Nelson was without a label. In 1965, Liberty's catalog wound up in the hands of a reissue label named Sunset, which was taken over by United Artists in 1971. Sunset released *Hello Walls* in 1966, and United Artists, hoping to capitalize on Nelson's new stardom released *Country Willie* (not to be confused with RCA's *Country Willie: His Own Songs*) in 1975 and *There'll Be*

Willie performs at KPHO TV in Phoenix, Arizona, on December 14, 1962.

Willie Nelson
***The Untitled Third Liberty Album* (Liberty)**
Recorded: 1963
Released: 1994 on *The Early Years: The Complete Liberty Recordings*
Willie Compositions: 1/11
Top 40 Singles: NA
Album Charts: NA

Nelson's unreleased third album for Liberty contained only one Nelson composition, a string-smothered "You Wouldn't Even Cross the Street." On the positive side, Allsup encouraged Nelson to sing country music classics by George Jones, Floyd Tillman, Hank Williams, Hank Thompson, and Ray Price. Price had titled his 1968 album after Boudleaux Bryant's brilliant song, "Take Me as I Am (Or Let Me Go)," and Nelson's version here is so good that not even Allsup's arrangement can ruin it. **Grade: C+**

Teardrops Tonight in 1978. These Sunset/UA reissues were a hodgepodge of released and unreleased songs from the Liberty vaults with little explanation of what was what.

Much better was a 1994 compilation, *The Early Years: The Complete Liberty Recordings Plus More*, which collected all the singles and album tracks released by Liberty, plus the unreleased third album, plus additional unreleased tracks. The latter include some of Nelson's new songs, ignored in favor of lesser material, more Shirley Collie duets, and more country standards.

The Early Years: The Complete Liberty Recordings Plus More gives us all this music, with plenty of session and release information plus a contextual essay by Joseph F. Laredo. There's a lot to like here if you're willing to pick through the misfires. Liberty didn't give Nelson the best showcase, but it did get him started on a real recording career. To be fair, it's hard to think of a Nashville major label that could have done a better job in 1961–1963.

Willie Nelson
***The Early Years: The Complete Liberty Recordings Plus More* (Liberty)**
Recorded: 1959–1963
Released: May 3, 1994
Willie Compositions: 34/61
Top 40 Singles: "Willingly" (#10), "You Took My Happy Away" (#33)
Album Charts: NA

This is the only package you'll need from the Liberty years. The two-CD, sixty-one-track compilation collects all the tracks from Nelson's two albums on Liberty, plus the planned-but-never-released third album, plus all the non-album singles, *plus* all the unreleased tracks that first surfaced on the budget albums *Hello Walls, Country Willie*, and *There'll Be Teardrops Tonight*, plus much more unreleased material. Highlights include eight hard-to-find, superbly done, close-harmony duets with his then-wife Shirley Collie Nelson. **Grade: B+**

The Winning Hand

Though he blew a lot of his newfound money on airplane tickets, hotel penthouses, and parties for his friends, Nelson saved enough money to buy a ranch house on seventeen acres in Ridgetop, twenty-two miles north of Nashville. The settlement date was November 22, 1963—and later that day, John F. Kennedy was assassinated in Dallas. It was not an auspicious omen.

Without a record contract and with most of his income coming from songwriter royalties, Nelson decided to retire to write songs and raise pigs in rural Tennessee. He did both, but the income from the new songs was modest, and the income from the pigs was negative. What he did manage to do was reassemble his family—both biological and musical—around him in Ridgetop.

One by one, they moved onto Nelson's property or nearby: his four children, his current wife Connie, his first wife Martha and her new husband, Willie's father and stepmother and their two sons, Willie's mother and her new husband, Willie's fiddler Wade Ray and his wife, and Willie's drummer Paul English and his wife. It was a re-creation of Abbott forty-five minutes from Music Row.

By the summer of '64, however, Nelson was restless and ready to end his short-lived retirement. He signed a three-year contract with Fred Foster's Monument Records, home for nineteen of Roy Orbison's twenty-one Top 40 singles. It only lasted for two July recording sessions, eight songs, and one single, "I Never Cared for You" backed with "You Left a Long, Long Time Ago." But that single was one of Nelson's best, and Foster was his most sympathetic producer until the singer met Jerry Wexler seven years later.

"Fred was the one who'd produced Roy Orbison," Nelson writes in *It's a Long Story: My Life*, "an artist who, like me, wasn't easy to categorize. I had heard how Fred let Roy be Roy. He promised to do the same for me at Monument Records. Fred seemed willing to follow me off the beaten track."

"I Never Cared for You" is one of Nelson's finest songs. It uses the reverse psychology of saying one thing to mean another. The sun is made of ice; the sky was never blue; stars are only raindrops, Nelson croons, "and I never cared for you." He's not the first writer to use such a device, but he's the first to justify it with a verse that tells his departing lover, if you think I only tell lies, well, listen to these.

The lyrics are terrific, but the music is even more ambitious. He opens with the chorus, sung slowly and dramatically as if a Tex-Mex corrido or flamenco *cante jondo*, then the music shifts to a syncopated dance rhythm for the verse and succeeding choruses, reverting to the slow drama for the tag. Foster was imaginative enough to hire a classical guitarist and marimba player to reinforce the Mediterranean

Willie Nelson, Kris Kristofferson, Dolly Parton, and Brenda Lee
***The Winning Hand* (Monument)**
Recorded: 1964–1982
Released: December 1982
Willie Compositions: 4/20
Top 40 Single: "Everything's Beautiful (In Its Own Way)" (Country #7)
Album Charts: Country #4, Pop #109

Monument Records took old and unreleased tracks from its vaults (including five of its rare 1964 recordings with Nelson), added some new performances, and with some overdubbing and creative editing allowed each of the four singers to do one or two duets with each of the others. That adds up to a dozen duets, which are supplemented by eight solo vocals. Lee's tracks are over-sung, and Kristofferson's are under-sung, but Parton and Nelson sound great together on lightweight material. Fred Foster's production covers the seams with sweetening strings. For such a misbegotten project, it's better than might be expected. **Grade: B-**

Publicity photo of Willie and Dolly Parton, circa 1982.

flavors. It still sounds exotic today—and it was extremely exotic in 1964. It was a #1 hit in Houston but a flop everywhere else.

Nelson's 1964 tracks for Monument would not be released on an album until 1982 when Foster released *The Winning Hand*, a jerry-rigged assemblage of old and new recordings in the style of *Wanted! The Outlaws*. Nelson, Dolly Parton, Kris Kristofferson, and Brenda Lee sing a dozen duets with one another and add eight solo performances. Five of Nelson's eight 1964 tracks are featured, three in their original solo versions and two as overdubbed duets with Kristofferson and Lee. In addition, Nelson sang on four new duets: one apiece with Kristofferson or Lee, and two with Parton. The duet on the Parton composition, "Everything's Beautiful (In Its Own Way)," was a string-laden hit.

Monument represented the kind of creative freedom Nelson said he wanted, but it failed to deliver the economic payoff he needed. His twin goals were often in conflict, and that's why it took him so long to attain either one. Convinced it wasn't going to happen with Foster, he invented a controversy over a badly printed photograph in an ad and declared he was leaving Monument to sign with RCA. He thus consigned himself to six years of purgatory at the bigger but less accommodating label.

Foster could have blocked Nelson's move to the larger label by holding him to his contract, but Monument's owner decided he'd rather lose Nelson as an artist and keep him as a friend than the other way around. That attitude paid off when Nelson asked Foster to produce him in 2006 and 2007 on a Cindy Walker tribute and a trio project with Merle Haggard and Ray Price, two albums that were nominated for Grammies.

On November 28, 1964, Nelson made his first appearance on the Grand Ole Opry, the live radio show taped in Nashville's Ryman Auditorium every weekend. He made thirty-five dollars, far less than he could make in the Texas dance halls. He hadn't moved to Nashville to make *less* money. Something had to change. He quit the Opry and a few weeks later signed with RCA.

Before leaving Monument, Nelson played Foster a Christmas song he'd just written, "Pretty Paper," a very short but charming tale about a poor guy sitting on the corner, trying to sell gift-wrapping paper to passing December shoppers. Foster passed the song on to his biggest artist, Roy Orbison, who turned it into a #15 pop hit. Nelson's first single for RCA? His own version of "Pretty Paper." It was not a hit for the man who wrote it.

CHAPTER 2

My Own Peculiar Way

IN PURGATORY WITH RCA, 1965–1972

It seemed like a good idea at the time. The partnership between Willie Nelson and Chet Atkins should have worked, but it became one of the greatest mismatches in country music history.

Atkins, the head of RCA Records when he signed Nelson at the end of 1964, was a masterful guitarist who would go on to win seven CMA Awards as Instrumentalist of the Year. He had signed with RCA in 1947 and landed a job as second guitarist for Mother Maybelle Carter and the Carter Sisters (June, Helen, and Anita) in 1949. Atkins was named head of RCA's Nashville division in 1957 and helped design the legendary RCA Studio B. He recorded twenty-two mostly instrumental Top 40 country albums between 1957 and 1978.

He also joined fellow producer Owen Bradley in crafting the "Nashville Sound," later called "Countrypolitan," on bestselling records by Jim Reeves, Don Gibson, and Skeeter Davis. This approach downplayed traditional markers of country twang such as fiddles and steel guitar and replaced them with orchestras and cooing backing singers. This boosted country sales and crossovers to the pop charts. When asked to define his genre, Atkins jingled the change in his pocket and said, "That's what it is. It's the sound of money."

Nelson hoped to get some of that money for himself. For one, he needed to do better by his family that was always scrambling to pay the bills. For another, his mission to become a preacher for broken hearts disguised as a hillbilly singer only made sense if he had a congregation to preach to. He had a following in Texas, but he wanted more than that. But so far, the capital of country music, Nashville, had found him too weird for radio.

If anyone could help him move from an outsider on Music Row to an insider, it would be Atkins. The producer admired the singer's songwriting (though not his guitar-playing) and figured if he could just wrap those songs in a thick blanket of sound, listeners would like the tunes, too.

Atkins was "the ultimate Nashville insider," Nelson told *Country Music: An Illustrated History*. "He saw me as an outsider writing outsider songs and singing in an outsider style. . . . . Even though his vision and mine were different, I couldn't get mad at a man who believed so deeply in my talent."

This beefier, bearded version of Willie was from the end of the RCA years.

Ultimately, it didn't work because Atkins was trying to fit Nelson's songs into the musical format that was dominating country radio at the time. Nelson was trying to fit those same songs into his contrarian vision of what country music should sound like. Here were two men who actually admired each other but who had completely different ideas of how to make a successful country record in the mid- and late-'60s. Their mutual admiration kept them together, even as their opposing philosophies pulled them apart. Nelson tried to swallow his unhappiness, and Atkins tried to be patient with his eccentric client. It was an awkward situation for both.

"I had great respect for Chet Atkins's musicianship and accomplishments as a guitarist and producer," Nelson writes in *It's a Long Story: My Life*, "but in working with Chet, the now eluded us. Because Chet was convinced I could be a superstar, it was hard to walk away from his operation. I had stars in my eyes. . . . Yet his way of producing, for all its technical wonders, fenced me in. I knew it, but blinded by ambition, I accepted his formula. I should have known better, but the truth is that it took me a long time—all of the '60s in fact—to finally see the light."

The circumstances were further complicated by Nelson's own inner conflicts. He craved financial success, not only for the stability it would bring his family but also for the respect it would bring him in the music industry. But he wanted to do it on his terms, with his sound. He wouldn't be satisfied with one or the other; he had to have both. This was a recipe for frustration—until, suddenly in 1975, it wasn't. But that was ten years away.

Willie backstage at *Arizona Hayride* TV show in Phoenix in November 1964.

Country Willie: His Own Songs

The Nelson/Atkins partnership actually got off to a promising start with their first album together, *Country Willie: His Own Songs*, released at the end of the summer of 1965. His first album for RCA not only duplicated the approach of his first album for Liberty, but it even recycled four songs from 1962's *. . . And Then I Wrote* and added five more from the early-'60s Pamper demos. This made sense, for if the country audience knew Nelson at all, it was for the hits he'd written for other artists. His first two RCA singles ("Pretty Paper" and "She's Not for You") were excluded from the debut, but both sides of the third single were terrific new compositions that launched side one.

The two songs were ballads, but they were given a lightly swinging, guitar-and-brushes bounce that seemed at odds with the drawn-out melancholy of the lead vocal. But that tension is essential, for both numbers try to find the silver lining in a cloudy situation. On "One Day at a Time," the narrator hopes that by ignoring yesterday's disasters and tomorrow's unlikely prospects, he can focus on the present, like a sparrow who finds "a hatch of sunshine" poking through the gray sky.

On "My Own Peculiar Way," he readily admits to his angry partner that his way of loving her is unconventional, even unreliable—but he hopes she will appreciate its earnestness. Most of us have at one time or another tried to recover from mistakes with convenient amnesia or the eccentricity excuse. Nelson's songs allow us to see ourselves making those moves.

Compared to what was to come, Atkins' production was remarkably restrained on this project. Nelson sings effectively against the steady beat; his ironic tales of stoicism in the face of romantic disaster come through clearly in all their subtlety. When Nelson sings to a woman that he loves her in "my own peculiar way," the listener can believe not only in his sincerity but also in the woman's skeptical reaction. Both the new songs and the old captured this rich paradox—richer than anything else in country music at the time.

Nonetheless, there were no charting singles. And that was a problem. The whole point of Nelson's partnership with RCA was to create hit singles, and on that score the album was a failure. That it succeeded in other ways was of little importance to the principals involved.

Chet Atkins, seen here with his Gretsch guitar, enjoyed instrumental hits both before and after he produced Willie.

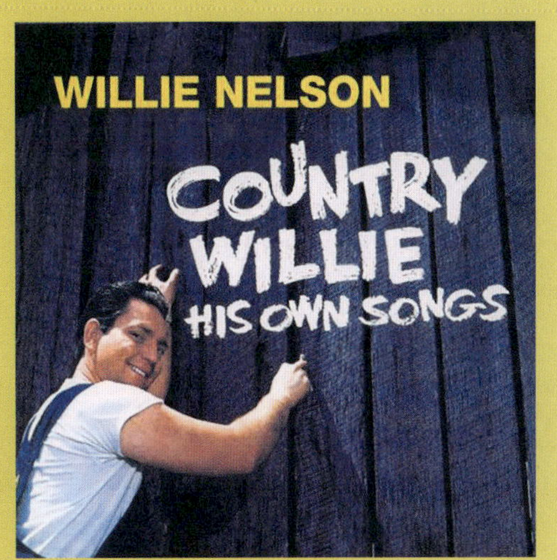

Willie Nelson
***Country Willie: His Own Songs* (RCA)**
Recorded: April 1965
Released: August 30, 1965
Willie Compositions: 12/12
Top 40 Singles: NA
Album Chart: Country #14

Nelson's RCA debut puts the emphasis on his already impressive resume as a songwriter: his own versions of the songs he'd written for other singers and a sampling of the Pamper demos. Even two of the new songs are strong, and Chet Atkins' production is more understated than it would be on Nelson's later RCA sessions. The virtuoso picking of Jerry Reed, Jerry Kennedy, and Pete Drake shine through, especially on the bluesy "Night Life" and "Are You Sure." On the other hand, the echo is heavy-handed, the rhythm section is annoyingly metronomic, and there were no hits. **Grade: B**

Country Favorites Willie Nelson Style

Even better was the second RCA album, *Country Favorites Willie Nelson Style*. Ernest Tubb had been a hero to Nelson ever since the former had a massive country hit with 1941's "Walking the Floor over You," which married the jazz-inflected singing of Jimmie Rodgers to the Western swing of Bob Wills. That was the combination that Nelson devoted his career to, and the younger man became a regular guest on Tubb's Nashville-based TV show, which debuted in 1965.

At that point, Tubb's band, the Texas Troubadours, was the best band in country music east of Bakersfield. The band included two instrumental legends—guitarist Leon Rhodes and steel guitarist Buddy Charleton—as well as two musicians destined to become successful singers: drummer Jack Greene and guitarist Cal Smith. It was an ensemble that could instinctively follow Nelson's every delay and rush in his phrasing. He loved their playing, and they loved his singing—so Nelson suggested to Atkins that he make an album with the Troubadours.

Nelson didn't write any of the dozen tunes, opting instead for three songs made famous by Bob Wills and two written by his old compadre Hank Cochran, including one made famous by his old employer Ray Price. Filling out the roster were songs linked to George Jones, Leon Payne, Bill Monroe, Guy Mitchell, Bobby Helms, Jenny Lou Carson, and Kitty Wells.

The album divides neatly into six slow heartbreak ballads, four insanely fast swing numbers, and two mid-tempo songs. The up-tempo tracks are musically dazzling, with tongue-twisting acrobatics in Nelson's vocals and hot solos by Rhodes, Charleton, and Nelson's longtime fiddler, Wade Ray. The ballads are well sung, but Nelson chooses higher keys and a smoother delivery in pursuit of pop crossover. These are less interesting than his later ballads and a bit too close to the famous, original versions of these songs.

Only the version of Hank Cochran's "Go on Home" provided a glimpse of the more dramatic interpretive singing to come. On this song, the narrator turns away a married woman, even though he clearly burns with passion for her, and Nelson's vocal captures the fierce wrestling between the narrator's desire and his conscience.

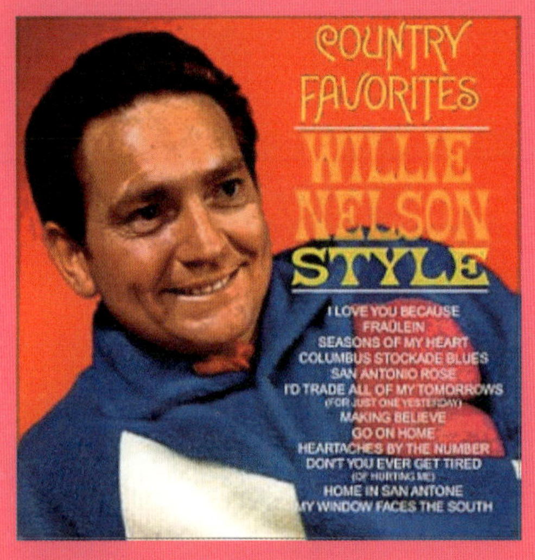

Willie Nelson
***Country Favorites Willie Nelson Style* (RCA)**
Recorded: December 15-16, 1965
Released: April 18, 1966
Willie Compositions: 0/12
Top 40 Singles: NA
Album Chart: Country #9

Nelson convinced producer Chet Atkins to let him record an entire album of old country standards with Ernest Tubb's Texas Troubadours without strings or female vocals. This resulted in high-speed romps through Bob Wills and Bill Monroe tunes, with hot solos from the band and heartbreak ballads sung in a sleek tenor that didn't allow Nelson to quite put his stamp on the material. This album—not the more famous but much later *Stardust*—marks the true beginning of Nelson's career as an interpretive singer. But only "Go on Home" hints at the dramatic singing to come. **Grade: B+**

Make Way for Willie Nelson

The album didn't yield any Top 40 singles, but it was Nelson's first Top 10 album on Billboard's country chart, and it stayed on the chart for seventeen weeks. Album sales didn't mean as much in the '60s as they would in the '70s, but it was hopeful sign. RCA followed it up with a very similar record in 1967: *Make Way for Willie Nelson.*

There were some important differences. Atkins was busy, so he turned the project over to Felton Jarvis, the young producer who'd been working with Elvis Presley. The Texas Troubadours were replaced by Nashville's A-Team session musicians—including

Ernest Tubb, a country hitmaker in the '40s, '50s, and '60s, had a TV show on which Willie was a frequent guest.

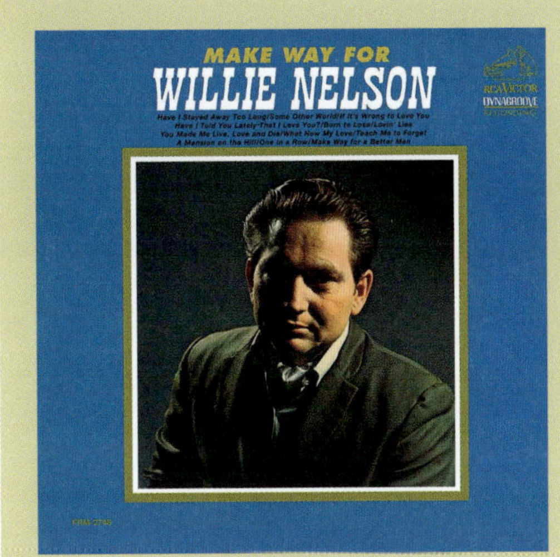

Willie Nelson
***Make Way for Willie Nelson* (RCA)**
Recorded: June–November 1966
Released: April 24, 1967
Willie Compositions: 1/12
Top 40 Single: "One in a Row" (Country #19)
Album Chart: Country #9

This sequel to *Country Favorites Willie Nelson Style* is also mostly devoted to Nelson's interpretations of other writers' songs. This one mixes in more pop material and pop arrangements with fewer hot solos, but producer Felton Jarvis allows Nelson more freedom to sing low and against the beat. The best songs are the hard-country numbers, but the one original, "One in a Row," gets the lushest pop treatment with strings and singers and became the only hit single. **Grade: B**

hot-shot guitarist Jerry Reed—though Nelson was allowed to bring three of his own musicians: fiddler Ray, drummer Johnny Bush, and steel guitarist Jimmy Day. The hot solos take a back seat, but Nelson is allowed to sing in lower, more comfortable keys with more freedom in his phrasing.

Gone were the high-velocity swing and bluegrass numbers; in their place were tunes by Broadway songwriter Frank Loesser and French chanteur Gilbert Bécaud. Loesser's "Have I Stayed Away Too Long?" was recorded by both Tex Ritter and Perry Como in 1943, and it often sounds as if Nelson and Jarvis were aiming for a sound halfway between the cowboy singer and the TV crooner. They usually nail it, but it's not the best use of Nelson's talents.

The title track, for example, boasts the snappy bravado of Nelson's hero Frank Sinatra. But more effective are two songs written by another hero, Floyd Tillman, where Nelson's career-long obsession with love gone wrong is allowed to grapple with mixed feelings. He's a singing preacher showing the congregation how it's done. He gets the same opportunity on Hank Williams' "Mansion on the Hill" and Lulu Belle and Scotty's "Have I Told You Lately That I Love You?"

The only Nelson composition on the album, a new song called "One in a Row," was also the first single. It received the most elaborate production: strings, backing vocals, and a stop-and-go rhythm. But the pop lushness took the sting out of Nelson's barbed lyrics, which dare a lover to stop telling lies for just one day. And if she can do that, he adds, that day will only be "one in a row." He never would release a version that captured the song's potential.

Nonetheless, the single went to #19 and the album to #9. That taught RCA the wrong lesson: It convinced them that Nelson needed bigger, poppier arrangements, not more understatement. It was the turning point in the singer's fraught relationship with the label. It was not a turn for the better.

Live Country Music Concert

Between the June and November sessions for *Make Way for Willie Nelson*, Jarvis recorded two Nelson concerts on July 9, 1966, at the Panther Hall Ballroom, home of the *Country Jamboree* radio show in Fort Worth, Texas. Even if the singer was struggling to gain traction in most of the world, he was a star in his home state. That anomaly was explained by the recording RCA released later that year as *Live Country Music Concert* (and again in 1976, post–*Red Headed Stranger*, as *Willie Nelson Live*).

The original show (later released intact in the box set *Nashville Was the Roughest of Them All*) featured Nelson on electric guitar, backed only by Wade Ray on bass and Johnny Bush on drums. Jarvis added some Chip Young guitar tracks back in Nashville, but the live experience comes through clearly. Bush, soon to emerge as a terrific singer and songwriter himself, was a limited drummer; but against his steady beat and Young's guitars, Nelson's guitar and Ray's bass roam restlessly and fearlessly.

This minimalist but flexible backing gave Nelson's voice room for a rhythmic spontaneity and an emotional depth that it had never had on vinyl before. It's rare for a band at a Texas dance hall to do more than a couple of ballads per set, but Nelson devotes most of his selections to slow tempos. He nonetheless commands the crowd's attention by singing so honestly about romantic love—how the thrill is inseparable from the anguish—that the Fort Worth dancers and record buyers everywhere were quieted by the surprise of having their own tangled experiences encapsulated so pithily.

"We were stars in Texas," Nelson told *Country Music: An Illustrated History*. "In Nashville, I was looked upon as a loser singer. [In Texas] I wouldn't have to change a thing. And they all liked what I did. So, I knew that what I was doing, I could do it forever, whether I pleased everybody in Nashville or not."

On "Night Life," Nelson plays the jazzy fills on electric rather than acoustic guitar. For his best-ever version of the overlooked Monument single "I Never Cared for You," Nelson belts out the proposition that the sun is made of ice over Ray's descending bass figure and then drops precipitously into a whisper for the equally unlikely claim of the title line. On one of his darkest songs, "I Just Can't Let You Say Goodbye," he is so distraught he strangles an ex-lover. He negotiates the tricky melody and wistful lyrics of "Yesterday," the Beatles' hit from the year before, as if it were an American Songbook standard.

"Touch Me," a neglected song from Nelson's debut album for Liberty, is stripped to the bones. It begins, as does "Hello Walls," with Nelson half-speaking, half-singing the title line, as if he were daring each person in the audience to touch him and feel the vibration of someone devastated by love, as if there were no other way to know what it's like. But there is another way, and it's to listen to his voice, backed by little but the suggestion of a rhythm section and bluesy guitar fills. The implication is that every listener has known romantic disappointment, but they can't really understand it till they hear it sung as nakedly as this.

The further implication is that Nelson couldn't sing or write this powerfully if he didn't have regular contact with an audience of working-class Texans, the people he grew up with, if he wasn't able to sense their reaction to each lyric line, each melodic line, as they stood in front of the stage. These live shows not only kept him financially afloat as a musician, they also sustained his creativity. And we can hear that process in the cheers from the crowd as soon as Nelson sings the two words of the song's title.

Live Country Music Concert is an invaluable document, a snapshot of how Nelson spent most of his

Willie plays his Stratocaster on the *Arizona Hayride* TV show in Phoenix in November 1964.

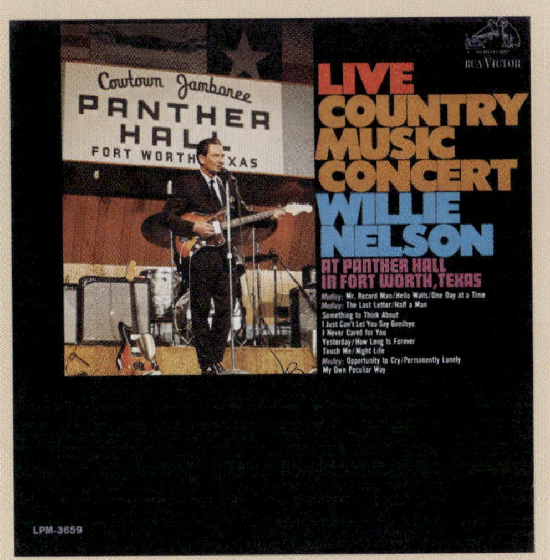

Willie Nelson
***Live Country Music Concert* (RCA)**
Recorded: July 9, 1966
Released: 1966 (re-released as *Willie Nelson Live* in 1976)
Willie Compositions: 10/11

On the one hand, this documents a typical Willie Nelson show in Texas in the 1960s. On the other hand, it's his finest recording of the decade. Despite some Nashville overdubs by guitarist Chip Young in Nashville, the stripped-down sound of Nelson's trio comes through. Ballads dominate the setlist, and the minimalist arrangements and sympathetic backing coax Nelson into some of his best singing ever. Here is the first indisputable recorded evidence of Nelson's genius. **Grade: A**

Willie records in the RCA Victor Studio in Nashville, circa 1965.

days during the 1960s, performing in person for an appreciative blue-collar audience in Texas. Each recording session in Nashville took up only a few days per quarter, but the live shows happened again and again. And those shows outstripped the studio performance in nearly every aspect but sonic cleanliness. Here is proof that Nelson had it figured out musically long before he captured that in the studio.

"You know, I always thought I could sing pretty good," he told *Scheer Intelligence* in 2017. "And it kinda bothered me that nobody else thought so. . . . The music I played on a bandstand was better than the music I played in the studio. For one thing, I'd be using my own band, and we'd have a better feel for it, be more relaxed. It just felt more comfortable. And we'd have an audience to play for. And it was just a whole lot more fun."

"The Party's Over" and Other Great Willie Nelson Songs

By the end of 1966, Nelson had released four albums for RCA: three pretty good studio projects and one terrific live recording. This contradicts the pervasive myth that Nelson's RCA years were an artistic wasteland, that he was a victim of misguided production that buried his gift under an avalanche of strings and singers. In fact, as we will discover, Nelson made good albums and bad for every label he ever worked for. At RCA, he started promisingly and ended strongly—but the middle years were a disaster, and that's what everyone chooses to remember.

If the first four RCA albums were a flawed but respectable start, RCA was disappointed with the poor sales results of the singles—and so was Nelson. Perhaps the ironies of his own songs weren't always easy to grasp on a first listen, especially when heard on a radio while a casual country fan was doing something else. Perhaps the bare-bones arrangements he preferred were too spare for such listeners. But that same audience responded to something in his voice when given half a chance. And so, Nelson found himself pulled in opposite directions by his artistic ambitions and his commercial aspirations.

"I'd get nervous," he told the *New York Times* in 1978. "I just didn't feel comfortable in that kind of situation. You'd walk into the studio, and they'd put six guys behind you who'd never seen your music before, and it's impossible to get the feel of it in a three-hour session. That was true for me, at least."

Willie publicity photo circa 1965.

Previously, Atkins and his protégé Jarvis had used strings sparingly on Nelson's records, but on *"The Party's Over" and Other Great Willie Nelson Songs*, the orchestra is slathered onto every track. It's no surprise that this ocean of violins constrained Nelson into the stiffest, least natural singing of his career thus far. He traded in his usual jazz approach to phrasing for a more classical method where every syllable had to hit its mark.

"Chet added the requisite sweeteners—heavy string sections and heavenly choirs that were supposedly making my work more palatable," Nelson writes in *It's a Long Story: My Life*. "It didn't work."

To make matters worse, these weren't "great Willie Nelson songs," no matter what the title claimed. These were a transparent effort to simplify his writing so the radio audience could get the point on the first listen. Gone were the tangled knots of grief, anger, and lingering affection that marked his best writing.

Now each song devoted itself to a singular emotion, usually a heartbroken martyr who chooses to "Suffer in Silence" and to tell his ex to "Go Away." One song was titled "To Make a Long Story Short (She's Gone)," and most of the material makes a complicated story simple. "Hold Me Tighter" and "Once Alone" are straightforward seduction numbers, and "I'll Stay Around" is an unambiguous pledge of love.

It's no coincidence that the album's three best songs—"The Ghost," "A Moment's Not Too Long," and "No Tomorrow in Sight"—were plucked from the stash of Pamper demos when Nelson was writing his

Willie Nelson
***"The Party's Over" and Other Great Willie Nelson Songs* (RCA)**
Recorded: June 1966–June 1967
Released: September 18, 1967
Willie Compositions: 12/12
Top 40 Singles: "The Party's Over" (Country #24)
Album Chart: Country #9

This is where the Nelson/RCA collaboration went south. Producer Chet Atkins swamped a dozen Nelson compositions in a sea of strings. The singer tried to accommodate the new approach with simpler songwriting and steadier singing, but that just weakened the album further. Nelson's latest compositions stuck to one emotion at a time, and his older, more ambitious compositions drowned in sugar. **Grade: D**

best mini-stories of lovers torn between desire and antagonism. But even the nightmarish "The Ghost," with its great opening line, "The silence is unusually loud tonight," is drowned in strings. And the new songs, including the album's title track and only hit single, offer no surprises in the verses that one couldn't expect from the title.

Texas in My Soul

Texas in My Soul, the next album, was another 180-degree change in direction. RCA decided to capitalize on Nelson's popularity in Texas by having him sing eleven songs about the state written by other people. Atkins produced with a band that mixed his own musicians (Grady Martin, Ray Stevens, Junior Huskey, and Buddy Harman) with Nelson's steel guitarist Jimmy Day. The strings and backing singers were sent home, though vibes and electric piano were added.

The songs were a mix of excellent (three Ernest Tubb numbers and the old folk song "Streets of Laredo") and embarrassing ("Dallas," "San Antonio," and "Remember the Alamo"). But good or bad, they were sung and played stiffly, as if Atkins were scared any hint of Texas swing would scare off non-Texan radio stations. Or maybe Nelson was so determined to have a hit, he would betray all his instincts and sing as predictably as Atkins requested. Whatever the cause, an album that should have been in Nelson's wheelhouse fell flat. Worst of all was the jingoistic, spoken-word track about the Alamo.

Good Times

The next album, *Good Times*, was an uneasy compromise between Nelson's and Atkins' inclinations. Drawn from six different sessions stretching from January 1965 to March 1968, the resulting record was split between seven understated songs in Nelson's preferred style and five overstated songs in Atkins' preferred style.

Willie Nelson
***Texas in My Soul* (RCA)**
Recorded: August 1967
Released: April 1, 1968
Willie Compositions: 0/11
Top 40 Singles: NA
Album Chart: NA

This should have been a much better album than it is. The concept of having Nelson sing eleven songs about his home state would seem a natural, but the singing and playing is anything but. Except on the three Ernest Tubb numbers, where Nelson loosens up a bit, he sounds stiff, as if he's straining to fit in with the Nashville musicians. Even worse, six of the songs are sappy, tourism ads for a state much more complicated than that. **Grade: D**

Side one is taken from sessions on December 12, 1967, and March 27, 1968, with three songs written by Nelson alone and three more written with his then-wife Shirley Collie Nelson. These sessions consisted of just four musicians: Nelson on vocals, Junior Huskey on bass, and Atkins and Grady Martin on guitars. Although the Anita Kerr Singers were overdubbed onto Mickey Newbury's "Sweet Memories," the other five songs were left unadorned. The album's title track, a #44 single, is too sentimental for its own good, but the other four songs are four of the best tracks Nelson recorded during the 1960s.

"December Day," an old Pamper demo, boasts one of Nelson's most elegant melodies, one that seems to reach again and again for happiness, only to fall back into wistfulness. The lyrics reinforce this by comparing a love affair to the seasons of the year—so hopeful in spring and so resigned in the winter. Nelson does full justice to this marvelous song, half-whispering, half-warbling the words as the two guitarists dance around him. He would do it justice again on 1971's *Yesterday's Wine*.

Just as good is the modest hit single, "Little Things," another Pamper gem, the musical equivalent of a Hemingway short story: two eight-line verses, each ending in a two-line refrain. But in those few words, Nelson brings to life a whole world as a husband on a business trip phones his ex-wife to see how she's doing and to muse on how much has changed.

Willie Nelson
***Good Times* (RCA)**
Recorded: January 1965-March 1968
Released: October 14, 1968
Willie Compositions: 10/12
Top 40 Single: "Little Things" (Country #22)
Album Chart: Country #29

What a weird album. Four of the tracks are among the finest songs Nelson ever wrote (three of them with his then-wife Shirley Collie Nelson) with some of his best singing ever. These four—plus two slighter numbers—are masterpieces of minimalism: just Nelson's voice, Junior Huskey's bass, and the guitars of Grady Martin and Chet Atkins. The other six songs are under-written, overproduced fiascos. Atop slight, sentimental material (four originals and two covers), producer Atkins piled strings and the Anita Kerr Singers. **Grade: B-**

Nelson leaves huge pauses in his vocal, as if to let the listener feel the weight of what's unspoken in this seemingly casual conversation.

That song was co-written with his then-wife Shirley, as were "Pages" and "She's Still Gone." The first finds the narrator ripping from his book of life the chapters referring to his ex, while the latter finds him hugging his pillow and listening to an empty room. In both cases, he holds out key words as if they were a judge's sentence on himself.

Then the album suddenly shifts from these bare-bones psychological dramas to the lightweight sentimentality of "Ashamed," puffed up with sweet violins and sweeter voices. Four of the next five numbers are in the same vein, twisting the arm of the listener to respond in a certain way rather than allowing us to make up our own minds. Interrupting the flow of syrup is one more understated tune, "Buddy," a slight Nelson original.

All in all, *Good Times* may well be the most schizophrenic album in country music history. The cover photo of Nelson with his arms around a mini-skirted model as if teaching her how to putt adds one more bizarre touch to the misbegotten project.

My Own Peculiar Way

In 1967 and 1968, Nelson recorded four singles that were never included on an RCA album until much later but which reveal the many ways he and RCA were trying to break through. First was a pop-folk rendition of Red Lane's murder-ballad "Blackjack County Chain," a brutally honest song about the reality of prison chain gangs that went to #21. It went no further because that same honesty caused some conservative radio stations to boycott it. This song about prisoners taking their revenge on a cruel sheriff, marked by a work-gang beat, Nelson's dryly understated vocal, and Grady Martin's acoustic guitar, was powerful stuff.

Equally political and controversial was the antiwar song "Jimmy's Road," recorded in 1968 but not released until the following year where it met a similar boycott during the Vietnam War. Upset that his long-time bandmate, the gentle guitarist David Zettner, had been drafted, Nelson wrote a kind of folk song about the step-by-step process of turning an innocent boy into a killer and then a dead man (Zettner himself didn't die and recovered to rejoin Nelson's circle). It's all the more chilling because of Nelson's deadpan vocal and Atkins' nightmarish, dissonant string chart. It remains one of the strangest—and strongest—singles Nelson ever released.

Recorded at the same July 8, 1968, session was a very different record, a cover of the old pop-jazz standard "Bring Me Sunshine," done in the style of a finger-snapping Frank Sinatra over a jaunty piano and a Billy May–like big-band arrangement. There was nothing ironic or discomforting about the lyrics' optimistic wish for love, and at #13, it was the highest-charting single during Nelson's stay at RCA.

Willie Nelson
***My Own Peculiar Way* (RCA)**
Recorded: November 1968
Released: February 10, 1969
Willie Compositions: 8/12
Top 40 Singles: NA
Album Chart: Country #39

On this album, unfortunately, Nelson was neither writing nor singing his "own peculiar way." Instead, he was simplifying both aspects to better fit producer Chet Atkins' heavy application of choirs, orchestras, and steady-as-she-goes rhythm sections. The few glimmers of originality–John Hartford's "Natural to Be Gone" and Nelson's own "I Just Dropped By"–were not enough to counter the big-band swagger, preachy message songs, and lachrymose ballads. **Grade: D**

Recorded at that same session was Nelson's version of the Dallas Frazier ballad "Johnny One Time," which finds the narrator warning his ex that her new boyfriend won't stick around very long—a story very much like a Nelson lyric. The lead vocal is strong, and the strings and singers are more tasteful than usual, and the single went to #36.

So, which of these singles would form the template for Nelson's next album? Not the political folk songs. No, the models would be the Sinatra-esque number and the string-buoyed ballad. The new album, *My Own Peculiar Way*, applied sweetening strings and/or singers to all dozen tracks.

The title track, an old Liberty song that Andy Williams had covered, set the tone with a sentimental vocal reinforced by the female oohs and violin vibrato. There was another string-laden Dallas Frazier ballad and a Nelson original, "That's All," that echoed the Sinatra standard "That's Life" and mimicked the brassy sound of "Bring Me Sunshine."

I don't mean to imply that strings and singers ruined every country record they touched. Singles such as Patsy Cline's "Crazy" and George Jones' "He Stopped Loving Her Today" are irresistible recordings because producers Owen Bradley and Billy Sherrill, respectively, knew how to reinforce the lead vocals without getting in their way—and because the singers knew how to use the voices and violins behind them as a boost rather than competition.

But the "Countrypolitan" sound was a poor fit for Nelson; it negated his best instincts and encouraged his worst. In these lush settings, he held out notes instead of using pauses, and he wrote songs that were blatant rather than ironic. And Atkins wasn't as subtle as Bradley. When he did back off a bit, Nelson relaxed and sang better. But most of *My Own Peculiar Way* was a victim of its mix of lightweight material and heavy-handed production.

Both Sides Now

You could see Nelson's pop-crossover hopes reflected in the photographs on his album covers. His first RCA release pictured him in overalls, it's true, but only to justify the title *Country Willie*. The other records presented him as a clean-shaven, neatly combed sophisticate in sweaters, blazers, and

Willie performs at the Palomino Club in Los Angeles on May 8, 1970.

Willie Nelson
***Both Sides Now* (RCA)**
Recorded: November 1969
Released: March 23, 1970
Willie Compositions: 4/11
Top 40 Singles: NA
Album Charts: NA

RCA's dogged attempts to put Nelson in every possible musical setting make this another head-scratcher of an album. He finally gets a chance to feature his road band and his new acoustic guitar Trigger, and that makes everything sound more comfortable. The two folk-rock tunes ("Everybody's Talkin'" and the title track) don't quite work, but Nelson's three new compositions (including "Bloody Mary Morning" and "I Gotta Get Drunk") get splendid treatments. "Once More with Feeling," the single, is overproduced; but the old songs associated with Hank Williams, Jimmy Wakely, the Carter Family and Ray Price are likable enough.
Grade: B-

leisurewear. He later complained about the strings and singers on his albums, but at the time he clearly wanted a place among Frank Sinatra, Perry Como, and Tony Bennett—big-band pop singers with jazz flavorings; urbane, adult subject matter; and highly polished arrangements. He said he wanted that, but he never felt comfortable with it.

Nelson could sing those rhythms and harmonies, but when he opened his mouth, he sounded like East Texas. When he let go of his premeditated plan and let his instincts take over, the music sounded nothing like a Manhattan cocktail party—it sounded like a Fort Worth beer joint. It was country music, and all his attempts to dress it up in white shoes and expensive sweaters couldn't disguise it. Yes, it was country music of unusual complexity in its lyrics, chord changes, and phrasing—but it was country music just the same. He wasn't going to break through until he accepted that fact, and that wouldn't happen until 1973.

Things had begun to change when his house burned down at the end of 1969. He moved to Texas, back to Tennessee, and finally back to Texas for good. In Austin, he connected with two different audiences: working-class adults and bohemian twentysomethings. Neither group wore sweaters and leisure suits or drank cocktails. One was a beer-and-whiskey crowd, the other a beer-and-pot bunch. Both wore jeans and bandanas and liked their music raw. Nelson changed his appearance to match theirs.

"It felt good to let my hair grow," he writes in *It's a Long Story: My Life*. "Felt good to get onstage wearing the same jeans I'd been wearing all damn day. Felt good to tie a red bandana around my forehead to keep the sweat from getting into my eyes. Felt good to no longer give a fuck about making a proper appearance. I liked being improper."

The music in Nelson's live show was growing improper as well. The stronger beat appealed to honky-tonk dancers and rock fans alike; the more aggressive solos did, too. The two audiences learned to tolerate each other at the former National Armory repurposed as a concert hall called the Armadillo

World Headquarters, then at the Austin Opry House, which Nelson bought and operated, and especially at the Willie Nelson Fourth of July Picnics, a kind of annual Hillbilly Woodstock.

While these rapid changes were happening in Texas, things had stagnated in Nashville. Everyone involved was frustrated. Nelson and RCA had tried everything, it seemed: stripped-down singer-songwriter performances, lavishly arranged pop, snappy big-band numbers, hardcore honky-tonk, weird originals, middle-of-the-road sentiment—nothing could break into the Top 10 singles chart.

"There was no slot that I fit in," he told the *Fresh Air* radio show in 1996. "My songs had a few chords in them, and country songs weren't supposed to have over three chords, according to executive decisions. And if it had more than three, then it wasn't country, and it shouldn't be recorded. And my voice wasn't exactly . . . I was nowhere near Eddy Arnold. My phrasing was sort of funny. I didn't sing on the beat. I had too many chords and I just didn't fit the slots, you know? And I wouldn't take orders."

It was a full twelve months before Nelson went back into a Nashville studio, with Atkins' sidekick, Felton Jarvis, behind the board. This time they'd try letting Nelson use his own band and his own guitar on country classics, Nelson originals, and contemporary folk-rock. In the meantime, he had made a major change in his musical approach.

Dan "Bee" Spears and pedal steel guitar great Jimmy Day listen to a playback at the Atlantic Records studios in New York City in February 1973.

In his early days on the Texas dance hall circuit, Nelson had played Fender Telecasters and Stratocasters, whose narrow necks made for easy fingering and whose piercing treble cut through the noisy ambience of the beer joints. In the '60s, he adopted a Baldwin electro-acoustic archtop, similar to Atkins' guitar, with a brushed-aluminum Baldwin amplifier. When a drunk broke that guitar's neck, Nelson took it to Scott Jackson's guitar shop in Nashville. Jackson advised against repairing the Baldwin and offered instead a vintage Martin guitar with nylon strings.

Willie with his daughters Paula and Amy in Las Vegas on June 18, 1980.

"When I got that guitar," Nelson wrote in *It's a Long Story: My Life*, "it sounded like Django Reinhart, the best guitar player who ever lived, so I kept playing it. [The Martin was] made of rosewood, an acoustic model with the richest, most soulful tone I'd ever heard. . . . Didn't take long for me to pick a hole in it. That's because classical guitars aren't meant to be picked. But that hole, along with the aluminum amp—aged by just the right amount of beer that'd been spilled inside—seemed to deepen its soulful tone. I named my guitar Trigger, thinking of the closeness between Roy Rogers and his beloved horse."

Nelson has played that guitar ever since. He has had it re-braced on the inside several times, but the exterior—including the pick-created hole—has never changed. He plays it onstage and in the studio; he keeps it near him on the bus, and he hid it from the IRS when the tax agents seized his property. He played as he sang (or, if you prefer, sang as he played), and that dialogue between voice and guitar, sliding around the beat or rising and falling in volume for dramatic effect, have become an indispensable part of Nelson's sound.

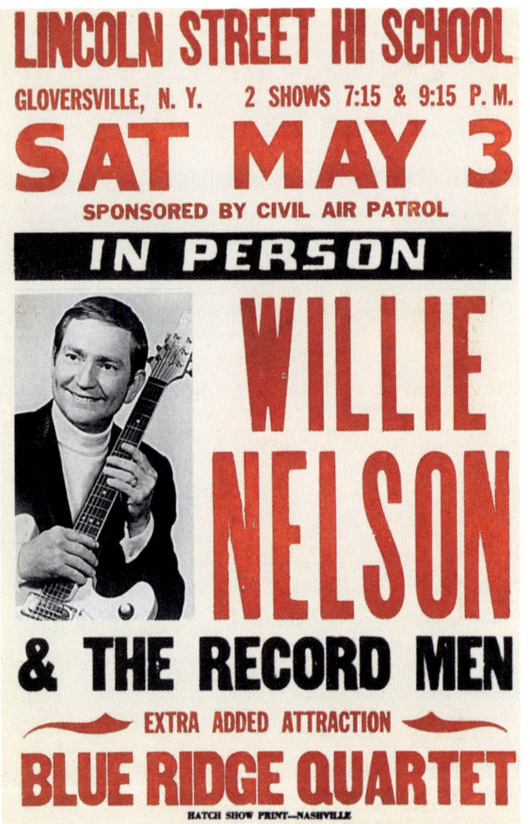

The resulting album, *Both Sides Now*, took its title from the Joni Mitchell composition, an almost perfect jewel of pop craftsmanship. It was joined on side two by another superbly written folk-rock number, Fred Neil's "Everybody's Talkin'." Except for a surprisingly good version of "Yesterday" on his RCA live album, Nelson had completely avoided the rock 'n' roll world that had been evolving rapidly from Elvis Presley to the Beatles to Bob Dylan. Nelson acted as if pop music still meant Frank Sinatra and Peggy Lee.

This made sense, for Nelson's music had presented adult subject matter to adult audiences from the time he joined a polka band in elementary school and a honky-tonk band as a teenager. He wasn't interested in electric guitars that roared with hormones; he was interested in steel guitars that moaned with hard lessons learned. He wasn't interested in the issues of dating—giddy infatuation and weepy breakups. He was interested in the issues of marriage—of "can't live with her and can't live without her." After all, he had been married himself since he was eighteen.

But nothing else had worked, so he decided to give the rock 'n' roll subgenre closest to him—folk-rock—a whirl. He convinced Jarvis to let him use most of his road band in the studio: guitarist David Zettner, steel guitarist Jimmy Day, Paul English's nineteen-year-old kid brother Billy on drums, and Nelson's wife Shirley on duet and backing vocals (and as a songwriter on the album's first single, "Once More with Feeling"). Only bassist Norbert Putnam represented the Nashville team.

But when Nelson tried to sing "Both Sides Now," as great a song as it is, he couldn't get a handle on it. Mitchell's ingenious metaphors were too different from the plainspoken monologues Nelson was used to. You could hear him feeling around for the syncopation in the Celtic melody and floundering when he couldn't find it. Something similar happens on "Everybody's Talkin'," the song sung by Harry Nilsson in the movie *Midnight Cowboy*. Jarvis even adds bongos to create a hippie vibe, all to no avail.

Nelson had better luck with the three new compositions he introduced on the album—his most impressive burst of songwriting in several years. The up-tempo number "I Gotta Get Drunk" and the mid-tempo tune "Bloody Mary Morning" would become staples of his live set for decades, with the latter functioning as the centerpiece of 1974's masterpiece, *Phases and Stages*. The original versions on *Both Sides Now* are quite likeable with Trigger unleashed for the first time in the studio. Even the overlooked ballad "It Could Be Said That Way" tells an ingenious story as a couple searches for euphemisms to describe the reasons for their breakup before admitting it's just time to go.

Because it would be released as the first single, Jarvis dresses up Shirley's composition in choirs and echo, suffocating its possibilities. She gets a better showcase in her duet vocal with her husband on Hank Williams' "Pins and Needles (In My Heart)." She never got the opportunities her talent deserved, and this would be her last collaboration with Willie.

Laying My Burdens Down

At the end of 1969, Shirley opened an envelope from the hospital and found a bill for Paula Nelson, a baby born to Connie Koepke and Willie Nelson on October 27, 1969. The two had been conducting an affair for more than a year since meeting at Larry Butler's 21 Club in Houston, and Nelson had foolishly given the hospital his home address at Ridgetop. Or maybe he wanted to be caught because he and Shirley were fighting so much.

Whatever the reason, he confessed all and Shirley moved out of Ridgetop as Connie moved in in early December. Willie and Connie finally got married on April 30, 1971, and Nelson lived as a bigamist until his divorce from Shirley came through that November. Shirley never remarried and never restarted her career.

Soon after Connie moved in, Willie's daughter Lana showed up with black eyes and bruises after being beaten up by her husband, Steve Warren. Willie went over to their house, slapped Steve around, and warned him not to do it again. When Steve and his brothers came back to Ridgetop, Willie was waiting for him with a shotgun. This is the origin story of the song "Shotgun Willie."

In mid-December, he bought his fiancée Connie a brand-new Mercury Cougar as an early Christmas present. A few days later at the mailbox, she forgot to set the brakes and the car rolled into the nearby woods. By the time the tow truck arrived, someone had stolen the front seats.

"Hank Cochran and I had been sitting in the basement writing songs," Nelson says in the book *Waylon & Willie*. "That year, I went through a divorce. I had four cars wrecked. We were kicking all this around and wrote a song, 'What Can You Do to Me Now?' The next day, my house burned down."

The new song "What Can You Do to Me Now?" captured the end-of-the-rope bewilderment of landing at rock bottom and hoping that it will, despite the pain, "make a man of me." Nelson had no idea how low bottom could be.

On December 23, he was at a party in Nashville when his nephew Randy Fletcher called and said, "Willie, your house is on fire. The house is melting." The uncle rushed home to find a "smoking black skeleton." Connie and Paula were safe, but Willie shrugged off the firemen's warnings and dived into the flaming structure. He emerged minutes later with a guitar case in each hand. In one was Trigger; in the other was his stash of "Colombia gold" marijuana.

The suddenly homeless family went to visit Nelson's sister, Bobbie, now relocated to Austin. Surrounded by family, new friends and old, the

Willie Nelson
***Laying My Burdens Down* (RCA)**
Recorded: June 1970
Released: September 14, 1970
Willie Compositions: 6/10
Top 40 Singles: NA
Album Charts: NA

Producer Felton Jarvis adds horns to the countrypolitan voices and strings to further weigh down Nelson's subtle writing and singing. A few songs, including the gospel title track, show enough restraint to shine. But most of the album is irredeemably overproduced, luring Nelson into some of the loudest and worst singing of his career. **Grade: D**

singer remembered how comfortable he felt living in Texas. He rented an abandoned ranch in Bandera, west of San Antonio. But he spent much of his time in Austin, soaking up the strange brew of rednecks and bohemia in the state capital. It would change the course of his career and his life forever.

The family returned to Ridgetop when it was rebuilt. But they quickly realized that they felt more at home in Texas than in Tennessee. It made more sense to drive from Austin to Nashville once a month for meetings or recording sessions than to drive from Nashville to Austin for live gigs three times a month. Eventually they bought a sprawling ranch with a nine-hole golf course near the Pedernales River in Spicewood. Willie would live there full- or part-time for the rest of his life.

Seven months later, Nelson and Jarvis reconvened at the RCA Victor Studio in Nashville. It was back to the countrypolitan formula: the Nashville A-Team musicians, massed voices, and soothing strings—with big-band horns now added. When this production overlay is dialed back, Nelson finds room to add the pauses and delays that make his singing so effective. When the production is dialed up, he tries to match it by singing loudly and badly.

The title track from the resulting album, *Laying My Burdens Down*, is one of the best gospel numbers Nelson ever wrote. It's handled with relative restraint and became a #68 single. The old Pamper demo "Happiness Lives Next Door" and a new composition, "When We Live Again," are also scaled back enough to reveal solid songs. On the other hand, promising originals such as "Following Me Around," "Minstrel Man," and "Where Do You Stand?" not only pile on the strings, voices, and horns but also bait Nelson into over-singing as the crescendos rise.

Willie Nelson & Family

The title and cover photo of Nelson's next album, *Willie Nelson & Family*, are misleading. "Willie Nelson and Family" was the name of his live band on the road, and the photo showed them gathered around a campfire. But Nelson was the only person in the picture heard on the vinyl album inside the sleeve. Once again, Jarvis was producing with his Nashville crew and the countrypolitan sound. The production wasn't as heavy-handed as on *Laying My Burdens Down*, but it was distracting as often as it wasn't.

Nelson had recently befriended two other country singer-songwriters, Merle Haggard and Kris Kristofferson, and recognized them as fellow travelers in his crusade to bring irony and swing to country music. He recorded Haggard's "Today I Started Loving You Again" and Kristofferson's "Sunday Morning Coming Down," planting seeds that would blossom in 1979's *Willie Nelson Sings Kristofferson* and 1983's *Pancho & Lefty*.

Nelson's vocals on those two songs for *Willie Nelson & Family* are so vigorous and freewheeling that they keep the strings at bay and let the feelings of his down-on-their-luck characters shine through.

Willie Nelson
***Willie Nelson & Family* (RCA)**
Recorded: November 1970
Released: March 1, 1971
Willie Compositions: 5/10
Top 40 Singles: "I'm a Memory" (Country #28), "Fire and Rain" (Country #29)
Album Chart: Country #43

This is another schizophrenic album. Producer Felton Jarvis added strings and/or choirs to nearly every track, but he loosened the reins for side one, allowing Nelson to sing with more finesse and freedom on songs by Kris Kristofferson, Hank Williams, James Taylor, and Nelson himself. Side two is overproduced, forcing Nelson to over-sing on some originals, including the single, "I'm a Memory." **Grade: C+**

Something similar happens on Hank Williams' "I'm So Lonesome I Could Cry" and James Taylor's "Fire and Rain," the latter more successful than the Joni Mitchell and Fred Neil songs on the previous album. Nelson had to sing more forcefully than he might have desired to overcome the orchestrations, but he did prevail.

It helps that Nashville bassist Norbert Putnam was finally getting the hang of Nelson's phrasing, and his bubbling bass lines loosen up the songs to the benefit of both the singer and the listener. The backing singers finally serve a useful purpose by morphing into a church choir on "Kneel at the Feet of Jesus," a rollicking Nelson original. Another new composition, the up-tempo boast, "I'm a Memory," by contrast, gets buried under the onslaught of horns and strings. Of course, RCA picked that track as a single.

The Words Don't Fit the Picture

Nelson's next release was *Yesterday's Wine*, a concept album so brilliant and prescient that it stood out from everything else he did at RCA. For that reason, we'll discuss it in the next chapter about concept albums. It was as much a commercial flop as it was an artistic triumph, but Jarvis was impressed enough to give Nelson more leeway on the subsequent project, 1972's *The Words Don't Fit the Picture*.

Nelson, too, had been inspired by *Yesterday's Wine* to write a batch of strong new songs. All ten of the tracks for the follow-up were originals, and only four were from the heap of early demos. Among the new songs was one of his best ballads, "Stay Away from Lonely Places," advice to the brokenhearted with a deliciously melancholy melody and a sexually explicit couplet, reminding us that even in this busy, seemingly impersonal world, "Someone's outstretched arms are waiting/To stay with you at least till dawn."

"London" is a strange, eerie mood piece, describing the stark difference between a quiet city late at night and a loud one during the day. "If You Really Loved Me" tells a lover how their relationship would be if they really loved each other, implying that they really don't. All these songs look at the timeless problem—desire bumping up against incompatibility—from a different angle, giving listeners multiple perspectives on the same riddle.

"Good Hearted Woman" is Nelson's version of a song he co-wrote with Waylon Jennings. Nelson contributed only the couplet "Through teardrops and laughter they'll pass through this world hand in hand" during a poker game, but Jennings liked it so much, he gave Nelson half the credit. This is a likable, rousing rendition, but the song wouldn't reach its potential until the co-writers recorded it as a duet.

Willie Nelson
***The Words Don't Fit the Picture* (RCA)**
Recorded: May–October 1971
Released: February 7, 1972
Willie Compositions: 10/10
Top 40 Singles: NA
Album Charts: NA

Producer Felton Jarvis gives Nelson a more sympathetic setting on this session, and the singer responds not only with more expressive singing but also better songwriting. He wrote all ten songs, and six of them are new, including such underrated gems as "Stay Away from Lonely Places," "London," and "If You Really Loved Me." The backing vocals are restrained, the strings are banished, and the Nashville pickers are more responsive, both on the ballads and the up-tempo two-step, "Good Hearted Woman." This is Nelson's second-best RCA album but a commercial dud. **Grade: B+**

Jarvis displays a light hand in the control room. The backing vocals are restrained, and the strings are absent, replaced by Weldon Myrick's more personal steel guitar. Many of the songs are enhanced by the interplay between David Kirby's acoustic guitar and Charlie McCoy's harmonica, echoing the interaction between Trigger and Mickey Raphael's harmonica in Nelson's road shows. Nashville was finally getting used to Nelson, and Nelson was finally getting used to Nashville—but it was too little too late.

The Willie Way

As 1971 dawned, it seemed as if Nelson and RCA were so disillusioned by the singer's sales history that they were reluctant to invest in the full countrypolitan treatment for Nelson's tracks. Ironically, this low-budget approach allowed Nelson's potential to blossom as never before.

His final three RCA albums—*Yesterday's Wine*, *The Words Don't Fit the Picture*, and *The Willie Way*, almost entirely recorded between May and October 1971—are by far the best of his thirteen original studio albums for the label. Producer Jarvis dialed back the frills and let the pauses in Nelson's vocals remain pauses and the words fall out of that silence. Finally, one could hear Nelson's performances as he intended them. If *Yesterday's Wine* is justly remembered as the best of the lot, the other two are unjustly overlooked, for they are nearly as good.

The final RCA album of new recordings, *The Willie Way*, borrows material from different sessions but remains unvarnished and thus more impactful. From the May 1971 sessions for *Yesterday's Wine*

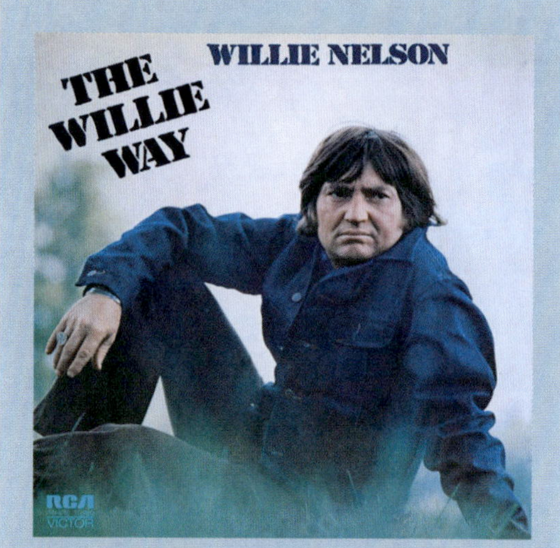

Willie Nelson
The Willie Way **(RCA)**
Recorded: May 1971-April 1972
Released: July 17, 1972
Willie Compositions: 8/10
Top 40 Singles: NA
Album Chart: Country #34

This grab bag of songs left over from the 1971 sessions for *Yesterday's Wine* and *The Words Don't Fit the Picture* is surprisingly strong. Producer Felton Jarvis didn't add the usual frills and allowed Nelson's voice—sure of itself at last—to come through unimpeded. The songs aren't quite as good as on the two previous albums, but they include a marvelous ballad, "Wonderful Future"; a moody blues, "Wake Me When It's Over"; two lively swing tunes from the Pamper demos; and a splendid version of Kris Kristofferson's "Help Me Make It through the Night." **Grade: B+**

come three leftover tracks: the ingenious Nelson ballad "Wonderful Future" (key line: "I've got a wonderful future behind me"); Nelson's organ-and-harmonica-fueled blues lament, "Wake Me When It's Over"; and his brilliant interpretation of Kris Kristofferson's "Help Me Make It through the Night."

From the October 1971 sessions for *The Words Don't Fit the Picture* come six more leftovers, including sparkling versions of two jewels from the Pamper demos—"Undo the Right" and "A Moment Isn't Very Long"—both given a jaunty Texas swing. And from his final RCA session, in April 1972, comes his spirited, barroom singalong version of "Mountain Dew," an Appalachian folk song credited to Bascom Lunsford and Scotty Wiseman.

At that same session, RCA recorded Nelson's first attempt at the *Phases and Stages* material—but once again, they didn't know what they had and never released it. The songwriting on *The Willie Way* isn't as strong as on *Yesterday's Wine*, *The Words Don't Fit the Picture*, and *Phases and Stages* (that's why these songs were leftovers)—but the performances are. With his final RCA trilogy, Nelson had at last found his voice and his sound. Now he just needed someone to connect him to a large audience outside of Texas.

Willie Nelson & Danny Davis with the Nashville Brass

RCA released a dozen studio albums with Nelson between 1965 and 1972 and never had a Top 10 single. When he became a superstar for Columbia, a miffed RCA kept inventing new ways to repackage its old Nelson recordings to make some belated money. Refusing to believe that the overproduction of Nelson's albums was the central problem, they overdubbed the Nashville Brass onto the original recordings and released the results as *Willie Nelson & Danny Davis with the Nashville Brass*.

Willie Nelson & Danny Davis with the Nashville Brass
Willie Nelson & Danny Davis with the Nashville Brass
(RCA)
Recorded: 1965–1980
Released: 1980
Willie Compositions: 10/10
Top 40 Single: "Night Life" (Country #20)
Album Chart: Country #14

Though Nelson graciously wrote a positive liner note for the album, he was otherwise uninvolved in the overdubs. Davis, the RCA producer that Waylon Jennings so often fought with, creates horn arrangements that resemble those for old-fashioned TV variety shows. The blaring horns are so disconnected from Nelson's vocals and lyrics that it's almost like listening to two different radio stations at once on your car radio. If Mickey Raphael's revelatory remix of Nelson's RCA tracks is justly titled *Naked Willie*, Davis's obscurantist mix could be called *Overdressed Willie*. **Grade: F**

The Essential Willie Nelson

Many Willie Nelson fans have long believed that there are some terrific performances buried beneath the overproduction RCA applied to his releases. Music critic Colin Escott was one, and Nelson's harmonica player Mickey Raphael was another. Escott picked out his favorite twenty songs from the RCA years and wrote an essay to justify his choices on the single-disc anthology, *The Essential Willie Nelson*.

Willie Nelson
***The Essential Willie Nelson* (RCA)**
Recorded: 1965–1972
Released: August 1, 1995
Willie Compositions: 16/20
Top 40 Singles: NA
Album Charts: NA

Nelson often discounted the eleven albums he made for RCA between 1964 and 1971, and he did labor under unsympathetic production for most of that era. For this compilation, however, country historian Colin Escott picked 15 of the more understated productions, where Nelson got the chance to do things "My Own Peculiar Way," as one song puts it. Included are the original recordings of songs such as "Me and Paul" and "Funny How Time Slips Away." The set ends with the non-album single "Phases, Stages, Circles, Cycles and Scenes," a glimpse into the post-RCA future. **Grade: B+**

Naked Willie

Raphael had the leverage to get permission from both Nelson and RCA to remix seventeen of the original RCA tracks by taking away the strings, choirs, horns, and more mechanical rhythm tracks. He called the process "un-producing" and he called the resulting album *Naked Willie*.

"What I've learned from Willie, working with him over the past three decades," Raphael writes in the 2009 liner notes, "is that less is more. . . . This is what it might have sounded like had Willie produced his own recording sessions for RCA."

Raphael wisely focuses exclusively on the most problematic material: the recording sessions after June 1, 1966, and before May 1, 1971—that is, after the first three of Nelson's studio RCA albums and before the last three. Those six titles prove that his tenure at the label was far from the wasteland it's often dismissed as. Raphael tries to prove the same of the seven albums in between—and he often succeeds.

Benefiting the most are his ironic, post-mortem ballads of lost love: "Following Me Around," "Happiness Lives Next Door," "I Just Dropped By," "When We Live Again," and "What Can You Do to Me Now?" Stripped of soothing strings and voices, the pain and anger underneath his seemingly stoic attitude emerge and create the drama these songs require. Outlier songs such as the gospel hymn "Laying My Burdens Down," the blues "If You Could Only See What's Going through My Mind," and the antiwar folk song "Jimmy's Road" are more effective in their starker states.

On the other hand, the peeled-back remixes reveal that Nelson's vocals were sometimes part of the problem. In trying to make himself heard over the wall of sound, he sometimes sang too loudly, too theatrically for his own good.

For Nelson, the RCA era was over. He had made some really good albums and some not-very-good albums, but none of his singles had reached the Top 10. And he felt as if the sound he had perfected on the stages of Texas's honky-tonks had never been captured in the studio. Now he was looking for another chance with another company.

"I never had any doubts about what I was trying to do, my songs or my music," he told *Rolling Stone* in 1978. "I just felt it was good. I had some discouraging moments as far as record labels were concerned, and I thought about droppin' out and quittin' and never doin' it again. In fact, I did quit several times. But it wasn't because I didn't think the music wasn't good. I just thought it was the wrong time for me."

Willie Nelson
***Naked Willie* (RCA/Legacy)**
Recorded: June 1966-November 1970
Remixed: 2008
Released: March 17, 2009
Willie Compositions: 14/17
Top 40 Singles: NA
Album Charts: Country #29, Pop #193

When Nelson's longtime harmonica player Mickey Raphael got permission to go back and "un-produce" the singer's problematic RCA catalog, Raphael removed the strings, backing vocals, horns, and extraneous instruments to reveal Nelson's marvelously subtle singing. Sometimes this works beautifully, especially on the romantic ballads and the blues, gospel, and folk material. But sometimes this reveals Nelson, caught up in the grandiose production, over-singing to make himself felt—and no amount of remixing can change that. Still, this is so much better than the original fiascos. **Grade: B+**

CHAPTER 3

Red Headed Stranger

CONCEPT ALBUMS & STARDOM, 1973–1978

Many of Nelson's best songs are short stories—very short stories, usually less than three minutes and twenty-five lines. But they're narratives with a beginning, middle, and end. In "Hello Walls," the plot begins with a jilted lover alone in his house, talking to the walls. As it develops, he's talking to the window, wondering if the water running down its surface is rain or tears. The narrator is clearly on the edge of sanity. But in the final verse, he pulls himself together and admits to himself that "she'll be gone a long, long time."

A lot of his songs tackle similar themes, overlapping in their effort to answer the same question: How does one cope with busted hopes? Each song made an impact, but what if Nelson stitched them together to tell a longer, fuller story? After all, rock 'n' rollers such as the Beach Boys and The Who were releasing loosely unified albums like *Pet Sounds* and *Tommy*. Nelson's hero Frank Sinatra had done something earlier with *In the Wee Small Hours*, and country artists Marty Robbins and Johnny Cash had done the same with *Gunfighter Ballads and Trail Songs* and *Bitter Tears: Ballads of the American Indian*. Why couldn't Nelson do it, too?

Well, for one reason, Nelson didn't have the commercial track record that the above artists did when they convinced their labels to release their atypical projects. But he was never one to let commercial reality stand in the way of his artistic ambitions. When he showed up at RCA's Nashville studio on May 3, 1971, he brought along his road-band buddies David Zettner, Dave Kirby, and Pete Wade to join the Music Row A-Team on a series of old and new songs that told a story. Producer Felton Jarvis had no choice but to roll the tape on what became *Yesterday's Wine*.

Willie plays a show at the Aragon Ballroom in Chicago on October 28, 1978.

Yesterday's Wine

"I think it's one of my best albums," Nelson writes in his autobiography, "but *Yesterday's Wine* was regarded by RCA as way too spooky and far out to waste promotion money on. . . . I was looked upon as a loser singer. They wouldn't let me record with my own band. They would cover me up with horns and strings. It was depressing. But as some athlete said, 'I hung my head high.'"

He was right to stand proudly. With *Yesterday's Wine*, Nelson proved how effective he could be in stripped-down arrangements, how powerful he could be when an album was unified by a sequence of songs that told a story. This was a different kind of concept album than a collection of hits he wrote for others or of songs about Texas. This was an ambitious song cycle, unified in theme and sound, that was part autobiography and part philosophical reflection. As such, it created the template for such landmark albums to come as *Phases and Stages*, *Red Headed Stranger*, and *Tougher than Leather*.

It begins with the voice of God at the Pearly Gates, asking a new arrival, "You do know why you're here?" Nelson answers in his speaking voice, "Yes, there's great confusion on Earth, and the power that is has concluded the following: Perfect Man has visited Earth already, and his voice was heard. The voice of Imperfect Man must now be made manifest." In other words, Jesus and Buddha were great, but who can relate to flawless Messiahs? We need to hear from someone as screwed up as ourselves. And who's more screwed up than Willie Nelson?

Nelson was already known for his exploration of spiritual issues, both in the Protestant church and in such dubious romantics as Kahlil Gibran and Edgar Cayce. But what makes *Yesterday's Wine* the best of Nelson's RCA albums is not its theology. Rather, it's the way it brings us inside the mind of a man who wants to be good but can't be good and wants to know why. Most of us have felt that way at times, and it's a thrill to have it reflected back to us.

"I was looking at that famous painting *Nighthawks* by Edward Hopper," Nelson writes in his book, *Energy Follows Thought: The Stories Behind My Songs*. "It's 1942. We're gazing into the window of a diner. A man and a woman sit next to each other on stools. A third sits apart. His back is to us. We don't know anything about these people. But we feel

Producer Arif Mardin, guitarist Doug Sahm, Willie, and producer Jerry Wexler gather in the Atlantic Records studios in New York City in February 1973.

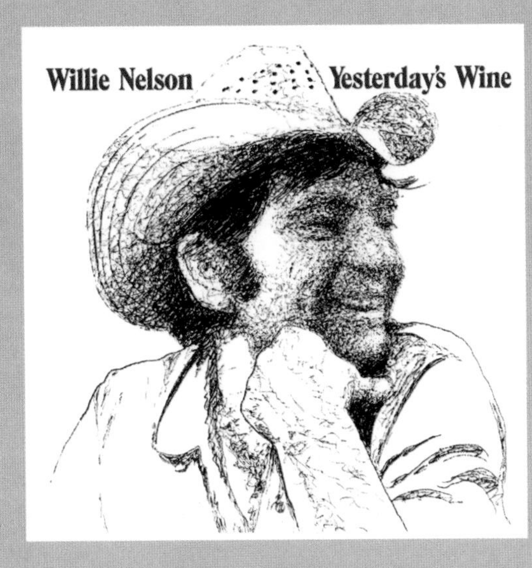

Willie Nelson
Yesterday's Wine **(RCA)**
Recorded: 1971
Released: November 15, 1971
Willie Compositions: 10/10
Top 40 Singles: NA
Album Chart: Country #43

Nelson's first attempt at a concept album was the best of his RCA releases. Side one is a suite of seven songs that has Nelson dying, conversing with God, and returning to Earth to try again. Side two begins with three splendid ballads about crumbling love (Nelson had just divorced his first wife), continues with a bouncy salute to the musician's life ("Me and Paul,") and ends with "Goin' Home," a song about attending his own funeral. The writing is sharp, the arrangements restrained, and the singing intimate. **Grade: A-**

loneliness in the air. We're drawn into a story that isn't being told. So we make up the story. We fill in the blanks. That's what I hope folks do when they hear "Yesterday's Wine." Make the story their own."

It helps that the music is understated and conversational, with the vocals and acoustic instruments out front, as if Nelson were talking with us, not at us. This was a sharp departure from the strings and choirs that made most of his early records so overbearing. It was a window into the future.

After God has sent the album's recently deceased narrator back to Earth, the latter rediscovers his "Family Bible" (Nelson's first national hit, in the form of Claude Gray's 1960 single) and folkloric aphorisms such as "Lend a hand, if you can, to a stranger." God lets him know that "It's Not for You to Understand," but the narrator keeps on trying anyway, attempting to figure out how and why the "difficult times" coexist with the "good times."

That's side one, and in 1971 the act of turning over a vinyl LP was a kind of intermission in the storytelling. On side two, Nelson applies the spiritual conundrums of the first side to his favorite topic: the transience of romance. "A short time is better than no time," he sings on "Summer Roses." But roses are doomed to fade, and you inevitably arrive at love's ending on a "December Day." Yet ex-lovers might meet up "in the strangest of places" and drink up their memories like "Yesterday's Wine," somehow improved with age.

If such love is unstable, friendship can provide a less intense but more consistent connection, as Nelson sings on "Me and Paul," a tribute to his longtime drummer Paul English. On "Goin' Home," the narrator, like Huckleberry Finn, gets the opportunity to attend his own funeral, where friends and family are "crying and talking for hours about how wild that I was."

Yesterday's Wine demonstrates how to make a concept album work. The individual songs have to be self-sufficient enough when they're out of context to satisfy a listener's need for a coherent story with equally strong emotional underpinning from the music. But each song also needs to have a strong enough connection to those around it that it gains something extra from the resonance. The sense that each number is adding narrative and emotional information to the previous one heightens the impact of both songs. That's what this album does again and again.

"They said my ideas, the songs were too deep," he told *Rolling Stone* in 1978. "I don't know what they meant by that. You have to listen to the lyric, I think, to appreciate the song. If you can hear one line of a song and have captured the whole of it and you can hum along for the rest of it, then those are more commercial. But mine usually tell a story."

Nelson thought it was his best album, RCA thought it was his worst, and their relationship never recovered. The label would record and release two more albums (see Chapter Two). But it was too late to save a partnership that had frustrated both parties for so long.

"I knew what I wanted to do; I knew my music better than they did," Nelson told *Scheer Intelligence* in 2017. "I knew my audience better than they did. I was playing to people every night at beer joints all over Texas, Oklahoma, New Mexico, Louisiana—I knew what they liked. And I got tired of trying to convince the people in Nashville, because they did not know at that time what I was doing down there. They was trying to tell me how Nashville does it, and that's cool, but it wasn't what I was doing. So I left Nashville and keep doing what I'm still doing, the same thing. It wasn't Nashville's fault; they have their own way of doing things."

Shotgun Willie

During the week of the Country Music Awards in 1971, Nelson joined a picking party at Harlan Howard's house and at 2 a.m. pulled out the songs for his next, as-yet-unrecorded concept album, *Phases and Stages*. When he finished, according to Nelson's autobiography, a stranger came up and said, "I'm Jerry Wexler. We're starting a country division at Atlantic, and I run it. I'd love to have the album you just sang." Nelson replied, "I have been looking for you for a long time."

Wexler, one of five key figures at Atlantic (along with owners Ahmet and Nesuhi Ertegun and producers Arif Mardin and Tom Dowd), had already produced classic recordings by Ray Charles, the Drifters, Solomon Burke, and Aretha Franklin. Wexler could hear what Nelson shared with those soul legends, despite the superficial differences. He had the same soulfulness in his voice and elasticity in his phrasing as Charles, who would become a recurring collaborator. Wexler and Nelson worked out a contract that compensated for a small advance with great creative freedom.

That freedom paid off on Nelson's first Atlantic album, 1973's *Shotgun Willie*. This wasn't a concept album—it was a "clearing of the throat," as Nelson later put it. It allowed him the autonomy to finally find his own sound—and the sound of the about-to-emerge outlaw country movement. It was country at its core, but it was the country of Texas in the 1950s, when the beat kept dancers on the floor and the steel made them cry. Additional flavors from 1950s Texas—the R&B of Bobby "Blue" Bland, the swing of Bob Wills, the Tex-Mex of Santiago Jiménez, and the blues of T-Bone Walker—were added to the recipe.

Nelson used his regular road band, which had learned how to flow with his idiosyncratic vocal phrasing. At long last, he was allowed to play acoustic guitar as a lead instrument in the studio as he did in his shows. He didn't have a lot of new songs, so he holed up in his hotel to write something.

"I paced from corner to corner," he writes in his autobiography, "listening to the radio waves, the old sensation of need surging through me. Then I went to the bathroom and sat down. I saw a sanitary napkin envelope on the sink. I picked up the envelope and started writing."

Willie Nelson
***Shotgun Willie* (Atlantic)**
Recorded: February 1973
Released: June 11, 1973
Willie Compositions: 7/12
Top 40 Single: "Stay All Night (Stay a Little Longer)" (Country #22)
Album Charts: Country #41, Pop #205

This was the blueprint for Nelson's future live shows, introducing the rhythm section (Paul English, Bee Spears, and Bobbie Nelson) and the traditional opening song ("Whiskey River"). Produced by R&B legends Arif Mardin and Jerry Wexler and featuring guests such as Waylon Jennings, the Memphis Horns, David Bromberg, Doug Sahm, and Donny Hathaway, here was the first sign that Nelson's view of American music was as inclusive and insightful as Ray Charles'. The material included two Bob Wills tunes, two Leon Russell numbers, and seven so-so Nelson originals, all sung with the relaxed swing that pointed the way to the triumphs ahead. **Grade: A-**

The results show up on the album's title track. Nelson's trusty Martin guitar plays an easygoing twelve-bar blues, and he sings, "Shotgun Willie sits around in his underwear, biting on a bullet and pulling out all his hair." The track was not designed to get played on country radio; it was designed to get whoops out of the stoner crowd at the Armadillo in Austin. The title was inspired by the incident when Nelson took a shot at his son-in-law's car after the latter had beaten up Nelson's daughter.

Wexler produced only the two Bob Wills numbers, "Stay All Night (Stay a Little Longer)" and the Cindy Walker–penned "Bubbles in My Beer." Both prominently featured Doug Sahm and his band, also Atlantic artists, and "Stay All Night" became a #22 hit for Nelson. That song and the title track were the only two that remained in Nelson's live set for very long.

Atlantic's Arif Mardin produced the rest with help from J. J. Cale producer David Briggs. Included were two compositions by Nelson's new friend, Leon Russell, a like-minded Oklahoman, and the best of Nelson's seven originals: "Sad Songs and Waltzes," an infectious slow waltz that laments such songs "aren't selling this year." Despite the uneven material, *Shotgun Willie* was the bestselling album of Nelson's career. He was forty, an age when most artists begin selling less and less. As in so many aspects of the music biz, Nelson was contrarian in this, too.

Bob Wills, seen here in 1944, was a founding father of Western swing and a major influence on Willie.

Willie Nelson: The Complete Atlantic Sessions

At least thirty-two songs were recorded during those February 1973 sessions in New York City. A dozen wound up on *Shotgun Willie*. Eleven were released three years later by Columbia as *The Troublemaker*. Another nine came out on two box sets: 1993's *Willie Nelson: A Classic & Unreleased Collection* (see Chapter One) and 2006's *Willie Nelson: The Complete Atlantic Sessions*.

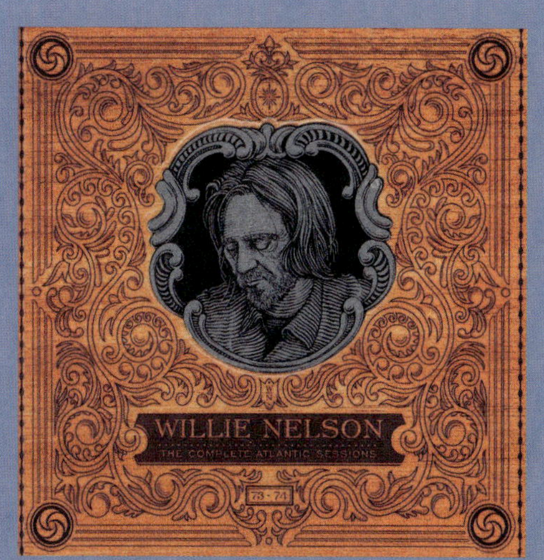

Willie Nelson
Willie Nelson: The Complete Atlantic Sessions
(Atlantic/Rhino)
Recorded: 1973–1974
Released: June 20, 2006
Willie Compositions: 46/61
Top 40 Singles: NA
Album Chart: Pop #80

This three-CD box set contains most of the songs recorded by Nelson during his two-year stay on Atlantic Records. Included are the two released studio albums—*Shotgun Willie* (plus twelve bonus tracks) and *Phases and Stages* (plus ten bonus tracks)—as well as the planned but never released *Live at the Texas Opry House, 1974* album (plus five bonus tracks). Not included are the eleven gospel hymns that were released as *The Troublemaker* on Columbia. Here is Nelson entering his peak period. **Grade: A+**

The Troublemaker

The Troublemaker, a kind of sequel to *Yesterday's Wine*, wasn't a concept album but a collection of traditional gospel hymns transformed by the rollicking, loosey-goosey musicians. It was as if Nelson, in the guise of the Imperfect Man, was demonstrating how these religious songs could be relevant to a sinner like him if you just shook the dust and sobriety off them and allowed them to be as human and spontaneous as they wanted to be. The title track portrayed Jesus as a nonconformist, much like the singer. It was as if Nelson was bridging the sacred and the secular by combining these holy worlds with his honky-tonk rowdiness.

"Uncloudy Day," made famous by the Staple Singers, became a #4 country single. Unfortunately, neither the single nor the album were released in 1973, the year they were recorded. Atlantic had it scheduled as its third Nelson studio album, but the company pulled the plug on its country experiment before that could happen. It's too bad, for this is the first recording to truly showcase Nelson's sister, Bobbie, on piano and his new harmonica player, Mickey Raphael, both of whom became pillars of the singer's sound well into the twenty-first century.

Willie Nelson
***The Troublemaker* (Columbia)**
Recorded: February 1973
Released: September 20, 1976
Willie Compositions: 0/11
Top 40 Single: "Uncloudy Day" (Country #4)
Album Charts: Country #1, Pop #60

During the same 1973 sessions that yielded *Shotgun Willie*, Nelson also cut eleven hymns for a gospel album that Atlantic never released. After the multiplatinum success of *Red Headed Stranger*, Columbia was all too happy to release those songs and was rewarded with a #1 country album. The mostly traditional material had been staples of Southern Protestant churches for decades, but Nelson and his unruly honky-tonk band (Doug Sahm, Jimmy Day, Sammi Smith, Mickey Raphael, and Bobbie Nelson) gave the material an enthusiastic, raucous treatment. The CD reissue adds live versions of four of these songs as bonus tracks. **Grade: A-**

Phases and Stages/Live at the Texas Opry House, 1974

Instead of releasing *The Troublemaker*, Atlantic put out *Phases and Stages*, the song cycle that first convinced Wexler to sign Nelson. Wexler decided to produce the album himself in Muscle Shoals Sound Studio in Sheffield, Alabama, using the studio's house band. This was the studio and band that had cut legendary records by Aretha Franklin, Mavis Staples, Wilson Pickett, and Leon Russell. Nelson was so unhappy about the decision that he re-recorded the album with his own band in Nashville. He and Wexler fought over the two versions, and Wexler won.

Maybe Wexler had a point. The Swampers, as the Muscle Shoals rhythm section of keyboardist Barry Beckett, bassist David Hood, and drummer Roger Hawkins became known, played with such economy and feeling that they gave Nelson's vocals more room and more sympathy than any band on any record

Nelson had made up to this point. With Bob Wills' fiddler Johnny Gimble and Conway Twitty's steel guitarist John Hughey adding country flourishes, it was the best-sounding Nelson record so far. These guys, accustomed to the improvisational phrasing of church-schooled soul singers, had no trouble following Nelson's unconventional singing.

Phases and Stages offered the strongest concept of all of Nelson's concept albums: a look at a divorce, with side one devoted to six songs (squeezed into five tracks) from the wife's point of view, and side two devoted to six from the husband's perspective. A thirteenth number, the brief "Phases and Stages (Theme)," was inserted five times to reinforce the continuity.

By the time he wrote these songs about divorce, Nelson had done a lot of research on the topic. He wrote them in the wake of his second divorce, from Shirley Collie Nelson, in 1971, so he could marry his third wife, Connie Koepke. He had divorced his first wife, Martha Matthews Nelson, in 1971, after nearly ten years of marriage, to marry Collie.

"I was going through a tough period when I wrote a lot of those songs, some traumatic experiences," Nelson told *Rolling Stone* in 1978. "I was going through a divorce, split-up, kids involved and everything. Fortunately now I don't have those problems. But I went through those thirty negative years, wallowing in all kinds of misery and self-pity and guilt and all that shit. But out of it came the knowledge that everybody wallows in the same old shit—guilt and self-pity—and I just happened to write about it. There's no way to write a sad song unless you had really been sad."

But he claimed that the album wasn't autobiographical. He was a real writer, he insisted, and could imagine the experiences of characters other than himself. "I'm not writing about myself or any

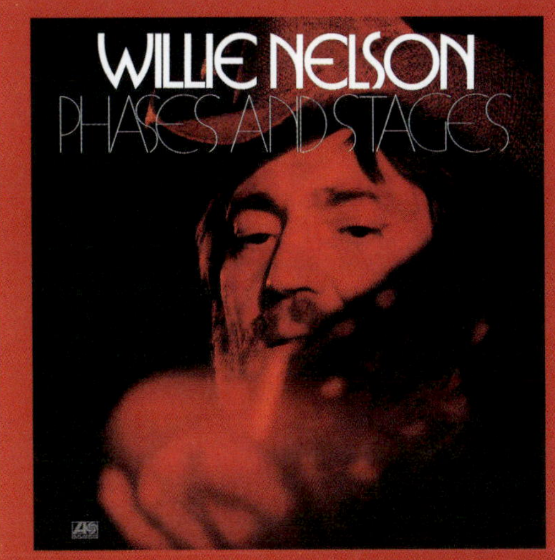

Willie Nelson
***Phases and Stages* (Atlantic)**
Recorded: October 1973
Released: February 25, 1974
Willie Compositions: 13/13
Top 40 Single: "Bloody Mary Morning" (Country #17)
Album Charts: Country #34, Pop #187

Produced by Jerry Wexler, this song cycle tells the story of a troubled marriage, beginning with six songs from the wife's perspective and ending with six from the husband's, all connected by a brief, repeating theme. In retrospect, it is even stronger than the subsequent *Red Headed Stranger*, for it contains Nelson's finest writing about country music's most ubiquitous theme: marriage. Songs such as "Pick Up the Tempo," "Bloody Mary Morning," and "It's Not Supposed to Be That Way" have become standards because they capture the sound of spouses under stress with such unerring accuracy. **Grade: A+**

relationship of my own," he wrote in *Energy Follows Thought*. "I take on the perspective of a woman I know only in my imagination and the voice of a man who's the composite of a million men I've met."

It's not surprising that Nelson does a good job of telling the man's half of the story on side two of *Phases and Stages*. What's surprising is how well he tells the woman's half. After a brief bit of the title theme, he begins the album with "Washing Dishes," the portrait of a wife wondering why she's still scrubbing floors and washing shirts for someone who doesn't even bother to hide the lipstick stains on the collars. The tone of the song, though, is more sad than mad, a slow waltz with a forlorn fiddle.

Bobbie Nelson in the Atlantic Records studios in New York City in February 1973.

Willie performs on *The Midnight Special* TV show on August 2, 1974.

That song ends with the line, "Someday she'll just walk away," and after a brief return of the theme, the next song is a more decisive waltz that declares, "Walkin' is better than runnin' away, and crawlin' ain't no good at all." Two songs later, on "Sister's Coming Home," the title character moves back in with her mother and before too long is "Down at the Corner Beer Joint," wearing her tightest jeans and managing her own recovery program. The jaunty optimism of the two-step music indicates she'll soon be loving someone else.

After the listener has flipped over the LP, a rambunctious banjo lick kicks off the man's point of view on the album's hit single, "Bloody Mary Morning." The up-tempo shuffle creates the sound of forward motion, even as Nelson sings of flying from Los Angeles to Houston to leave behind the memory of the woman who left him the night before. He originally recorded the song for RCA in 1970, but that stiff version pales next to the lubricated propulsion of this one. Moreover, the track proves the worth of the concept album, for the song takes on added meaning this time without changing a single word.

The next song flashes back to the night before when he found her farewell note claiming she no longer loved him. Over a swaggering blues, he insists there had been "No Love Around" for a long time—but the more he insists, the less convincing he becomes. That becomes clear on the next two aching ballads, "I Still Can't Believe You're Gone" and "It's Not Supposed to Be That Way." By the end of the album, though, he's asking the band to "Pick Up the Tempo" and carry him into the next phase or stage of his life.

Maybe he matched it a few times, but Nelson never made a better album than *Phases and Stages*. It had the tightest narrative of all his concept albums. It had great songs ("Pretend I Never Happened" was a #6 country hit for Waylon Jennings; "Pick Up the Tempo" was recorded by Jerry Jeff Walker and "Sister's Coming Home" by Emmylou Harris), great playing, great singing, and great sound. This should have been the record that made Nelson a star, but Atlantic didn't know how to work with country radio, so the singles never had much chance. Not enough people heard the music.

Wexler recorded Nelson with his own band at the Texas Opry House in Austin on June 29–30, 1974, for a planned live album on Atlantic. It was never released until 1995 on *A Classic & Unreleased Collection* (see Chapter One), then with six additional songs in 2006 on *Willie Nelson: The Complete Atlantic Sessions*, and finally as a stand-alone album, *Live at the Texas Opry House, 1974* in 2022. It's an invaluable snapshot of an ensemble that was fast

Willie Nelson
Live at the Texas Opry House, 1974 **(Rhino)**
Recorded: June 29–30, 1974
Released: April 23, 2022
Willie Compositions: 9/19
Top 40 Singles: NA
Album Charts: NA

The terrific live album of Nelson and his 1974 band (the Nelson siblings, Jimmy Day, Johnny Gimble, Mickey Raphael, Paul English, and Bee Spears) that Atlantic taped but never released, eventually emerged in the 2006 box set, *The Complete Atlantic Sessions*, and then as this 2022 stand-alone album. **Grade: A**

becoming one of the greatest live bands in country music history. They had found their sound and lineup during the sessions for *Shotgun Willie*, and they performed four songs from that album. They also did three from *Phases and Stages*, giving a hint of what their abandoned Nashville version of that album might have sounded like.

Red Headed Stranger

"I was getting up in years," he told *Hustler* in 1978. "When you hit 40, for a picker, it's getting pretty close. If you haven't made it by then, a lot of people are gonna start saying you're over the hill and you're not gonna do it. I already had a lot of success as a songwriter, so I could've laid down, but I guess I was just too stubborn. I wanted to pick and sing, and I wanted to be known as a good picker and a good singer. I wasn't satisfied just being a songwriter."

Nelson had reason to despair about record labels. RCA had frustrated his desires at every turn. His relationship with Monument fell apart after one single. First Liberty—and later Atlantic—had shut down their country music divisions just as he was gaining some momentum. When he turned in his first album to his next label, Columbia Records, the company's reaction was not encouraging.

They weren't happy that it was yet another Willie Nelson concept album, an approach with a lousy commercial track record so far. They weren't happy that the tunes resembled anachronistic cowboy songs, with tales of horse thieving, Montana shootouts, and Denver barrooms. They weren't happy that the sound was so stripped down that it resembled a home demo more than a studio master. They weren't happy that it didn't really showcase Nelson's songwriting. They weren't happy that you could hear buzzing strings and squeaky drum pedals. But Nelson was adamant: It wasn't a demo—it was the album. Columbia decided to teach him a lesson by releasing it as it was.

Willie opens his July 4th Picnic at the Texas World Speedway in College Station, Texas, in 1974.

Nelson had conceived the album on a drive from Steamboat Springs, Colorado, to Austin, Texas, in January 1975. His wife, Connie, had reminded him of an old cowboy song, "Red Headed Stranger," that he used to sing to kids. Why not flesh it out into a fuller story with some new songs and some borrowed songs? By the time they reached Austin, he mostly had it.

This was the story: A blue-eyed, red-haired Montana preacher is suspicious that his wife is being unfaithful and is devastated when he learns that it's true. Riding a black stallion into Blue Rock, he finds the happy couple in a tavern and leaves them still smiling as he shoots them dead. Filled with remorse, the preacher's soon crying in the rain.

He rides away with his late wife's bay pony trailing behind him. When a blonde in a brothel begins to stroke the pony, the preacher shoots her on the spot. The man and his two horses drift down the Rockies, and he meets another woman in another tavern, in Denver. This time it's true love, and the preacher is finally able to let the memory of his dead wife go and sleep in the arms of someone new.

Like most concept albums, this one lacks the careful plotting of a stage musical. Instead, it drops some helpful hints and allows listeners to fill in the gaps. But there's enough continuity for each song to resonate with those around it and thus provide an extra measure of pleasure. Nelson wrote only three of the nine vocal numbers on the album (he also wrote one of the three instrumentals, and his "Time of the Preacher" is inserted three times, much like the theme for *Phases and Stages*).

Armed with this song list, Nelson took the band into Autumn Sound Studio outside of Dallas. At first they played as boisterously as they had on *Shotgun Willie*, but Nelson stopped them. He had something else in mind. "This is more of a solitude-sounding thing," he told them, according to his biographer, Joe Nick Patoski. "I tell you what: Put your instruments down and let me play it solo. Just play along only if you feel like you can add something to it."

As a result, *Red Headed Stranger* was the leanest, starkest recording of Nelson's career. It didn't make sense to the suits in Nashville, but it made perfect sense to a rock 'n' roll audience that was used to artists such as Bob Dylan and Joni Mitchell going from quiet, acoustic guitars to noisy, full bands and back again. By 1975, the Eagles, Byrds, and Linda Ronstadt had converted enough listeners to country-rock that audiences were prepared to accept the adventurous edge of country music itself. Nelson was just what they were looking for. Texas audiences already knew that, and the other forty-nine states were about to find out.

The stone that got the avalanche going was the first single, "Blue Eyes Crying in the Rain," a 1947 hit for Roy Acuff. Written by Hank Williams' producer Fred Rose, it married country emotion to swing elegance, a fusion right up Nelson's alley. He sang it beautifully, and when listeners went looking for the album it came from, they found a collection that sounded like nothing on contemporary country radio. It sounded so folkloric, so old-fashioned that it seemed radically new.

"Blue Eyes" was Nelson's first #1 country hit, and the second single, a remake of Lulu Belle and Scotty's 1948 hit, "Remember Me (When the Candle

Willie Nelson
***Red Headed Stranger* (Columbia)**
Recorded: February 1975
Released: May 26, 1975
Willie Compositions: 4/12
Top 40 Singles: "Blue Eyes Crying in the Rain" (Country #1/Pop #21), "Remember Me (When the Candle Lights Are Gleaming)" (Country #2)
Album Charts: Country #1, Pop #28

This is the first album Nelson produced himself with his own band, and the stripped-down arrangements yielded a #1 country album and two hit singles. Today the album seems marred by its undernourished arrangements, the misogyny of the title track, and the poor fit of some of the country standards within the overarching concept. Nonetheless, the decluttered arrangements allow the glorious singing to shine through, and the record bursts with the enthusiasm of a new era dawning. The 2000 CD reissue added four bonus tracks. **Grade: A-**

Lights Are Gleaming)," went to #2. Other key songs included Jeannie Seeley's 1973 hit "Can I Sleep in Your Arms" (written by her then-husband Hank Cochran) and "Hands on the Wheel," by young Texas songwriter Bill Callery. It wasn't Nelson's songwriting that was creating the breakthrough. It was his singing—the very thing that Nashville had thought problematic all along.

Perhaps the minimalist production had forced listeners to focus on that voice and all the overtones and displaced accents it contained and to marvel at its expressiveness. *Yesterday's Wine* and *Phases and Stages* may have been better albums, for they combined the splendor of that voice with the drama of his writing. And there were problems with *Red Headed Stranger*: The arrangements do seem undernourished, the old country standards don't always fit the storyline, and the lyrics' casual treatment of violence against women is discomfiting. But it was the right record at the right time to grab an enormous audience that no one had recognized before.

The album changed not only Nelson's career but country music itself. For a genre that had always considered a gold record (five hundred thousand copies sold) a huge hit, the platinum record (one million copies sold) for *Red Headed Stranger* raised everyone's expectations. Then it went double-platinum. Meanwhile, another album, *Wanted! The Outlaws*, featuring Nelson, Waylon Jennings, Jessi Colter, and Tompall Glaser, went double platinum as well.

Willie promotes his *Red Headed Stranger* album at Peaches Records in Atlanta on October 28, 1975.

Wanted! The Outlaws

This was RCA's way of making up for its missed opportunity with Nelson. The label had never known what to do with this eccentric artist, and now that Columbia, against its own better judgment, had stumbled into double-platinum success with him, RCA wanted some of the action.

Jerry Bradley, the son of legendary producer Owen Bradley and Chet Atkins' successor as head of RCA, had an idea. Hazel Smith, office manager at the Glaser Brothers' studio near Music Row, a hangout nicknamed Hillbilly Central, had come up with a label for Jennings and Glaser: They were the "outlaws" of country music. It struck a chord, and Jerry Bradley had his art department draw up an Old West wanted poster, with the faces of Nelson, Jennings, Colter, and Glaser plastered on what looked like sepia parchment nailed to a tree. Printed across the top were the words: "Wanted! The Outlaws—Reward."

Now all he needed was the music to justify the cover. Jennings and Glaser were still signed to RCA, which still owned the rights to all the songs Nelson had recorded for them. Colter was signed to Capitol, but she was Jennings' wife—and Bradley was sure something could be worked out. He pulled two songs from the much-neglected *Yesterday's Wine* (the title track and "Me and Paul"); got two previously unreleased songs apiece from Jennings, Colter, and Glaser; and paid for Nelson to overdub a new vocal onto Jennings' unreleased live version of "Good Hearted Woman." A few more recycled tracks were added and, *voilà*, a new album.

Despite its cobbled-together mix of old and new music, it sold like gangbusters. A new movement was stirring within country music; Smith gave it a name, and Bradley gave it an image. Suddenly "outlaw country" was a phrase everyone knew and many embraced. It gave audiences a vehicle for vicarious rebellion, it gave artists an excuse for doing things their way, and it gave the labels a new source of cash. Everyone was happy.

"We thought it was the best thing that happened to us," Nelson told *Country Music: An Illustrated History*." 'Hey, they're calling us outlaws.' Everybody who's in the creative business has to have a little outlaw in them. I think there's a lot of people in the audience who have a little outlaw in them, too. So, they were willing to forgive us, as long as the music was good."

The Sound in Your Mind

Columbia was just as eager to cash in on Nelson's newfound celebrity. The label obtained the rights to *The Troublemaker*, the unreleased gospel album he had recorded for Atlantic, and released it in 1976. They also rushed out a new album, *The Sound in Your Mind*, that contained only two new songs written by

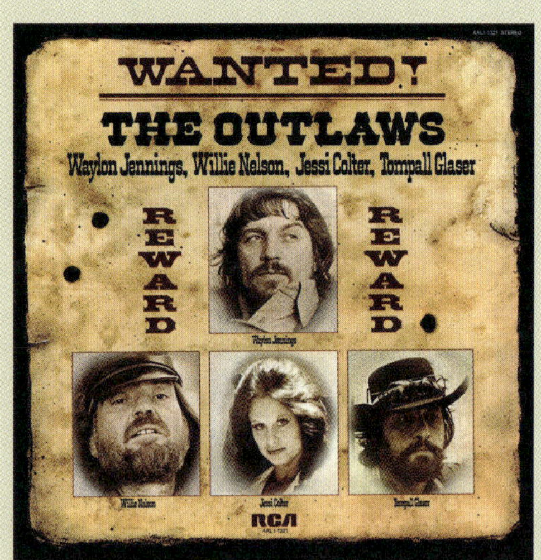

Willie Nelson, Waylon Jennings, Tompall Glaser, and Jessi Colter
***Wanted! The Outlaws* (RCA)**
Recorded: 1970–1975
Released: January 12, 1976
Willie Compositions: 4/11
Top 40 Singles: "Good Hearted Woman" (Country #1, Pop #25), "Suspicious Minds" (Country #2)
Album Charts: Country #1, Pop #10

After its old artist Nelson went to #1 for Columbia, RCA realized that maybe he and his scruffy friends such as Jennings, Glaser, Colter, Billy Joe Shaver, and Kris Kristofferson were on to something after all. It was a movement without a name till RCA scrounged up seven previously released tracks and four unreleased ones and slapped them together under Hazel Smith's label for the performers: The Outlaws. The name and the music struck a chord with the public, and this unlikely compilation became the first-ever country album to be certified by the RIAA as a million seller. The hit singles were both Jennings duets: with Nelson on "Good Hearted Woman" and with Colter on "Suspicious Minds." When it was reissued on CD in 1996, nine more old tracks were added plus a version of Steve Earle's "Nowhere Road" sung by Nelson and Jennings. **Grade: B+**

Willie Nelson
***The Sound in Your Mind* (Columbia)**
Recorded: December 1975
Released: March 1, 1976
Willie Compositions: 6/11
Top 40 Singles: "I'd Have to Be Crazy" (Country #11), "If You've Got the Money I've Got the Time" (Country #1)
Album Charts: Country #1, Pop #48

In response to RCA's hodgepodge of material on *Wanted! The Outlaws*, Nelson recorded eleven disconnected songs with his band for this album, including a new version of "The Healing Hands of Time" that trumped the older version on *Wanted! The Outlaws*. Only two new Nelson songs were included—both of them fine examples of his romantic-post-mortem ballads—and the nods to Louis Armstrong and Lefty Frizzell are fine. Despite some jarring electronic effects and mood shifts, the singing and playing are splendid. **Grade: B**

Nelson himself: the title track and "Thanks Again." Also included were "Healing Hands of Time" (originally done for the first RCA album and recycled on *Wanted! The Outlaws*) and a studio version of the live-show medley of "Funny How Time Slips Away/ Crazy/Night Life." To flesh out the new album, "Amazing Grace," Stephen Fromholz's "I'd Have to Be Crazy," plus three vintage songs were added.

Though the eleven songs (squeezed into nine tracks) were recorded with Nelson's road band in one go at Autumn Sound, the album had the same grab-bag feel as *Wanted! The Outlaws*. There was little continuity in theme or sound from song to song, and annoying electronic effects on Jody Payne's guitar and Fromholz's vocal mar several songs. On the other hand, Nelson is singing with more confidence than ever, and it's a coming-out party for Mickey Raphael, Bobbie Nelson, and Trigger (Willie Nelson's acoustic guitar) as three of country's best instrumentalists. Just listen to the way Raphael's harmonica shadows the lead vocal on the Frank Sinatra/Louis Armstrong number, "That Lucky Old Sun," and the way sister Bobbie's piano fuels the romp through Lefty Frizzell's "If You've Got the Money."

Willie relaxes in Luckenbach, Texas, in 1976.

To Lefty From Willie

Willie Nelson
***To Lefty from Willie* (Columbia)**
Recorded: February 1977
Released: June 13, 1977
Willie Compositions: 0/10
Top 40 Single: "I Love You a Thousand Ways" (Country #1)
Album Charts: Country #2, Pop #91

Lefty Frizzell had his biggest hits when Nelson was an impressionable teenager, and the latter pays tribute to the former with this glowing album of ten songs recorded by Frizzell (seven of them written or co-written by him). These are classic country songs, and Nelson and his road band don't gussy them up but present them with great clarity. If anything, the performances are a bit too respectful and understated. **Grade: B**

Lefty Frizzell had died July 19, 1975, and Nelson decided to spend his newfound commercial capital on a different kind of concept album: *To Lefty from Willie*, an album devoted to ten of his favorite Frizzell songs (seven written or co-written by Frizzell), from the latter's first single in 1950 to his penultimate album in 1973. Yes, Frizzell was the first to record songs such as "That's the Way Love Goes" (a hit for Merle Haggard and Johnny Rodriguez), "I Love You a Thousand Ways" (John Anderson), "Always Late with Your Kisses" (Dwight Yoakam), and "I Never Go Around Mirrors" (Keith Whitley). And, yes, Frizzell recorded "Railroad Lady" by Jerry Jeff Walker and Jimmy Buffett near the end of his life.

Nelson recorded all these songs, for he was immensely influenced by his fellow Texan, borrowing not only Frizzell's resonant tone and elastic phrasing but also his ability to write realistic mini-dramas about troubled marriages. As a result, *To Lefty from Willie* is more than just an act of gratitude; it's a revelation of sources. On the other hand, it's often a bit too reverential, too polite—too much like Lefty Frizzell and not enough like Willie Nelson.

Accepting gold records for *Wanted! The Outlaws* in 1976 are (from left) Tompall Glaser, Waylon Jennings, Jessi Colter, Kenneth Glancy, Jerry Bradley, Willie, and Chet Atkins.

Waylon & Willie

Thanks in large part to the blockbuster success of *Wanted! The Outlaws*, the phrase "Waylon & Willie" became as universal and as indivisible as "Abbott & Costello" or "Butch Cassidy & the Sundance Kid." Jennings and Nelson really were good friends and songwriting partners offstage, but onstage they had become the personification of the outlaw country mythology, two larger-than-life characters unbound by rules and having the time of their lives.

The myth was a gratuitous combination of image and music. The two men seemed to have the whole spectrum of mid-'70s social rebellion covered, with the black-clad Jennings swaggering around like a Phoenix biker, and the bandana-wearing Nelson smiling beatifically like an Austin stoner. Just as important was the musical contrast, with Jennings' growling baritone offset by Nelson's crooning tenor. Like all good showbiz, the divergence was as crucial as the similarity—and it helped that real talent lay below.

The best way to keep that myth alive was to release vocal duets that became hit singles, and the music industry was eager to oblige. There was a problem, though. Jennings was signed to RCA and Nelson to Columbia, and each label wanted to keep their prize artist to itself. On the other hand, Neil Reshen was the manager for both men, and he convinced both the labels and the artists that everyone would make bushels of money if they bent the rules and made the duets happen. He was right.

The first proof of concept was the overdubbed live version of "Good Hearted Woman" from *Wanted! The Outlaws*, which won a CMA Award for Best Country Single of 1976. A confirmation of the formula came on Jennings' 1977 *Ol' Waylon* album, which led off with the Jennings-Nelson duet on " Luckenbach, Texas (Back to the Basics of Love)," which went to #1, stayed there for six weeks, and became Jennings' bestselling single ever. A new record credited to both of them seemed preordained.

Waylon & Willie was the inevitable title for the inevitable album. There were only five actual duets; each man contributed three solo numbers to flesh out the track list. But the first single, "Mamas Don't Let Your Babies Grow Up to Be Cowboys" by Ed Bruce and Patsy Bruce, ingeniously used reverse psychology to become the anthem for the outlaw country movement. The more Jennings and Nelson warn mothers about cowboys who waste their lives on Lone Star beer, loose women, battered guitars, and broken-down trucks, the more enviable they make the lifestyle seem. It was a massive hit.

Downtown Luckenbach, Texas.

Willie Nelson and Waylon Jennings
***Waylon & Willie* (RCA)**
Recorded: November 1977
Released: January 9, 1978
Willie Compositions: 3/11
Top 40 Singles: "Mamas Don't Let Your Babies Grow Up to Be Cowboys" (Country #1), "I Can Get Off on You" (Country #1), "The Wurlitzer Prize" (#1), "If You Can Touch Her at All" (Country #5)
Album Charts: Country #1, Pop #12

Presented as a duo album, this record included only five actual duets. The record was fleshed out by three vocals by Nelson alone and another three by Jennings alone. Despite its misleading marketing and its thrown-together nature, this is actually a terrific listen. The results included three #1 singles, including the outlaw country duet anthem "Mamas Don't Let Your Babies Grow Up to Be Cowboys,"), the tongue-in-cheek anti-drug duet "I Can Get Off on You," and Jennings' solo ode to a jukebox, "The Wurlitzer Prize," plus another Top 10 hit, Nelson's incandescent solo version of Lee Clayton's "If You Can Touch Her at All." Additional treats included two more duets on Kris Kristofferson compositions and Jennings' electric-piano-framed version of Stevie Nicks' "Gold Dust Woman." **Grade: A-**

Willie plays dominoes against the residents of Luckenbach, Texas, in 1977.

The two men used a similar strategy on the co-written and co-sung "I Can Get Off on You," which had the singers promising their women that they were giving up cocaine, pot, and alcohol because they got a natural high from love. The more they promised, the more inebriated they sounded. The other three duets included a lively version of "Pick Up the Tempo" from *Phases and Stages* plus two Kris Kristofferson compositions.

Jennings' solo numbers included another *Phases and Stages* song, "It's Not Supposed to Be That Way," and "The Wurlitzer Prize," a lament about a broken-hearted man feeding coins into a voracious jukebox. Nelson's solo efforts included one of his greatest vocals on Lee Clayton's "If You Can Touch Her at All," an awestruck description of the no-man's-land between sex and love. Somehow Nelson maintains a mood of bewildered wonder without ever losing hold of the lovely melody or lapsing into mere leering.

Waylon & Willie is often underrated because of its transparently commercial motivation and its shoving together material from three different sources. It's counterintuitive, but it's true: Commercial greed can sometimes inspire great art as effectively as it subverts it. In this case, box-office demand created a body of music that's actually a much better listen than *Wanted! The Outlaws*, *Ol' Waylon*, and *The Sound in Your Mind*.

Stardust

Like many singer-songwriters, Nelson found his writing declining in both quantity and quality as he became more successful. This isn't surprising, for fame reduces both the motivation and the free time needed for creative work. With stardom comes more demands on your time—live appearances, TV appearances, interviews, business meetings, and all the travel from one to the other. With stardom also comes less incentive to wrack your brain for the idea that might make you break through to a larger audience.

Unlike most singer-songwriters, Nelson had an alternate career path available. Not only could he excel as a performing songwriter such as Merle Haggard or Paul Simon, but he could also excel as an interpretive singer such as Elvis Presley or Aretha Franklin. Every performing songwriter covers outside material occasionally, and every interpretive singer writes an original now and then. But it's hard to think of anyone who has assumed both roles as equally and as successfully—both artistically and commercially—as Nelson has.

The hyphen in the label "singer-songwriter" may well be the most overrated punctuation mark in modern culture. After all, the two halves of that combo

are two very different activities that require very different kinds of thinking. Songwriting is all about "slow thinking," of standing back from the moment, of searching the mind for just the right phrase—musical or verbal—jotting it down and then reconsidering it to see how it might be improved. By contrast, singing (or playing an instrument) is all about "fast thinking," of being in the moment, acting instinctively in real time, to keep up with the flow of the music.

And interpretive singing makes different demands than singing one's own material. Instead of playing yourself, you have to play someone else. And to play someone else, you have to find some connection between that character and your own experiences. And to make your version of someone else's song different enough to justify a second (or tenth) version, one has to bring something new to the song without abandoning what made the song appealing in the first place.

Nelson had that rare combination of skills. At the beginning of 1977, though, that wasn't obvious to many people. From the time Faron Young topped the charts with "Hello Walls," people understood Nelson's songwriting ability. And with *Phases and Stages* and *Red Headed Stranger*, observers finally grasped that Nelson's unconventional vocal style on his own songs was a virtue, not a flaw. But except for the few people who had bought 1966's *Country Favorites* or 1967's *Make Way for Willie Nelson* and those who had paid close attention to his recent remakes of gospel and old country numbers, Nelson's interpretive genius wasn't apparent. It was about to become unmistakable.

Willie Nelson
Stardust **(Columbia)**
Recorded: December 1977
Released: April 17, 1978
Willie Compositions: 0/10
Top 40 Singles: "Georgia on My Mind" (Country #1), "Blue Skies" (Country #1), "All of Me" (Country #3), "September Song" (Country #15)
Album Charts: Country #1, Pop #30

It wasn't the novelty of a country star singing the songs of Hoagy Carmichael, Duke Ellington, and Irving Berlin that made this album a platinum triumph. It was the inspired freshness of Nelson's approach to these American Songbook standards. In contrast to the theatrical earnestness of the pop-jazz singers who usually tackled this stuff, Nelson provided a totally natural but utterly unpredictable phrasing as well as a disarming, glowing tone. He sounded not as if he were singing about a bygone musical era but about a particular woman shining with stardust. The CD reissue included a second disc of ten songs in the same vein from Nelson's subsequent albums. **Grade: A+**

In the two and a half years since *Red Headed Stranger* catapulted him to stardom, Nelson had been busy with touring and duets with Jennings. He hadn't been writing much, so now was the time to pursue another dream, a different kind of concept album: a transformation of the American Songbook. His recent albums *Red Headed Stranger*, *Wanted! The Outlaws*, and *Waylon & Willie* had all landed in the Top 30 on the Billboard pop charts, so there was pressure for Nelson to cross over to pop music.

He crossed over so far that he flew over contemporary rock 'n' roll and landed half a century earlier in 1928 when Don Redman recorded the first version of Hoagy Carmichael's "Stardust," the song that became the title of Nelson's next album. *Stardust* was a collection of American Songbook numbers, those sophisticated show tunes and Tin Pan Alley numbers by Carmichael, Irving Berlin, George Gershwin, and others from the mid-twentieth century that jazz musicians have been singing and playing ever since. These tunes had been as much a presence on the radios and nightclubs of Nelson's youth as the honky-tonk songs of Ernest Tubb, Bob Wills, and Floyd Tillman.

"When you played a club in Texas back then," Nelson told the *New York Times*, "you had to do 'San Antonio Rose' and you had to do 'Stardust,' because those people didn't know what was country and what wasn't. They still don't; they haven't been educated that music is separated. They still think it's all music. Back then you just took requests, and if you knew the song, you played it."

Lefty Frizzell was the subject of Willie's first tribute album, *To Lefty from Willie*, in 1977.

On the *Stardust* album, however, Nelson plays these well-worn songs as no one had ever played them before. Johnny Gimble's instrument sounds more like a fiddle than a violin; Booker T. Jones's instrument sounds more like a church organ than a jazz piano; Mickey Raphael's instrument sounds more like a juke joint harmonica than muted trumpet, and Nelson's own two instruments sound more like a campfire guitar than big-band archtop, more like an East Texas drawl than a Manhattan croon.

Jones, the former leader of the brilliant soul music instrumental quartet Booker T. & the MGs was the producer. He crafted arrangements that were as minimalist as those for *Red Headed Stranger* without sounding as threadbare. As Otis Redding's longtime organist, he knew how make a harmony sound full without becoming obtrusive—and he made sure the strings and reeds were just as tastefully restrained. As a result, these well-known songs for the first time sounded conversational rather than declamatory, but if you listened carefully, you heard behind Nelson's redolent vocal shimmers of organ, fiddles, and horns.

The breakthrough song was Carmichael's "Georgia on My Mind." Never has Nelson's seemingly reluctant delivery served him better. It's as if he's hesitant to admit to how much he misses the South now that's gone North, and Jones's elegiac organ reinforces the notion that something invaluable has been left behind. Raphael's harmonica solo is suffused with longing, and Nelson sings of the roads that lead back home with a yearning any homesick listener will recognize. When the horns finally emerge at the very end, the repeating riff seems to fade like a landscape in the rearview mirror.

Willie and Waylon Jennings in New York City on February 5, 1978

Willie performs songs from *Red Headed Stranger* with the Family in 1975.

Willie and Family Live

In many ways, the success of *Stardust* (three Top 3 country singles) was even more surprising than that of *Red Headed Stranger*. The latter fit into an already established appetite for country-folk-rock, but there was no evident clamoring for country-jazz versions of fifty-year-old songs. It was as if Nelson had convinced his large audience to follow him wherever he wanted to go. His road show played larger and larger venues with shows that ranged across the broad spectrum of Nelson's recordings. His road band, ever more skilled and more attuned to its impulsive leader, now added a second drummer, Rex Ludwig, to join Paul English.

This was the octet that recorded *Willie and Family Live* at Harrah's in Lake Tahoe, Nevada. Drawing songs from the Pamper demos through the RCA purgatory and the Atlantic salvation, from the concept albums and Jennings collaborations to the yet-to-be-released tributes to Kris Kristofferson and Leon Russell, the singer and his mates shift gears smoothly and give each song a different treatment while always sounding like the same band. Raphael, Payne, and the Nelson siblings all play terrific solos that they probably never played before and likely never played again.

Studio albums have the virtues of sound control and second guessing that live albums lack, but live albums can catch the spark of playing in the moment as bandmates and audience egg each player on. Neither studio albums nor live albums alone can provide a complete picture of an artist's work, and that's why *Willie and Family Live* is such an invaluable document.

Willie and Family Live was released a dozen days before Nelson's forty-fifth birthday, and he was at the height of his box-office power. He had climbed the mountain, but he knew he hadn't climbed it alone. Rather than reinvesting his newfound commercial clout in his own career, he used a big slice of it to repay debts to those who had inspired him and/or helped him along the way. He invested another big chunk into risky artistic gambles: movies, neglected repertoire, songwriter tributes. As usual, Nelson wouldn't follow the expected career path of a country or pop star; he would go his own way.

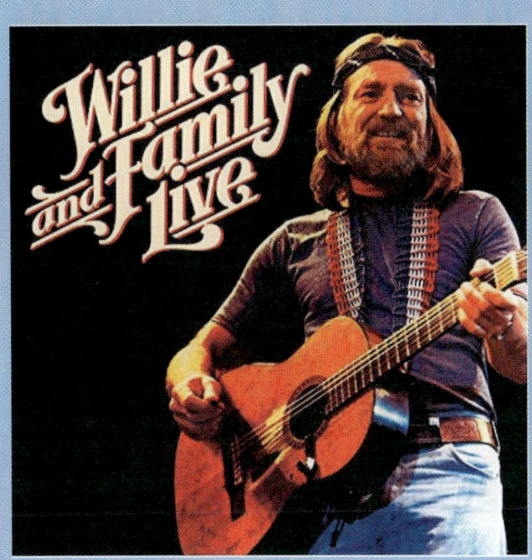

Willie Nelson
Willie and Family Live **(Columbia)**
Recorded: April 17, 1978
Released: November 1978
Willie Compositions: 12/32
Top 40 Single: "Whiskey River" (Country #12)
Album Charts: Country #1, Pop #32

Willie Nelson and Family was one of the greatest live bands in the history of American music, especially in the late '70s and early '80s, when they were at the peak of their powers. That's well documented in this concert taped at Harrah's in Lake Tahoe, Nevada. No matter what corner of his many-roomed career the singer decides to visit, his seven backing musicians are right there with him, as aggressive or as restrained, as tasteful or as inventive as required. Emmylou Harris and Johnny Paycheck add guest vocals. Originally released as thirty-four songs on two vinyl albums, it was later reissued as thirty-six songs on two CDs. **Grade: A**

Willie and Waylon perform at the Omni Coliseum in Atlanta on March 2, 1978.

CHAPTER 4

Old Friends

TRIBUTES, DUETS & SOUNDTRACKS, 1979–1982

Willie Nelson puts out albums as often as many men get haircuts.

Between 1976 and 1991, Bruce Springsteen released six albums, and the Rolling Stones seven. During those same sixteen years, Willie Nelson released thirty-eight. In the five years of 1979–83, he released seventeen new studio albums, which included two soundtracks, two American Songbook albums, a Christmas album, a gospel album, a tribute album, a contemporary pop album, one album of new songs, and eight collaborations with old friends.

Nelson's philosophy about releasing albums was obviously different than his rock contemporaries. Springsteen, for one, was known for his perfectionism and wouldn't let go of a project until he was happy with every bar of music. Nelson, by contrast, was ready to move on to the next project while the last reel of tape on the previous project was still flapping around the capstan. His approach was: If I'm feeling it, why not put it out? Why leave it to the bootleggers and the box-set compilers to release good music when its moment had already passed?

Bruce Lundvall, the president of Nelson's label, Columbia Records, begged to differ. He felt his top country artist was diluting the value of any one release by flooding the market with too many titles. Only the most dedicated fan could keep up with the avalanche of albums, and the casual fan might tune out altogether. But Nelson had creative freedom written into his contract, and he was going to take advantage of it. If Lundvall had had his way, he would probably have kept the most commercial projects and would have canceled the quirkiest side projects; he might have sacrificed quality in the cause of scarcity.

The best albums are often also bestsellers, of course, as in the case of *Willie Nelson Sings Kristofferson*, *San Antonio Rose*, *Always on My Mind*, *Pancho & Lefty*, and *Me and Paul*. But one can easily imagine Columbia shelving such terrific albums as *Old Friends*, *In the Jailhouse Now*, *Angel Eyes*, and *Music from Songwriter* in favor of such mediocrities as *WWII*, *Take It to the Limit*, *City of New Orleans*, the first Highwaymen album, and the *Electric Horseman* soundtrack.

Willie accepts the top honor of Entertainer of the Year at the CMA Awards in Nashville on October 8, 1979.

Sugar Moon/ Willie Sings Hank Williams

Such decisions might have been good for Sony's bottom line but disastrous for hardcore music fans. As it was, the label did turn down such completed albums as the *Sugar Moon* collaboration with Merle Haggard's Strangers and a *Willie Sings Hank Williams* tribute—superb recordings that only emerged on box sets in the '90s.

Nelson's admiration for his duet partner Merle Haggard extended to Hag's terrific road and studio band, the Strangers, the only real rivals to Nelson's Family band in the '70s and '80s. Nelson liked the way they played so much that he recorded with them even when Haggard wasn't around. It was a way for Nelson to present himself with new challenges and keep himself on his toes in the studio.

Maybe Columbia felt old country and western hits weren't as enduring as the songs of Hoagy Carmichael and Harold Arlen (who supplied the title tracks for the platinum albums *Stardust* and *Somewhere over the Rainbow*). If so, the label was sadly mistaken. Songs such as Williams' "Cold, Cold Heart," Bob Wills' "Sugar Moon," and Floyd Tillman's "Each Night at Nine" are near-perfect matches of vernacular language and popular music and are as appealing today as they ever were. And in Nelson's understated, Sinatra-esque delivery, these tunes are given a whole new interpretation and thus take on a whole new life—much as he once reinvigorated the Carmichael and Arlen numbers

Nelson seemed to enjoy himself in the studio, hanging out with his band and other friends, playing his latest compositions and his overlooked older compositions, the songs he'd grown up with and the contemporary songs that impressed him. As long as no one stopped him, he was going to keep doing it. Advisers could suggest a different approach, but they weren't having much luck slowing him down.

Willie, Emmylou Harris (center), and Joan Baez perform at the Circle Star Theatre in Palo Alto, California, in 1974.
Opposite: Willie in 1985, around the period he recorded a Hank Williams tribute album that went unreleased until 1993.

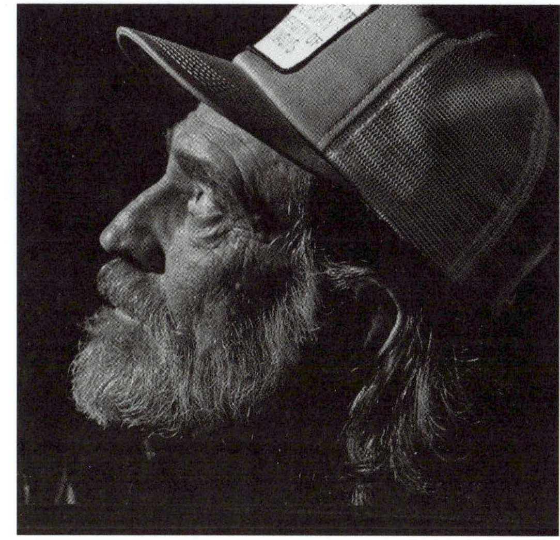

Willie Nelson
Willie Sings Hank Williams **(Rhino)**
Recorded: Mid-'80s
Released: 1993 on *Willie Nelson: A Classic & Unreleased Collection*
Willie Compositions: 0/10
Top 40 Singles: NA
Album Charts: NA

This tribute to Hank Williams is a nod to a profound influence on Nelson as both a songwriter and a singer. All ten tracks are Williams' compositions, and Nelson leans on Jimmy Day, Williams' former steel guitarist, to do them the way Hank did. He's too faithful to the originals for his own good, but these are great songs done by a major apostle. Unreleased until a 1993 box set. **Grade: B**

Willie Nelson
Sugar Moon **(Rhino)**
Recorded: Mid-'80s
Released: 1993 on *Willie Nelson: A Classic & Unreleased Collection*
Willie Compositions: 0/10
Top 40 Singles: NA
Album Charts: NA

When Merle Haggard didn't show up for a session at Nelson's home studio, the latter impulsively decided to record some vintage jazz and Western swing tunes with Haggard's band, the Strangers. The chemistry is astonishing on the crisp, surging momentum. The Strangers' two horn players—Don Markham and Gary Church—give the singer a rare chance to interact with sax and trombone—and he takes full advantage, especially on the early-jazz numbers by Louis Armstrong and Earl Hines. Unreleased until a 1993 box set. **Grade: A-**

One for the Road

His first release of 1979 was a two-LP set co-credited to Leon Russell, *One for the Road*. It was the first time Nelson would share credit on an album, but it would be far from the last. At the end of the '70s, many listeners thought of Russell as English because he had first made his name as the pianist and music director for Joe Cocker's band, Mad Dogs and Englishmen. But Russell was actually from

Willie Nelson and Leon Russell
One for the Road (Columbia)
Recorded: March 1979
Released: June 11, 1979
Willie Compositions: 0/20
Top 40 Single: "Heartbreak Hotel" (Country #1)
Album Charts: Country #3, Pop #25

Unlike most of Nelson's duet partners, Russell is a gifted player, so the give-and-take on this project is as much instrumental as vocal—indeed Nelson handles most of the vocals himself. Originally released as two vinyl LPs (since reissued as a single CD), the first half is a loosey-goosey jam on songs associated with Elvis Presley, Roy Rogers, Hank Williams, and more. The second half features Nelson singing ballads by Irving Berlin and Harold Arlen over Russell's electric keyboards. The second-half synths sound dated in a way the first-half piano doesn't. Vocalist Maria Muldaur and slide guitarist Bonnie Raitt make guest appearances. **Grade: B**

Tulsa, Oklahoma, just north of Texas, and shared the same honky-tonk, jazz, blues, showtunes, and gospel influences as Nelson.

Nelson's then-wife Shirley had given her husband an eight-track tape of Russell's third solo album, 1972's *Carny*, and he instantly recognized their common sensibility. Just as Nelson had gone to Nashville to find success as a songwriter but not as a singer, Russell had moved to L.A. to find success as a backing musician but not as a singer. Just as Nelson had returned to Texas to establish himself as a frontman, Russell had returned to Oklahoma to do the same. Nelson had even recorded two of Russell's songs on *Shotgun Willie*.

Recording *One for the Road* in Burbank, California, with Nelson's Family band backing them, Nelson and Russell sang twenty songs written before 1960. There were no originals by either man. Alongside the pop-jazz standards by Cole Porter, George Gershwin, and Harold Arlen were hillbilly standards by Hank Williams, Gene Autry, and Jimmie Davis. The glue holding these two halves of American music together was the country-swing of Bob Wills, the groundbreaking bandleader who grew up in Texas but who enjoyed his greatest success leading the house band at Cain's Ballroom in Tulsa.

To replace the absence of Wills' fiddles and steel, the arrangements leaned heavily on Trigger and Mickey Raphael's harmonica. "Arrangements" may be too presumptuous a word, for these sessions have the feel of two friends playing their favorite old songs and making it up as they go along. That's both the limitation and the charm of this set—they could have called it *Mad Dogs and Red Dirt Cowboys*. The superior first half emphasizes a lively dance hall feel anchored by Russell's acoustic piano. The less rewarding second half is dominated by Nelson singing ballads over Russell's synths.

Willie Nelson Sings Kristofferson

Nelson made another new friend in 1972. He and Kris Kristofferson bonded during the Dripping Springs Reunion that year, and Nelson was impressed by Nashville's newest hot songwriter and his way of working literary moves into authentic-sounding country songs. It didn't matter that Kristofferson really couldn't sing; he was obviously trying to push country songwriting in the same direction as Nelson—more realism, more irony, more subtlety. These songs truly came alive in the mouths of great singers such as Sammi Smith, Johnny Cash, Waylon Jennings, and Jerry Lee Lewis. Why not Nelson himself?

He had recorded one Kristofferson song on each of his final two RCA albums and two more as duets on *Waylon & Willie*. Now he wanted to do a whole album of his new friend's songs, producing them just the way he heard them. *Willie Nelson Sings Kristofferson*, this summit meeting of a brilliant writer and a brilliant singer, proved an artistic peak for both men.

Except for a handful of guest appearances, the album was just Nelson and his road band, which at this point featured two guitarists (Nelson and Jody Payne), two drummers (Paul English and Rex Ludwig), and two bassists (Bee Spears and Chris Etheridge), as well as pianist Bobbie Nelson and harmonicaist Mickey Raphael. This doubling of nearly every instrument—each playing a slightly different version of the rhythm—created a push-and-pull dynamic that gave Nelson's Texas swing an even knottier tension.

You can hear this especially on the mid- and up-tempo songs such as "Me and Bobby McGee," the lusty comedy of "You Show Me Yours (And I'll Show You Mine)," and the quiet-verses/louder-chorus approach of "Sunday Morning Coming Down." It allows every listener to measure the tension in their own lives between Bobby's "freedom" and "nothing," between the hope of "Sunday Morning" and the regrets of "coming down" from Saturday night.

Willie Nelson
Willie Nelson Sings Kristofferson **(Columbia)**
Recorded: April 1979
Released: October 22, 1979
Willie Compositions: 0/9
Top 40 Single: "Help Me Make It through the Night" (Country #4)
Album Charts: Country #5, Pop #42

Kris Kristofferson is a superb songwriter but a notoriously underwhelming singer, and on this album nine of his best songs come alive as never before, thanks to Nelson and the Family band, both operating at the peak of their powers. Nelson treats these songs with the same respect and affection that he gave the American Songbook numbers on *Stardust*, and because Kristofferson was an old running buddy (and backing singer on several songs), Nelson has never sounded more invested as an interpretive singer. When he suddenly rises from his low-key storytelling on "Help Me Make It through the Night" into a high-register wail of pain, the effect is chilling. **Grade: A+**

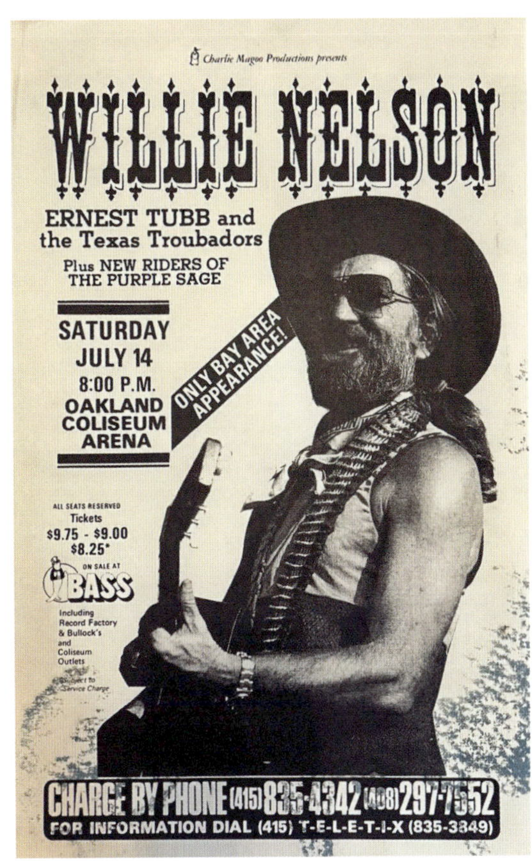

This latter track, considerably more restrained than the RCA version, was a great leap forward, setting up an extended instrumental coda that takes the conflict beyond words.

The ballads were just as good. On "Please Don't Tell Me How the Story Ends," Nelson asks his partner in a crumbling relationship to ignore the problems and enjoy the time they have left. But when he describes the feel of her touch, suddenly he lets go of a high-tenor, nearly falsetto cry that betrays the pain beneath the narrator's stoicism.

Something similar happens in "Why Me." On the verses, the narrator asks what he has done to deserve God's blessings, but knowing the answer, he leaps into a quivering high tenor to beg for yet more help. In contrast to Kristofferson's thin-voiced hit version, Nelson's plump vocal sounds blessed on the verses—and that allows his chorus desperation to cut all the more deeply.

Kristofferson's songs fit so well with Nelson's voice only because the former's songwriting aligned perfectly with the latter's lifelong project: elucidating in song how we all might retain our dignity even as we cope with loss. Nelson's songwriting had long searched for fresh, new ways of examining this inexhaustible issue—and here was a batch of songs that served the purpose well without requiring Nelson to pull out a pen.

Willie and Kris Kristofferson play some songs at Tootsie's Orchid Lounge in Nashville in 1982.

When a relationship ends, Kristofferson writes, it's easy to dwell on the bad times—but maybe it's better to have one more roll in bed "For the Good Times." It's a song Nelson might have written himself, and his vocal pulls out the sadness and the pleasure in this scenario as Kristofferson's voice never could.

Nelson's albums devoted to Kristofferson and Lefty Frizzell—like Merle Haggard's salutes to Bob Wills and Jimmie Rodgers—legitimized the concept of tribute albums in country music, building on the example of Ella Fitzgerald's *Songbook* albums in jazz and anticipating the trend in pop music later in the century. All such efforts acknowledge the oft-overlooked reality that the song's composer is often as important as its singer—an inconvenient truth for music marketing departments but an important reminder for listeners.

Pretty Paper

Willie Nelson
***Pretty Paper* (Columbia)**
Recorded: Summer 1979
Released: November 6, 1979
Willie Compositions: 2/12
Top 40 Singles: NA
Album Charts: Country #11, Pop #73

For his obligatory country-music Christmas album, Nelson approached the traditional carols the same way he did the standards from the American Songbook: as elegant swing tunes to be understated by his road band. Booker T. Jones, who produced *Stardust*, is behind the knobs and adds his trademark organ to songs like "White Christmas" and "Winter Wonderland." "Christmas Blues" is a slow-blues instrumental by Nelson and Jones. **Grade: A-**

The Christmas record is the most old-fashioned of concept albums, one that every country label expects its artists to do. Instead of seeing it as an obligation, however, Nelson saw it as an opportunity. He could reunite with *Stardust* producer Booker T. Jones to further explore the pre-Elvis American Songbook. It was another chance to revisit the music of his childhood, and he did so with an older-but-wiser detachment that looked fondly on the uninhibited joy of those days, while realizing he could never be that carefree again.

The *Pretty Paper* album achieved that effect by stripping the holiday songs down—sometimes to the very bones of an organ, a bass, and an acoustic guitar—so every pause and whispery stretch of a syllable could be heard clearly. The song selections aren't surprising—the popular holiday songs of the '30s were not so different from those of the '70s—but the arrangements are. Tunes such as "White Christmas," "Winter Wonderland," and "Santa Claus Is Coming to Town" are usually delivered with bubbly enthusiasm; but Nelson gives them a wistfulness that underlines how irretrievable childhood really is.

The title track, a Nelson composition that became a pop hit for Roy Orbison and Nelson's first single for RCA, is given a new, more tender reading that allows us to sympathize with the legless peddler of gift wrapping without blaming the busy shoppers who ignore him. The whole album contains some of Nelson's finest singing.

Family Bible

Another old-school concept album was the gospel record, something country labels used to ask for until sales drooped. Columbia released Nelson's first gospel project, *The Troublemaker*, in 1976, but allowed him to release the second, *Family Bible*, on MCA's short-lived Christian Music label Songbird. This was clearly a labor of love for the singer, a chance to reunite with his sister, Bobbie (who shares

Willie Nelson
Family Bible **(Songbird)**
Recorded: June 1980
Released: September 1, 1980
Willie Compositions: 3/11
Top 40 Singles: NA
Album Chart: Country #26

There's a stark elegance to this collection of eleven gospel songs sung by Nelson accompanied by nothing but his own acoustic guitar and his sister Bobbie's piano. This is religious faith proclaimed not as a proselytizing boast but as a quiet, confident declaration. Most of the tunes are traditional hymns, but the record also features three Nelson originals (including the 1957 title track) and the reggae hymn "By the Rivers of Babylon" made famous by Jamaica's Melodians.
Grade: A-

the cover photo with him), on the religious music of their childhood (the album is dedicated to Mama Nelson). As on *Pretty Paper*, Nelson whittled the arrangements down to the fundamentals: his voice, his guitar, and his sister's piano. Those three elements are all these songs need.

The Electric Horseman

Nelson was so famous by 1979 that movie stars were reaching out to him, not the other way around. One of them was Robert Redford, who invited Willie and Connie to ride horses with him at his Utah ranch. While there, the actor asked the singer if he'd ever considered acting. No, he replied, but how different could it be from singing, which was really another kind of acting? When Nelson sang "Hello Walls," he wasn't the person talking to the furniture in his now-empty house—that was a character he had created and was now speaking through.

"Acting is like singing," he says in *Willie Nelson: An Epic Life*, "except there's no melody. There's a lot of one-liners in movies, every now and then a zinger, with a conversation in between. In a song, you have to condense the whole story in two minutes or less."

Willie in a promotional still from the 1979 movie *Electric Horseman*.

Now that he had the clout to pursue almost any creative outlet, he dove into film. If his mission was to help his audience survive life's catastrophes not with denial or hysteria but with composure, why not do it through cowboy movies? How was that any more of a stretch for a honky-tonk singer than jazz records and gospel records? Nelson and his Austin pal, journalist Bud Shrake, had already been working on a movie script based on *Red Headed Stranger*, and Nelson was willing to put that off for a while to get his feet wet acting in someone else's picture.

Director Sydney Pollack (*They Shoot Horses, Don't They*) agreed to cast Nelson in *The Electric Horseman*. Redford plays a cowboy-turned-cereal-pitchman on the skids; torn between a wife and a lover, he absconds with a valuable racehorse into the desert. Jane Fonda is the lover, and Nelson is the cowboy's manager. It's actually a good movie, and Nelson acquits himself in a small role. He sang five cowboy songs for the film (including one new composition, "So You Want to Be a Cowboy"). But the rest of the music (for both the movie and the subsequent soundtrack album) was incongruous jazz-rock by Dave Grusin.

Willie Nelson
***The Electric Horseman* (Columbia)**
Recorded: September 1979
Released: December 1979
Willie Compositions: 5/11
Top 40 Singles: "My Heroes Have Always Been Cowboys" (Country #1), "Midnight Rider" (Country #6)
Album Charts: Country #3, Pop #52

Nelson made a surprisingly impressive acting debut in *The Electric Horseman.* The soundtrack was another matter. Side one had Nelson breezing through five cowboy songs, including two Top 10 country singles: "My Heroes Have Always Been Cowboys" and a remake of Gregg Allman's "Midnight Rider." Side two was devoted to Dave Grusin's forgettable jazz-disco score.
Grade: C

Honeysuckle Rose

Pollack was so impressed by Nelson's screen presence that he agreed to cast him as a lead in *Honeysuckle Rose*, a movie that Pollack would produce with Jerry Schatzberg directing. The plot is similar: A cowboy is torn between his wife and lover as he tries to keep his flagging career afloat. This time Nelson is the cowboy, Amy Irving the lover, and Dyan Cannon the wife. The film wasn't as good as *The Electric Horseman*, but the soundtrack was decidedly better.

On a plane ride, Pollack suggested to Nelson that he write a new song for the picture about a musician's life on tour. The singer instinctively responded by scrawling onto a barf bag the lyrics for the chorus of "On the Road Again." When he got home and put it together with its earworm melody, it captured the giddy, forward motion of a bus on the highway, carrying a traveling circus of nonconforming artists.

That chorus is so jangly and catchy, so bouncy and easy to sing along to, that live audiences can't resist. And when they join in—whether they're on-key or not—they feel as if they're on Nelson's bus rolling down the highway to the next adventure. As an unabashed celebration of the camaraderie of life on the road, it was atypical of most of Nelson's writing, a departure from his ongoing examination of loss.

More typical was another new song, "Angel Flying Too Close to the Ground," one of his greatest compositions. The superb version on the *Honeysuckle Rose* soundtrack begins quietly, just voice and acoustic guitar, as the narrator explains how he found a fallen angel and patched up her "broken wing," knowing full well that she might leave him as soon as she recovered. The song points out that our efforts to help the needy are seldom entirely selfless, while honoring the effort nonetheless. After all, the person being helped may have angelic qualities, but he or she is rarely blameless for crashing and burning.

Caught between the narrator's desire to heal the angel and his equal desire to hold on to her, the song coils with tension. As the tension builds, so does the arrangement, as Bobbie's piano and Mickey Raphael's harmonica join; the drums get stronger much as the healing angel does and prepare for liftoff. That sets up the heartbreaking refrain: "Leave me if you need to; I will still remember." Bob Dylan admired the song so much, he recorded it as the B-side of his 1983 single "Union Sundown."

Willie Nelson and Family
***Honeysuckle Rose* (Columbia)**
Recorded: Fall 1979
Released: July 18, 1980
Willie Compositions: 4/12
Top 40 Singles: "On the Road Again" (Country #1, Pop #20), "Angel Flying Too Close to the Ground" (Country #1)
Album Charts: Country #1, Pop #11

The movie *Honeysuckle Rose* found Nelson playing the lead role of a country singer caught between a wife back home (Dyan Cannon) and a young singer onstage (Amy Irving). The film was better than expected, but the somewhat ramshackle soundtrack reprised much of *Willie and Family Live* less persuasively. Nelson wrote three new songs for the movie, including one of his most popular, "On the Road Again," and one of his best, "Angel Flying Too Close to the Ground." Emmylou Harris and Hank Cochran sound great on their songs; Cannon and Irving less so on theirs. **Grade: B**

Almost as good is the third new song: "I've Come to Live Here in Your Eyes," a ballad of finally admitting to oneself that one has fallen in love despite one's stubborn resistance. The rest of the soundtrack album is a mixed bag, an uneasy mix of too-fast tempos, buzzing guitars, live tape, studio tracks, and overdubbed crowd noises. Emmylou Harris sounds terrific in a duet with Nelson on Rodney Crowell's "Angel Eyes" and in a solo version of "So You Think You're a Cowboy," the *Electric Horseman* song.

San Antonio Rose

Nelson's insight into the similarities between singing and acting served him well in his newfound enthusiasm for duets. He discovered that the back-and-forth in musical duets resembled the dialogue in movies—one assumed a character and engaged another character in conversation, directing each vocal line to one's partner and seeming to respond to their reply. Here was a whole new way of furthering his mission to create musical scenarios where the protagonist responds to crisis.

Opposite: Willie and Amy Irving in a promotional still from the 1980 movie *Honeysuckle Rose*.

It also enabled him to hang out with his friends and make music. He had never done a lot of duets before RCA overdubbed his voice on "Good Hearted Woman" for *Wanted! The Outlaws*. He had recorded a handful with his second wife, Shirley—and one of them, "Willingly," even became a Top 10 country hit—and "After the Fire Was Gone," his duet with Tracey Nelson was the flip side of "Bloody Mary Morning" and was nominated for a Grammy. But the success of his duets with Waylon Jennings on *Wanted! The Outlaws* and *Willie & Waylon* gave Nelson a taste for it, and the more he did it, the more he enjoyed it.

Between 1979 and 1982, Nelson would record eight duet albums with Leon Russell, Ray Price, Hank Cochran, Hank Snow, Webb Pierce, Waylon Jennings, Roger Miller, and Merle Haggard (two weren't released till 1983, and one was released under Cochran's name). Some of these were more successful—commercially and/or artistically—than others, but together they represent a major departure from Nelson's standard operating procedure. Suddenly, he was willing to share the spotlight and experiment in singing dialogues rather than monologues. There were gems in every project, and sometimes everything gelled into one of his best albums.

"These guys were my heroes," he told *Goldmine* in 1995. "To be able to afford to go into the studio with Faron Young, Hank Snow, Webb Pierce, Roger Miller, Ray Price and do albums and have 'em come out? That's amazing. I was not only singing with my friends, I was singing with guys that I had listened to growing up. . . . I thought they needed to be recorded. I loved those songs, and I know a lot of other people do."

He released a double album with Leon Russell in 1979 and sang duets with Emmylou Harris and Amy Irving on the *Honeysuckle Rose* soundtrack in 1980. That same year, he recorded an album of duets with Ray Price, the man who had hired an unknown Nelson as a bassist, had signed him to a publishing deal, and had turned his composition "Night Life" into a country hit. In 1961, Price had recorded the

Ray Price, a longtime star himself, made two duet albums with Willie and a trio album with Willie and Merle Haggard.

Willie Nelson and Ray Price
***San Antonio Rose* (Columbia)**
Recorded: January 1980
Released: May 19, 1980
Willie Compositions: 2/11
Top 40 Singles: "Crazy Arms" (Country #16), "Faded Love" (Country #3), "Don't You Ever Get Tired (Of Hurting Me)" (Country #11)
Album Charts: Country #3, Pop #70

Now a superstar, Nelson reunites with his former employer to sing two compositions apiece from Nelson, Bob Wills, and Hank Cochran, plus five more deep-country classics. Price's singing is as smooth as a satin sheet, Nelson's as rumpled as a quilt, and an all-star band plays superbly. There are no new songs, but the two leaders bring two lifetimes of experience to their masterful phrasing. Crystal Gayle sings on Wills' "Faded Love." Two bonus tracks were added to the CD reissue. **Grade: A-**

album *San Antonio Rose: A Tribute to Bob Wills*, which featured Price's voice gliding smoothly over the propulsive swing of an all-star band that included Grady Martin, Jimmy Day, and an unknown acoustic guitarist named Willie Nelson.

That album opened with the title track, and so did a 1980 album called *San Antonio Rose*, which featured Price and Nelson singing over an all-star band featuring Nelson, Martin, Leon Russell, Johnny Gimble, Buddy Emmons, and the Family. The two lead vocals—Price's silkily precise and Nelson's as unpredictable as ever—created just enough difference between them that one can enjoy the give-and-take, as if they were two old guys in a barbershop trying to top each other's story about romantic hard luck. Beneath the bravado, it's easy to pick up on the lingering pain. Here's an example of duets at their best.

"To me," Nelson told me in 2020, "Ray Price is the greatest country singer ever, followed closely by George Jones. Frank Sinatra is my favorite singer ever. First of all, they had great voices, but their phrasing is what made them great singers. You can just say the words, but that doesn't mean anything. It's how you phrase the words that lets people know how you feel about the words. You move the accent off the beat, and that adds some feeling."

Greatest Hits (& Some That Will Be)

"Faded Love" was the only song from *San Antonio Rose* that made it on Columbia's first compilation album, *Greatest Hits (& Some That Will Be)*. Nelson had only been recording for Columbia for six years by the end of 1980, but he had released so much with such success that this two-LP, 20-track *Greatest Hits* compilation, drawn solely from Columbia releases, seemed justified.

Willie Nelson
Greatest Hits (& Some That Will Be) **(Columbia)**
Recorded: 1975–1980
Released: August 21, 1981
Willie Compositions: 4/20
Top 40 Single: "Heartaches of a Fool" (Country #39)
Album Charts: Country #1, Pop #27

These twenty tracks on two LPs (later a single CD) gather up the biggest singles, the staples of the live show and a few astute album cuts. A re-recording of "Heartaches of a Fool," a song that Nelson sold to Paul Buskirk in 1960 along with "Night Life," was previously unreleased and became a modest hit. That's the only surprise in a package with minimal notes but smart choices. **Grade: B+**

Make the World Go Away

It has always seemed strange that Nelson never did a duet album with Cochran, one of Nelson's oldest friends, the man who sacrificed his own pay raise so Nelson could work at Price's Pamper Music. But he did; it just wasn't credited as such. If you squint at the liner notes on Cochran's 1980 album, *Make the World Go Away*, you'll find that Nelson sang on half of the ten tracks. Ironically, he didn't sing on his own composition, "Angel Flying Too Close to the Ground," the only track on the album that Cochran didn't write or co-write.

Hank Cochran, a friend and songwriting partner since Willie arrived in Nashville in 1960, is seen here in the mid-'80s. Opposite: Willie tours in support of the album *Willie Nelson Sings Kristofferson* in Los Angeles in January 1980.

Instead, Nelson joins in on four Cochran compositions that were hits for other artists, "I Fall to Pieces" (Patsy Cline), "A-11" (Johnny Paycheck), "You Comb Her Hair Every Morning" (George Jones), and "A Little Bitty Tear" (Burl Ives), as well as "Sally Was a Good Old Girl," a hit for Cochran himself. Cochran is a likable singer, much better than Kristofferson or Tom T. Hall, for example. He was fine on the verses, but on the choruses he lacked a higher gear to shift into. On their duets, Nelson provides that overdrive—and those are the album's highlights. On the other songs, Cochran's vocals struggle to compete with the country-rock production with its fattened and pumped-up drums and electric guitars.

Hank Cochran
***Make the World Go Away* (Elektra)**
Recorded: August 1980
Released: 1980
Willie Compositions: 1/10
Top 40 Singles: NA
Album Charts: NA

Though he's not credited on the front cover, Nelson sings five duets with his old friend Hank Cochran on this overlooked album. All five are hits that Cochran wrote for himself, Patsy Cline, George Jones, Burl Ives, and Johnny Paycheck—and Nelson's extra oomph pushes these versions across the finish line. By himself, Cochran sings four more of his old hits and Nelson's "Angel Flying Too Close to the Ground." The classic '60s material sometimes feels at odds with the country-rock arrangements, but the duets make the record a triumph. **Grade: B+**

Somewhere Over the Rainbow

Somewhere over the Rainbow draws its repertoire from the same well of pre-Elvis pop standards as *Stardust*, but the approach is radically different. Instead of working with his road band and producer Booker T. Jones, Nelson assembles a drummer-less, keyboard-less, acoustic string sextet featuring his old Houston pal Paul Buskirk on mandolin, Bob Wills' fiddler Johnny Gimble, two acoustic bassists, and Merle Haggard sidekick Freddy Powers on acoustic guitar and duet vocals.

The lack of percussion gives the session a floating feel that allows Nelson's vowels to hover above the ballads and to slip and slide their way through the up-tempo swing numbers. He takes full advantage of this sonic freedom to syncopate and improvise at will. Songs associated with Nat King Cole, Louis Armstrong, and Fats Waller sit comfortably next to those linked to Judy Garland and Connie Francis, with the country instruments bridging the gap between jazz and pop.

Cole's "Mona Lisa" and Garland's "Somewhere over the Rainbow" are filled with yearning for an

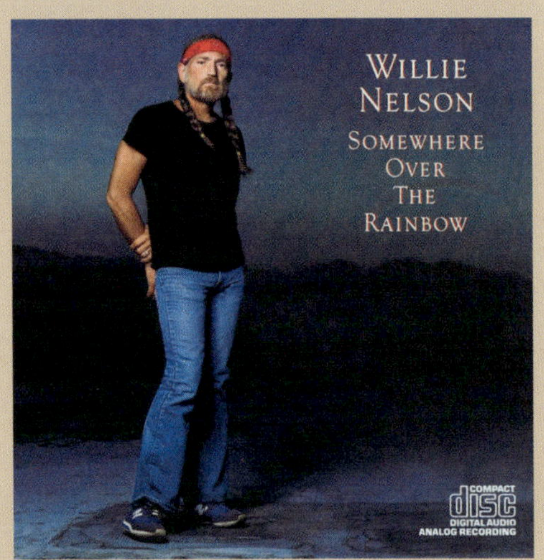

Willie Nelson
Somewhere over the Rainbow **(Columbia)**
Recorded: July 1980
Released: February 23, 1981
Willie Compositions: 0/10
Top 40 Singles: "Mona Lisa" (Country #11), "I'm Gonna Sit Right Down and Write Myself a Letter" (Country #26)
Album Charts: Country #1, Pop #31

Nelson reaches back before Pearl Harbor Day for these old pop standards, and he records them with an all-acoustic strings sextet that features fiddler Johnny Gimble and mandolinist Paul Buskirk. The results often suggest what Nat King Cole might have sounded like if he had grown up on a West Texas ranch and then moved to Paris to sing with Django Reinhardt and Stephane Grappelli. Freddy Powers sings duets on several numbers. **Grade: A-**

impossibly beautiful woman and an impossibly utopian land, and Nelson's vocals capture both the dream and its elusiveness. Nelson is at the peak of his vocal powers here and is given free rein to use them. Gimble's fiddle dominates the mix on many songs, lending a French cabaret feeling to the proceedings.

Always on My Mind

Nelson wrote few songs in these years (only two on this next album) but concentrated instead on improving as an interpretive singer. The work paid off, and *Always on My Mind* contains his best singing ever. If you want to understand why Miles Davis admires Nelson so much that he named a song after him, listen to Nelson sing the title song. The Texas hillbilly elongates the phrase, "You were always on my mind" till it fills up with regret and irony. He repeats the line three more times—now sad, now bitter, now hopeful—his breathy drawl curling up like smoke. Sound like a muted trumpet solo or what?

Nelson didn't write "Always on My Mind," but he could have, for it has all the elements of his best songs: a relationship reconsidered in the rearview mirror with a combination of regret and hurt. It was actually written by Mark James, Wayne Thompson, and John Christopher and had already been recorded by Brenda Lee, Gwen McRae, and Elvis Presley; but it was so close to his own songwriting that Nelson knew just what the song needed.

He begins with the song's opening apology, "Maybe I didn't treat you quite as good as I should have," and that tinge of guilt colors everything to come. When he reaches the title line, he elongates the phrase till it's clear that the blame is as much on his mind as the lingering love. When he begs for a second chance on the bridge, he sings as if he knows how much baggage he's carrying. It's one of his greatest performances.

Chips Moman co-wrote the lead-off track, "Do Right Woman, Do Right Man," a big hit for Aretha Franklin. Nelson has neither Franklin's lung power nor her lightning flashes of intuition; instead, he relies on smarts and phrasing. His alternating hoarse whispers and deep-throated yodels create the perfect

Willie Nelson
Always on My Mind **(Columbia)**
Recorded: October 1981
Released: March 1, 1982
Willie Compositions: 2/10
Top 40 Singles: "Always on My Mind" (Country #1, Pop #5), "Let It Be Me" (Country #2, Pop #40), "Last Thing I Needed the First Thing This Morning" (Country #2)
Album Charts: Country #1, Pop #2

This collection of showstoppers given larger-than-life renditions by previous artists—Elvis Presley's "Always on My Mind," Aretha Franklin's "Do Right Woman, Do Right Man," Simon & Garfunkel's "Bridge over Troubled Water," Procol Harum's "A Whiter Shade of Pale," and the Everly Brothers' "Let It Be Me"—are given life-size interpretations by Nelson. He never forgets the sins that necessitated these redemption anthems, and that tension makes these tracks thrilling. **Grade: A**

polar counterpart to Franklin's. Nelson gives the male take on mutual responsibility in a relationship with a balanced mix of R&B and country that is as satisfying as it is rare. Two other fine Moman compositions also bridge the gap between soul and country, and Nelson strolls across that span as confidently as Ray Charles once did.

Just when you thought you couldn't bear one more version of Paul Simon's "Bridge over Troubled Water," Nelson comes by and makes it sound brand new. On the best-known versions, Art Garfunkel and Franklin elaborated the religious romance with lung-bursting embellishments. Nelson takes the exact opposite approach. He strips the song of everything that isn't absolutely necessary. He carves out empty spaces that make his husky understatement all the more stark and affecting. He sustains the tension by accenting beats other than those the song calls for. His measured confidentiality brings a new sense of intimacy to the overly familiar lyrics.

It's an album of big, showstopper songs that are held back from bombast by Nelson's understated verses that patiently build toward the big choruses and thus justify them. He was still recovering from a collapsed lung, and that reduced capacity kept him from over-singing, allowing producer Chips Moman's band to create the huge climaxes with the singer's knowing irony in contrast to the arrangement. By holding back this way, Nelson is telling his listeners to avoid any attempt to obliterate the past with over-the-top emotion—not only does it distort reality, but it never works anyway.

Old Friends

A short while before he died in 1992, I saw Roger Miller play a small club in the D.C. suburbs, and his between-songs banter proved as funny as his comic songs. He introduced one number by saying, "Willie called me up one day and said, 'How'd you like to do an album with me?' I said, 'Oh, Willie, you do an album with everybody.' He said, 'That's not true; I'm only up to the M's.'"

Due to patter like that and hit songs such as "Dang Me," "Chug-a-Lug," and "Do-Wacka-Do," Miller had a reputation as a gifted comic—which he was. But there was another side to his talent: his wry dissections of broken marriages, not unlike those of Nelson and Cochran, his drinking and picking buddies at Tootsie's Orchid Lounge.

Some of these more serious songs were recorded by other singers: "Half a Mind" (Ernest Tubb), "Invitation to the Blues" (Ray Price), "Husbands and Wives" (Everly Brothers), and "When Two Worlds Collide" (Jerry Lee Lewis). These four songs plus six other Miller compositions were included on *Old Friends*, a 1982 album produced and co-sung by Nelson.

Fittingly enough, the album's only two comic numbers, "Aladambama" and "Sorry Willie," are sung by Miller alone with a tongue-in-cheek drollery.

Willie Nelson and Roger Miller
***Old Friends* (Columbia)**
Recorded: November 1981
Released: May 1982
Willie Compositions: 0/10
Top 40 Single: "Old Friends" (Country #19)
Album Charts: NA

This is a combination of a duet album like the ones Nelson did with Ray Price and a tribute album like the one Nelson did for Kris Kristofferson. The title song is done as a trio with Price and two songs are duets; Miller sings the two comic numbers alone, and Nelson sings the five heartbreak ballads alone. Because he's best known for his funny songs, Roger Miller is underrated as a songwriter. But his comic material as well as his more serious numbers was full of marvelous language and sneaky insights into human nature. And seldom have those songs been sung as gracefully as they are here. **Grade: A-**

The latter was based on an actual incident when Miller started dating Nelson's first wife before the divorce papers were signed. But the broken-marriage ballads ("When a House Is Not a Home," "When Two Worlds Collide," and "I'll Pick Up My Heart (And Go Home)") are sung by Nelson alone and are so close to the spirit and standards of his own songwriting that he gives them powerful readings.

In the Jailhouse Now

If the Miller and Nelson album was a summit meeting of great songwriters, its sequel—a duet album between Webb Pierce and Nelson—is a rendezvous of great singers. Pierce is a big man with a huge, nasal tenor that yelps, hollers, and swaggers through each song. His carefree gusto rubs off on Nelson, who sings more aggressively than usual. This can backfire on the subtler ballads, but the two men swing like crazy on the up-tempo honky-tonk, making each number vibrate with energy.

Long before Nelson and Jennings were labeled country outlaws, Webb Pierce was a Music Row renegade, rubbing the suits the wrong way with his blunt opinions, hard drinking, flamboyance, and undisciplined approach to music-making. That has kept him out of the Country Music Hall of Fame, where he clearly belongs, thanks to the excitement he brought to almost everything he recorded. That's certainly the case here.

Webb Pierce recorded a duet album with Willie, *In the Jailhouse Now*, in 1982.
Opposite: Willie at Caesars Palace in Las Vegas on June 18, 1980.

Willie Nelson and Webb Pierce
***In the Jailhouse Now* (Columbia)**
Recorded: June 1981
Released: June 28, 1982
Willie Compositions: 1/10
Top 40 Singles: NA
Album Charts: NA

Pierce, Nelson, and Nelson's band (plus ringers Leon Russell and Richard Manuel) cut loose on nine songs recorded by Pierce between 1951 and 1960, most of them country chart-toppers, as well as a boisterous new song, "Heebie Jeebie Blues." The title track is the Jimmie Rodgers classic that was a #1 hit for Pierce for twenty-seven weeks in 1955, and it's even more vibrant here. "There Stands the Glass" is one of the greatest drinking songs, as a brokenhearted alcoholic ruefully contemplates his first beer of the night. **Grade: A-**

WWII

Nelson's terrific duet projects with Miller and Pierce failed to chart, and so did the singles. Seeking a commercial rebound, Nelson turned to a sure bet: another duet album with Waylon Jennings. It yielded a Top 5 album and a Top 15 single, but it was an artistic disappointment. It followed the template of *Waylon & Willie*, but the magic was gone.

It was Jennings' label and Jennings' show. Nelson's participation was limited to the five duets, including his new composition, "Write Your Own Songs," soon to be done better by Nelson alone. Jennings sang all the solo tracks himself. Pop hits by Otis Redding and Jimmy Webb were mixed with country hits by Tom T. Hall and Barbara Fairchild without improving any of them.

This was the dilemma of the whole outlaw country movement. You had to create the persona of a rough-and-tough rebel with a sensitive heart. That outside/inside tug-of-war was what fascinated listeners, who wanted to believe they had a little of both. If the artist was too tough or too sensitive, the tension was spoiled and the appeal for the listener lost. On this album, Jennings' bristling, tough-guy character upset that balance and had that effect.

Willie Nelson and Waylon Jennings
***WWII* (RCA)**
Recorded: 1981–1982
Released: September 27, 1982
Willie Compositions: 1/11
Top 40 Single: "(Sittin' on) The Dock of the Bay" (Country #13)
Album Charts: Country #3, Pop #57

This follows the successful formula of 1978's *Waylon & Willie* by cobbling together five duets and five solo vocals and calling it a duo album. This time, though, all the solo cuts were by Jennings. These tracks were all new, but the Chips Moman–produced results were less satisfying. The song selections were questionable, and the backing by Moman's band seems under-rehearsed. The duet version of Otis Redding's "(Sittin' on) The Dock of the Bay" was a hit, despite its melodramatic reading. The album does include Jennings singing the rare Guy Clark song, "The Old Mother's Locket Trick." **Grade: C-**

First Lady Rosalynn Carter, President Jimmy Carter, and Willie on stage in the late '70s.

Pancho & Lefty

Merle Haggard wasn't as close to Nelson personally as duet partners Jennings, Miller, Kristofferson, Price, and Cash were—but Haggard was a better match artistically than anyone else on the planet. Just four years younger than Nelson, Haggard grew up in California. But his family was from red-dirt Oklahoma, and young Merle absorbed that Texahoma love of cowboy songs, dancehall swing, and honky-tonk heartbreak. Many of Nelson's vocal partners had a similar background, but only he and Haggard could write them as convincingly as they sang them.

Both men had made up rhymes as kids and songs as soon as they got guitars. Both recognized that seemingly simple structure of a country song could be a laboratory for examining all of life's setbacks: disappearing lovers, disappearing parents, poverty, prison, or changing times. The end of a love affair could become a surrogate for any other problem, and the reaction to such a breakup could be the response to any like challenge. And if a hint of syncopation and improvisation acknowledged the unpredictability of life, all the better.

Both men were as happy to sing someone else's song containing a similar drama as to sing their own. So, when they rendezvoused with co-producer Chips Moman at Nelson's Pedernales Recording Studio in Texas in early November 1982, they each brough a few of their own songs and a few old songs they were fond of.

As often happens when two people are so much alike, the small differences matter all the more. Haggard's baritone was marked by fatalistic pessimism, while Nelson's tenor was colored by a guarded optimism. There was enough mutual respect between the two singers that neither tried to dominate the other but instead made sure both approaches came through with understated finesse.

Haggard and Moman thought they were finished, but Nelson thought the album still needed an anchor song. His oldest child, Lana, suggested Townes Van Zandt's "Pancho and Lefty" and played him Emmylou Harris's brilliant 1977 version. "I love anything Emmylou does," Nelson writes in *It's a Long Story: My Life*, "but I could hear how the song lent itself to a duet sung by two men. . . . I loved the song's essential mystery. I saw it as a great Western, and I couldn't wait for Merle to hear it."

Willie Nelson and Merle Haggard
Pancho & Lefty **(Epic)**
Recorded: November 1982
Released: January 10, 1983
Willie Compositions: 2/10
Top 40 Singles: "Reasons to Quit" (Country #6), "Pancho and Lefty" (Country #1)
Album Charts: Country #1, Pop #37

Nelson and Haggard both boasted thick-textured, gravelly voices that expressed a confidence all the more impressive for being so slyly understated. They both had deep roots in the western half of the country-and western-tradition and knew how to make a cowboy's dream as appealing as it was elusive. Those factors made all these tracks shine—not just the classic Townes Van Zandt title tune but also the older songs by Nelson, Haggard, Bob Wills, and the singing cowboys Smiley Burnette and Stuart Hamblen. The studio band was a blend of musicians who'd worked with one of the three co-producers: Nelson, Haggard, and Chips Moman. *Grade: A-*

Willie and Waylon Jennings on stage together
in New York City in April 1978.

Merle Haggard and band perform at the White House in March 1982.

This was a tale of two outlaws in the Mexican desert: the local Pancho and the Ohioan Lefty. Perhaps it was only a coincidence that Lefty fled home with a mysterious influx of cash just before the Federales captured Pancho. Perhaps not. Perhaps it didn't matter. The police claimed they could have picked him up anytime they wanted.

But this bittersweet song is handled masterfully by these two men nearing fifty, evoking not only the friendship and adventure but also the betrayal and regret. Haggard wasn't part of the original, Nashville-based outlaw country movement. But unlike that crew, the Californian had actually served time in prison and knew how to scrub the romanticism off the genre.

Nelson released three more albums in 1983—*Tougher than Leather*, *Take It to the Limit,* and *Without a Song*—but they really belong in the next chapter, and we'll consider them there. But the fourteen albums discussed above—the commercial triumphs and flops, the artistic highs and lows—prove that the pluses can outweigh the minuses when you release all the music you have inside you while your creative juices are still flowing.

When artists become famous, they accumulate what I call "celebrity capital," the leverage to make demands of labels, venues, and media who now have reasons to keep you happy. Most artists use this capital to seek better financial terms. Nelson spent some of his on that, but he spent a big chunk of his new-won influence to make records with scant commercial prospects and to get them released on a major label. The biggest winners were the listeners who got to hear Nelson making terrific music with Webb Pierce, Roger Miller, Kris Kristofferson, Hank Cochran, and sister Bobbie that might never have existed otherwise. Money comes and goes, but recordings last forever.

Sharing songs on the Clarks' porch in Nashville in 1972 are (from left) Townes Van Zandt, Susanna Clark, Guy Clark, and Daniel Antopolsky. Willie recorded songs by Townes and Guy, and Susanna painted the cover art for the *Stardust* album.

CHAPTER 5

Tougher Than Leather

A NEW LEASE ON LIFE, 1983–1990

On August 13, 1981, Nelson was at his home on the Hawaiian Island of Maui, his getaway from the rigors of the road and the pressure of fame, a place where he could relax with family and a handful of friends to decompress and recharge. As he often did, he went for an hour-long run along the shore and then cooled off by diving into the ocean. But the sudden change from hot to cold proved too much for his 48-year-old body, and his smoking-stressed left lung collapsed.

Somehow he struggled through the waves to the beach where he lay for nearly half an hour in the sand to catch his breath before walking to a nearby hotel and calling the paramedics. When they arrived, they inserted a tube through his back and into his lung to reinflate it. They had to do this three times before the lung stabilized the next day at the Maui Memorial Hospital. It would be months before he'd be able to resume a normal life, much less his typically abnormal life.

Forced to stop moving so he might heal, he returned to an old habit he'd been neglecting: writing songs. But instead of describing how to cope with a divorce or romantic breakup, he wrote about a more dramatic breakup—with life itself. The stakes were higher, but the message was the same: You have to acknowledge how much hurts, but you have to retain enough self-possession to go on. He could have made the songs autobiographical, but that seemed self-indulgent.

Willie and Bobbie Nelson perform at their childhood church, the Abbott Methodist Church, for CBS TV on March 5, 1988.

Tougher than Leather

"The best time to write, of course, is when things are still," he told me in 1991, "and things haven't been still for a long, long time. . . . But my favorite albums are the ones where I wrote a lot of the songs: *Red Headed Stranger*, *Yesterday's Wine*, *Phases and Stages*, and *Tougher than Leather*. That last one got lost in the shuffle. I wrote that when my lung had collapsed, and I was laid up in the hospital. Again, when I was still."

Instead, he turned to the gambit he'd used for *Red Headed Stranger*; he'd make his narrator an Old West gunslinger for whom confrontations with death were part of the job description. Eventually he had enough of these gunslinger songs for an album that was released in 1983: *Tougher than Leather*, the most underrated of his great concept albums, following in the footsteps of the records mentioned above.

The opening song establishes the steady, somber tone of a dying man facing up to his fate. Nelson plucks his unaccompanied acoustic guitar and slowly drawls, "Was it something I did, Lord, a lifetime ago? Am I just now repaying a debt that I owe?" After a telling pause that implies a "yes" to both questions, Nelson muses, "Justice, sweet justice, you travel so slow," then stubbornly insists, "but you can't change my love for the rose."

Like those in *Red Headed Stranger*, these songs are arranged to form a narrative. Unlike that earlier celebration of rugged individualism, this new collection of songs is a somber mediation on the connections that matter more as death approaches. These deliberately paced, understated songs—seven originals, three of them done twice, and two covers—may lack the rousing punch and accessible sentiments of Nelson's more popular songs, but they gradually draw the listener in by focusing on hard questions with no easy answers.

The opening song depicts death as life's inescapable sentence. Yet the next, "Changing Skies," uses the metaphor of a bird flying through gathering clouds to describe love as another constant. Just the same, the gunman points out, love provides no freedom from the indifferent, ever-changing weather.

These two songs are told in the first person, but the title song switches to the third person to describe an aging gunfighter who shoots down a young challenger and then cruelly crumbles the rose of the dead man's sweetheart. Old Tougher than Leather (as Nelson calls him) rides off into the sunset but is haunted by the memory of the young woman and the kind of love he has long denied himself. Before he can find her, however, death hunts him down and delivers its own brand of justice.

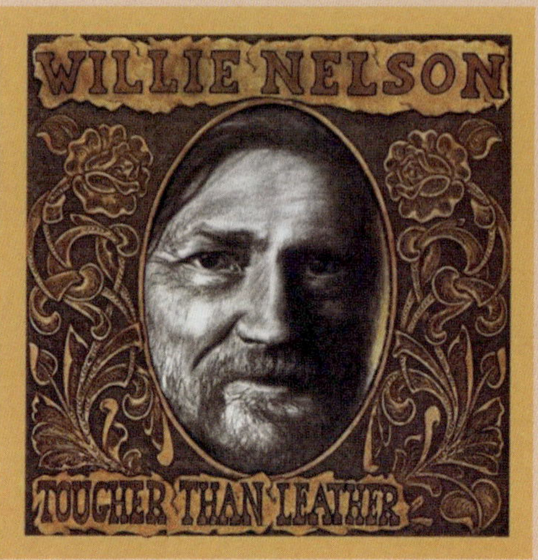

Willie Nelson
***Tougher than Leather* (Columbia)**
Recorded: August/September 1981
Released: February 14, 1983
Willie Compositions: 7/10
Top 40 Single: "Little Old Fashioned Karma" (Country #10)
Album Charts: Country #4, Pop #39

Forced to stay off the road for a month in 1981 while he recuperated from a collapsed lung, Nelson suddenly had both the time and inspiration for the biggest, best songwriting spurt of his middle career. The result was his most cohesive, most ambitious concept album. Most cohesive because all seven of the originals advance the narrative. Most ambitious because it drives home the sobering message that no one—not the fastest gunfighter, not the most elusive rider—escapes death. From the contrarian, lo-fi production of Nelson and bassist Bee Spears to the jazzy licks supplied by Johnny Gimble, Grady Martin, Mickey Raphael, and Nelson himself to the dark, literary lyrics, this record is best understood as an early, never-bettered alternative-country album. **Grade: A+**

The mirror reversal of this tale is "Somewhere in Texas (Part 2)," which depicts death's justice is as amoral as it is inexorable. Another young cowboy is arrested for a fatal stickup committed by someone who looks like him. Sentenced to die in the electric chair, he is sustained by the love of his girlfriend and sits with her rose in his cell. He dies just the same, though, for as Nelson puts it in the closing song, "Nobody Slides, My Friend."

We all live under a death sentence, Nelson implies, and there are no pardons. Love cannot provide freedom from that sentence but can offer some meaning in the face of it. In "Summer of Roses," recycled from *Yesterday's Wine*, Nelson faces up to this fact with a wistful, longing vocal over Johnny Gimble's slow fiddle solo. "A short time I have to be with you, my love," Nelson acknowledges, "but a short time is better than no time at all."

The album's only up-tempo tune is the first single, "Little Old Fashioned Karma," which sports a brisk, crisp Western swing. Gimble, pianist Bobbie Nelson, guitarist Grady Martin, harmonica player Mickey Raphael, and Nelson himself all get off smart solos, as if one could dance on one's own grave. But on the ballads that dominate the record, Nelson seems to let go of each syllable reluctantly, as if trying to collect his courage before the final hammer falls.

When Nelson performed at the Capital Centre in Maryland on March 16, 1983, he opened the show with a solo acoustic version of "My Love for the Rose" from *Tougher than Leather*. On this song of a dying cowboy, Nelson's voice contained resignation, regret, and perseverance, all in the same line. Gradually the band seeped into a medley of songs from the just-released album, and Nelson stripped away the easy sentimentality of most contemporary country music and revealed the more difficult paradoxes that shadow our lives.

Later in the show, he sang a song cycle from another, not-quite-as-good cowboy concept album, *Red Headed Stranger*. Mickey Raphael's harmonica evoked the "scream of the panther" and the "fiery black stallion." Sister Bobbie hid shyly behind her curtain of waist-length hair, but she added country-boogie piano to the fast songs and wistful arpeggios to the slow ones. Atop this backing, Nelson avoided melodramatic flourishes and reduced his singing to a deadpan drawl that almost suggested a casual speaking voice. There was nothing haphazard about this. Having taken us into his confidence, he gave the key phrases a resonant vibrato that was all the more riveting for the contrast.

Willie plays a guitar solo.

Take It to the Limit

Willie with his third wife, Connie Koepke Nelson, at the Astoria Hotel in New York in 1984.

It would have been nice if Nelson's songwriting renaissance on *Tougher than Leather* had carried over to his subsequent projects, but that wasn't what happened. Instead, Nelson hit the road again as soon as he was able, even though his damaged lung made him an audibly weaker singer. For his recording projects, he went back to his post–*Red Headed Stranger* habits: duet albums, soundtrack albums, tribute albums, American Songbook albums, and crossover-pop albums. Some of these were really good and some of them were mediocre, but none of them featured a major crop of new Willie Nelson songs.

In the mediocre category was *Take It to the Limit*, one more attempt to milk the cash cow that was the Waylon & Willie trademark. There was growing antipathy between the two partners. Jennings, originally the bigger star, felt eclipsed by Nelson's success and fed his resentment with cocaine. He sang a duet part on five of the ten tracks but had no solo numbers, allowing his partner to sing the rest of the album by himself.

This was, after all, the first Willie & Waylon project to be released by Columbia, Nelson's label, after the first two and a half (*Willie & Waylon*, *WWII*, and *Wanted! The Outlaws*) had been on Jennings' label, RCA. Each company was eager to showcase its own star on each outing. But Jennings sounds disengaged throughout this recording.

For his part, Nelson hadn't completely regained his vocal strength after his collapsed lung and faltered at key moments. And this was an anti-concept album, mishmashing pop-rock hits by Paul Simon and the Eagles with old honky-tonk classics by George Jones

Willie Nelson and Waylon Jennings
***Take It to the Limit* (Columbia)**
Recorded: October 1981–November 1982
Released: April 18, 1983
Willie Compositions: 1/10
Top 40 Singles: "Why Do I Have to Choose" (Country #3), "Take It to the Limit" (Country #8)
Album Charts: Country #3, Pop #60

This third duet album (not counting *Wanted! The Outlaws*) finds the collaboration losing steam. Maybe it's Jennings' rumored jealousy of Nelson's greater success; maybe it's the aftermath of Nelson's collapsed lung. Maybe it's the feeling that the sessions were so rushed that the singers never took the trouble to work out a real dialogue. There are a few nice moments, but producer Chips Moman tries to cover up the many problems with horns, loud guitars, and cooing female vocals that make it sound like a leftover RCA session. **Grade: C**

and David Allan Coe and songs recycled from past albums by each singer. "Old Friends," for example, was released as a duet with Roger Miller in 1982 and as a duet with Jennings in 1983.

There are a few good moments. Nelson's one new song, "Why Do I Have to Choose," is one of his better romantic-dilemma numbers; and his solo version of Jennings' "We Had It All" has a soulful R&B flavor. But producer Chips Moman tries to cover up the album's many flaws by adding so many sweeteners that he merely adds more problems.

"It's still me and Waylon singing," Nelson told me in 1991. "The arrangements might be a little different. We like each other. There's a lot of mutual admiration and respect. The only thing we're alike is that we're both stubborn; I laugh at his stubbornness, and he laughs at mine. We make a lot of really good music together. He probably doesn't want to admit he likes me that much. We used to fight a lot, but we've mellowed out a lot in the past few years."

Willie Nelson
***Without a Song* (Columbia)**
Recorded: April 1983
Released: October 24, 1983
Willie Compositions: 0/10
Top 40 Single: "Without a Song" (Country #11)
Album Charts: Country #3, Pop #54

R&B legend Booker T. Jones, who produced Nelson's classic *Stardust* album, reunites with the singer for this attempt at a sequel. But the attempt is undercut by an unfortunate cheesiness most obvious on "As Time Goes By," a duet with Julio Iglesias. For every successful song, such as the radiant versions of "Autumn Leaves" or the title track, there's a clunker like "Harbor Lights." **Grade: B-**

Without a Song

Just as it's usually a mistake to try to recapture the magic of a past love affair, it's often just as doomed to try recapture the special moment of a past recording session. That was proved on the follow-up duet albums with Nelson and Jennings and on *Without a Song*, an attempt to replicate the Kismet of the *Stardust* session.

Once again, the session focused on vintage, pre-Elvis pop standards from Hollywood films, Broadway shows, and Tin Pan Alley. Booker T. Jones once again produced, using Nelson's Family band. But this time, the material isn't as strong; instead of tunes from Hoagy Carmichael, George Gershwin, and Duke Ellington, this time we get numbers from James Monaco, Hugh Williams, and Herman Hupfeld. And the vocals are correspondingly less inspired.

It's bad enough that Julio Iglesias, the European superstar, provides a Spanish duet vocal on "As Time Goes By" that's all whispery smarm. It's worse that Nelson echoes him on that song and tracks such as "Harbor Lights" and "Once in a While." Booker tries to pump some feeling into this lazy sentimentality with heavy-handed strings and female vocals until it sounds like a Chet Atkins RCA session. Nelson does rouse himself into push-and-pull brilliance on a few songs—"Autumn Leaves," "I Can't Begin to Tell You," and the title track—but these few gems are not enough.

WILLIE NELSON and FAMILY CONCERT
AUG 3 1984
FRIDAY 8:00 P.M.
MISSISSIPPI VALLEY FAIR
Davenport, Iowa
Not Good For Admission To Fairgrounds No Refunds

Willie and Faron Young backstage at the 4th of July Picnic at the Pedernales Country Club west of Austin in 1980.

Angel Eyes

Nelson had much better luck with his follow-up album of pre-1950 pop standards, *Angel Eyes*, subtitled *Featuring the Guitar of Jackie King*. King was Doug Sahm's childhood friend in San Antonio and went on to back up jazz legends such as Chet Baker and Sonny Stitt on the West Coast. Nelson liked to sit around and pick with King when they were both in Texas, because they both liked Django Reinhardt and Gatemouth Brown. King even replaced Grady Martin in Nelson's road band at one point but proved a poor fit.

Out of that friendship, however, came this project, the first straight-ahead jazz album of Nelson's career. He certainly had the chops to hold his own with King's quartet of Texas jazz cats, and the interplay between Nelson's acoustic guitar and King's hollow-body electric—quicksilver runs alternating with vocal-like melodies—is dazzling.

Nelson seldom showcased his jazz guitar skills as explicitly as this, and that's what makes the album so important, despite its commercial failure. It reveals the weapons the singer kept in his back pocket—a fascination with and a mastery of elastic, elliptical phrasing and improvisation—that influenced everything he sang and played without revealing itself for more than brief moments. But that musical sense that nothing is foreordained, that the next moment is always up for grabs, is what makes Nelson's recordings so riveting even as he approaches the same subject matter again and again.

As listeners, we can't fully appreciate the full spectrum of Nelson's gifts until we approach him as a jazz artist as well as a country artist. This is not as far-fetched as it may first seem. After all, Miles Davis (who shared a manager, Neil Reshen, with Nelson) was so impressed with Nelson's unorthodox tone and phrasing that the jazz trumpeter titled a 1970 composition "Willie Nelson" and recorded it with John McLaughlin and Jack DeJohnette.

The same year Nelson released *Angel Eyes*, he made a surprise appearance on *Master of Suspense*, the new album by jazz trumpeter Jack Walrath. Walrath, who had played with such jazz greats as Charles Mingus, Hank Jones, and Sam Rivers, had created a freewheeling, Mingus-like arrangement of Hank Williams' "I'm So Lonesome I Could Cry"; and he knew the only person who could handle a post-bop arrangement of a honky-tonk standard: Willie Nelson.

Nelson was so intrigued by the idea that he delayed his departure for a long tour to do the session in Texas. It worked so perfectly that Nelson insisted that Walrath and pianist James Williams stick around and cut a version of the cowboy standard, "I'm Sending You a Big Bouquet of Roses." It's uncanny how Nelson's voice curls, dives, twists and climbs like a muted trumpet solo.

Willie Nelson
Angel Eyes **(Columbia)**
Recorded: Late 1983
Released: May 7, 1984
Willie Compositions: 0/8
Top 40 Singles: NA
Album Chart: Pop #116

This album carries the credit "featuring the guitar of Jackie King," and indeed the veteran Texas jazz guitarist is highlighted nearly as much as Nelson. Mixing jazz standards like "I Fall in Love Too Easily" and "There Will Never Be Another You" with country classics from Bob Wills and Spade Cooley, the album illustrates the crucial role of swing in both fields—at least in Texas. Playing acoustic guitar to King's electric archtop, Nelson also proved he could play a jazz solo as nimbly and as imaginatively as anyone. Ray Charles sings the duet part on the title track. **Grade: B+**

Nelson also appears on *Chalk Mark in a Rain Storm*, the 1984 album from Joni Mitchell, another musician who worked with Mingus. The album's best track is the jazz-rock fusion arrangement of the Sons of the Pioneers' old chestnut, "Cool Water." While Mitchell seems to strain a bit for the unusual jazz rhythms and harmonies of the arrangement, Nelson simply relaxes into it.

With minor changes, Nelson played basically the same songs at every show. But if you listened to his concerts as if they were jazz shows, where every improvised departure from the text creates a new story, the show became a lot more interesting. It certainly stood up to such scrutiny.

Harmonica virtuoso Mickey Raphael and legendary Nashville guitarist Grady Martin twisted the country songs through blues scales. Nelson used the bare minimum of notes to pull a song out of its accustomed moorings and into a much more revealing posture. His vocals too delayed an accent to build the tension and then release it in a flurry of syllables. There was a lot more going on at a Willie Nelson show than most people ever noticed. He could take off on a different daredevil improvisation every night, but even when he painted himself into a corner, he would carve a new door in the song's back wall and step through it into a chorus where the crowd could sing along.

City of New Orleans

After *Tougher than Leather*, Nelson's songwriting well ran dry again. After two albums of old pop standards, he turned to contemporary songwriters for his next album, *City of New Orleans*. Recorded in Nashville with producer Chips Moman using his own band, this was another mixed bag. The title track, written by Chicago folk-music hero Steve Goodman and memorably recorded by Arlo Guthrie, was a timeless train song—and Nelson give it a full-bodied treatment over a punchy railroad rhythm that makes the song's charm more obvious than Goodman or Guthrie ever could.

The rest of the album never comes close to that powerful opening. His only original song was "Why Are You Pickin' on Me," a bouncy, witty Pamper demo left over from the early '60s. Instead, he relies on songs associated with Michael Jackson, Elvis

Willie Nelson
***City of New Orleans* (Columbia)**
Recorded: October 1983
Released: July 16, 1984
Willie Compositions: 1/10
Top 40 Single: "City of New Orleans" (Country #1)
Album Charts: Country #1, Pop #69

The title track, Steve Goodman's indelible folk song, is transformed into an American anthem of the nation as seen from a moving train window, thanks to Nelson's seemingly off-handed vocal over a propulsive track. He does something similar with one of his older, wittier songs, but the rest of the album tries too hard. Nelson abandons his usual ironic detachment and pushes the maudlin side of ballads such as "She's Out of My Life" and "The Wind Beneath My Wings." Producer Chips Moman once again loads up the strings, horns, and backing voices till the tracks sag under the weight. **Grade: C+**

Presley, Neil Diamond, Danny O'Keefe, Buffy Sainte-Marie, Dave Loggins, Conway Twitty, and Faron Young that don't seem to inspire him that much. Much of this music is sentimental balladry, and Nelson too often gives in to its manipulative songwriting, squeezing a predictable response from the listener rather than wrestling with the paradoxes of real-life romance and letting the listener decide for oneself.

Music from Songwriter

When he was invited to co-star with Kris Kristofferson in a movie entitled *Songwriter*, Nelson concluded that perhaps he should actually write some new songs for it. Nelson and his longtime drinking buddy Bud Shrake, an Austin journalist and novelist, were sharing a bottle of tequila just before Christmas of 1977 when they came up with the whole storyline for *Songwriter*. It took them seven years to get the cameras rolling, but Sydney Pollack, the director of *Electric Horseman* and the producer of *Honeysuckle Rose*, agreed to produce the script with Robert Altman protégé Alan Rudolph directing.

Nelson would play Doc Jenkins, an aging star who quits songwriting and performing because he's been cheated out of his money so many times. Instead, he decides to manage his former singing partner, Blackie Buck (Kristofferson) and a young up-and-comer, Gilda (Lesley Ann Warren). The old-timers plot to get revenge on Doc's music publisher while helping Gilda go from awkward wannabe to poised pro. It's Nelson's best film, full of entertaining hijinks but as serious about musical creativity as it is irreverent about the music business.

That care for the music pays off in a terrific soundtrack album: *Music from Songwriter*. The two duets and four solo Kristofferson performances were written by Kristofferson. But the five solo Nelson tracks were all written by him, including three new songs and much-improved versions of "Write Your Own Songs" from *WWII* and "Good Times" from the RCA album of that name. Unlike most pop soundtracks, which usually have no more than a tangential relationship to the movie's subject, these songs by Nelson and Kristofferson crystallize the central themes of "Songwriter" far better than anything in the script.

In fact, side one of the vinyl LP is a kind of mini-concept album, centered on the challenges of the songwriter life. This is a variation on his usual theme: the challenges of the married life. Each life has its rewards, and each has its trials. If you are honest about both halves of that reality, you will be pulled in opposite directions by all the contradictions and paradoxes. The only way to survive that tug-of-war is through the art of irony, the ability to hold in

Willie Nelson & Kris Kristofferson
Music from Songwriter **(Columbia)**
Recorded: May/June 1984
Released: October 8, 1984
Willie Compositions: 5/11
Top 40 Singles: NA
Album Charts: Country #21, Pop #152

Robert Altman protégé Alan Rudolph created one of the best movies ever made about the pop music business when he filmed Nelson and Kristofferson as renegades trying to cope with sleazy concert promoters and music publishers. The two stars sang two duets for the picture, supplemented by five terrific originals from Nelson and four more from Kristofferson—all set to sparkling, minimalist backing that inspired some of Nelson's best singing and picking. Best of all was the acid-dipped remake of "Write Your Own Songs," a sweet suggestion where Nashville big shots can stick their contracts and a perfect summation of the movie's themes. **Grade: A-**

one mind the way things should be and the way things actually are.

The new song "Nobody Said It Was Going to Be Easy," co-credited to Nelson and Mickey Raphael, could apply to either life. In fact, it connects them by offering solace to the long-suffering wives of musicians. This sad, spare country waltz suggests we shouldn't be surprised by the title's philosophy, because "it was never easy before."

Another new song, "Who'll Buy My Memories," is a country lament about the songwriter's troubling dilemma: how can one turn one's most personal treasures—one's memories—into commodities that one can sell to pay the rent.

"Write Your Own Songs" is a patient but lethal assault on "Mr. Music Executive" and "Mr. Purified Country" who disparage songwriters' habits while getting rich off their labor. Yet another new waltz, "Songwriter" offers encouragement to all Nelson's despairing colleagues, urging them to "Write on, write on," no matter what the obstacles, lest "it all slip away." Nelson took his own advice and turned in his best writing since *Tougher than Leather*.

These last four songs are all delivered with the slow, sparse arrangements Nelson thrives in. His deep-grained voice holds each syllable until it has acquired a resonant hum before releasing it. His all-star band plays with admirable restraint, and producer Booker T. Jones adds just enough organ to reinforce the resonance.

On the other side, Jones uses much thicker arrangements to compensate for Kristofferson's vocal liabilities. Wrapping the songs in slide guitar, organ, phased guitar, and echoed harmony vocals, Jones achieves a dense atmospheric sound that casts an eerie spell. Recognizing that Kristofferson is a much better actor than singer, Jones focuses on the dramatic qualities of his voice with good results.

Kristofferson responds with his best songwriting in years. He draws on the old metaphor of the country music rebel as an outlaw into two songs about fugitives on the run: "Crossing the Border" and "Under the Gun." The ghostly vocals and unnerving slide guitar evoke both the freedom and fear of being an outsider. Billy Swan joins him for a duet vocal on the witty heartbreak song, "Down to Her Socks." Kristofferson ends the album with the somber, austere "The Final Attraction," a semi-autobiographical look at an aging singer-songwriter who somehow rouses himself from all his defeats to connect with his audience one more time.

Me and Paul

If he was having trouble writing new songs, Nelson could always reach into his storeroom of old songs, dust them off, shine them up, and put them on a new album. If he was frustrated by the production on the original version or disappointed that so few people heard the song the first time, he could give his favorite children a second chance. That's what he did for *Me and Paul*, an album that supplemented two new compositions with three from old RCA albums, two from the Pamper demos, and one each from his brief, commercially stunted days on Monument and Atlantic Records.

"I can't believe those songs weren't a hit the first time," he told the *Washington Post* in 1998. "So, I've given them another life, another chance, because I think they're better than the public acceptance would suggest. Maybe the arrangement wasn't right, or the production, or there wasn't enough promotion. All these things to blame it on. I think the song was good, and I just want to give it another chance."

To these nine originals, he added three Billy Joe Shaver songs that Waylon Jennings had recorded on his landmark 1973 album, *Honky Tonk Heroes*. All ten of the old songs were given new life by Nelson's more mature singing and by the slinky, virtuosic playing of his band—with guest electric guitarist Grady Martin and harmonica whiz Mickey Raphael providing especially tasty fills and solos. This was musical recycling at its most useful.

In contrast to Jennings' country-rock stomping, which emphasized the punchlines of Shaver's choruses, Nelson's country-jazz subtlety brings out the surprisingly elegant wordplay of Shaver's verses. Some of Nelson's own inventive language can be heard in the reverie of "I Let My Mind Wander," an old Pamper demo, and in the reverse psychology of "I Never Cared," a Monument single. From his first two concept-album masterpieces, the poor-selling *Yesterday's Wine* and *Phases and Stages* come the overlooked gems "Me and Paul," an ode to male friendship, and "Pretend I Never Happened," a plea that the singer is doing his best to undermine.

With all this high-quality songwriting lined up, Nelson's new songs had a high standard to meet. "She's Gone" is a respectable though slight ballad, but "Forgiving You Was Easy" is one of his best mid-tempo, two-step creations. The lyrics admit that pardoning is easy but forgetting is hard, and yet the music does everything it can to ease that pang. It's a reminder that whenever Nelson has the right material, the right band, and the right mood, he can still work wonders.

Willie and Neil Young onstage at the Farm Aid concert in Camden, New Jersey, on September 30, 2006.

Willie Nelson
***Me and Paul* (Columbia)**
Recorded: November 1984
Released: February 25, 1985
Willie Compositions: 9/12
Top 40 Singles: "Forgiving You Was Easy" (Country #1), "Me and Paul" (Country #14)
Album Charts: Country #3, Pop #152

This odd album takes seven of Nelson's early compositions from his pre-*Red Headed Stranger* years and adds two new originals and three Billy Joe Shaver songs, and gives them all the slinky, jazz-country treatment that his mid-'80s band was so masterful at. The results shed new, welcome light on all ten of the old songs, revealing them as more subtle than one ever knew. One of the new originals, "Forgiving You Was Easy," was so catchy that the music was the antidote to the lyrics' pain. **Grade: A**

Funny How Time Slips Away/Brand on My Heart

On April 22, 1985, Nelson released two more duet albums with aging country stars: *Funny How Time Slips Away* with Faron Young and *Brand on My Heart* with Hank Snow. With these, he seemed to have discharged his debt to the previous generation. He would continue to record duet albums with his contemporaries such as Haggard, Jennings, and Shaver; but these releases wrapped up his salutes to the previous generation. The two albums were recorded separately—the Young with Fred Foster producing a band of old-timers in Texas, the Snow with Chips Moman producing his own band in Nashville—but they felt like two sides of the same coin.

Nelson had stronger ties to Young, who once gave the starving young songwriter a big break by refusing his offer to sell "Hello Walls" for a pittance. Instead, Young recorded it and turned it into a #1 hit in 1961. Nelson also wrote the B-side, "Congratulations," which hit #28 on its own. The following year, Young had another Top 10 hit with Nelson's "Three Days." The singer and the writer reunite for duets on these three songs, four more Nelson originals, four more Young hits, and a Mel Tillis song. Joe Allison, producer of Nelson's debut album, wrote Young's smash, "Live Fast, Love Hard, Die Young."

Snow and Nelson had less of a personal connection, but they had both left small towns to travel far and wide. Snow captured the exhilaration of that escape and rambling on classic road songs such as "I've Been Everywhere," "I'm Moving On," and "Golden Rocket"—all #1 country singles. The record is filled out with more Snow hits such as "A Fool Such as I," the Ivory Joe Hunter blues "I Almost Lost My Mind," Jimmie Davis's 1938 hit, "It Makes No Difference Now," and Hank Locklin's 1954 hit, "Send Me the Pillow You Dream On."

By 1985, however, the baritones of both Young and Snow had lost their luster. Young tried to com-

Willie Nelson and Faron Young
***Funny How Time Slips Away* (Columbia)**
Recorded: April 1984
Released: April 22, 1985
Willie Compositions: 7/12
Top 40 Singles: NA
Album Charts: NA

This is a payback album. Young was one of the first singers to record Nelson's songs when the latter was an unknown newcomer to Nashville in 1961. Twenty-five years later, they hold an obviously affectionate reunion to sing duets on Young's Nelson-written hits "Hello Walls" and "Three Days," five more Nelson compositions, plus some other Young hits. Unfortunately, Young's excessive vibrato doesn't fit comfortably with the cleanliness of Nelson's delivery. **Grade: C+**

Ray Charles enjoyed a chart-topping country duet with Willie, "Seven Angels" in 1985.

Willie Nelson and Hank Snow
***Brand on My Heart* (Columbia)**
Recorded: September 1984
Released: April 22, 1985
Willie Compositions: 0/10
Top 40 Singles: NA
Album Charts: NA

Of all of Nelson's duet albums with older country stars, this is the weakest. His admiration for Nova Scotia's Snow is justified and surely sincere, but the two voices don't match up well. Snow's overly ornate delivery, full of quivers, is a poor match for Nelson's restrained approach. The repertoire is Snow's hits and an odd assortment of standards. **Grade: C**

Elvis Presley and Hank Snow, seen here backstage in 1955, shared the same manager in Colonel Tom Parker, and both had their songs reworked by Willie.
Opposite: Willie tours in support of *The Promiseland* album in Miami on June 27, 1986.

pensate by adding vibrato and embellishment in every nook and cranny, while Snow adds a hint of Jimmie Rodgers yodel to decorate his thinning instrument. By contrast, Nelson's vocals are a model of unfussy minimalism. Young would die in 1988 and Snow in 1999, so Nelson was lucky to record them when he could—but it was probably already too late.

Highwayman

During the July 13, 1985, Live Aid benefit concert for victims of the 1983–1985 Ethiopian famine, Bob Dylan suggested that maybe some of the money raised could go to America's family farmers, who were slowly but surely being squeezed out of existence by a consolidating agribusiness industry. Nelson, who had seen the slow-motion destruction in East Texas, was inspired by the comment to organize the first Farm Aid concert on September 22, 1985, in Champaign, Illinois. Joining him onstage were Dylan, Johnny Cash, Merle Haggard, John Fogerty, Billy Joel, B. B. King, Loretta Lynn, Roy Orbison, Lou Reed, Tom Petty, Emmylou Harris, and many more.

It came together so quickly not only because many artists felt the same way but also because Nelson and his team had been organizing large, multi-artist, outdoor concerts ever since they began their more-or-less annual Fourth of July Picnics in 1973. Nelson said

Waylon Jennings, Willie Nelson, Johnny Cash, and Kris Kristofferson
***Highwayman* (Columbia)**
Recorded: Winter 1984–1985
Released: May 6, 1985
Willie Compositions: 0/10
Top 40 Singles: "Highwayman" (Country #1), "Desperados Waiting for a Train" (Country #15)
Album Chart: Country #1

This is the kind of boisterous, barroom sing-along that sounds good at closing time, but not so great in the light of day. While Kristofferson has never had much of a voice, Cash and Jennings boast strong, distinctive instruments—but they lack the adaptability necessary for harmony singing. Nelson and guest vocalist Johnny Rodriguez have their moments, but this was as much an artistic flop as it was a box-office hit. **Grade: C-**

Above: Willie performs at the Cheyenne Frontier Days Arena in Wyoming on July 17, 1987.

he scheduled those shows in the middle of Texas's blistering summers so his redneck and hippie fans would be too hot to fight. But Farm Aid was inspired by nobler intentions.

"We have fewer farmers now," he told *No Depression* in 2004. "We used to have eight million. Now we're less than two million. We're losing 300–800 a week. And that's the plan of the powers that be; that's the way they set it up. Because they think fewer and bigger is better. I know that's not the truth. I know that when you take a farmer off his land, you also take him out of his home."

Nelson was invited to join his old compadres Jennings and Kristofferson on Johnny Cash's annual TV Christmas special in 1984. Cash didn't know Nelson that well but was a longtime pal of the other two, and the quartet soon bonded over guitars in a Swiss hotel. They enjoyed each other's company so much they agreed to make a record. Maybe they should have released a tape from that hotel lobby, for what came out was an overproduced and under-thought boondoggle titled *Highwayman* and credited to Waylon Jennings/Willie Nelson/Johnny Cash/Kris Kristofferson (they would adopt the Highwaymen name later).

On the front cover, the four faces float in a cloud above a desert landscape as if peering out from Mount Rushmore, and on the vinyl LP inside they sing as if from the bottom of the Grand Canyon, thanks to the booming echo producer Chips Moman added to everything. These are big voices that need room to maneuver, but here they are crowded in a small space and react by getting louder rather than freer. Nelson and Cash are on every track; Jennings and Kristofferson drop in here and there.

Johnny Cash wrote the only two originals—"Big River," one of his best, and "Committed to Parkview," one of his worst—and Cindy Walker is represented by one of her weakest, "Jim, I Wore a Tie Today." But even songs as good as Guy Clark's "Desperados Waiting for a Train" and Bob Seger's "Against the Wind" are done in by the over-singing and over-playing. Jimmy Webb's title track is overwritten. Tex-Mex singer Johnny Rodriguez adds a personal touch to Woody Guthrie's "Deportee," and Nelson leads Cash through a witty rendition of John Prine's "The Twentieth Century Is Almost Over." That's it for the bright spots.

Half Nelson

Nelson spent much of his time after *Stardust* singing duets with friends old and new. Many of them were full-album projects, such as *Pancho & Lefty* with Merle Haggard; but several were one-off collaborations that were released on the albums of his singing partners. *Half Nelson* gathers those scattered efforts onto a single disc. The title track from the Haggard album is joined by duets that originally appeared on albums by Neil Young, Ray Charles, Julio Iglesias, Carlos Santana, Mil Tillis, and Lacy J. Dalton.

Three songs make their debut here. Nelson adds his vocal and acoustic guitar to a recently discovered Hank Williams demo of "I Told a Lie to My Heart," the kind of post-breakup ballad of mixed feelings that Nelson might have written himself. It's a good song, but the original guitar part on the demo is so slow and stiff that the song never ignites. More successful are the duets with Leon Russell and George Jones on the Rolling Stones' "Honky Tonk Women" and Nelson's own "Half a Man."

And this reveals a truth about Nelson's duets: He's such a sympathetic partner that he will often adopt the affect of the other singer. He can become as maudlin as Iglesias or as cathartic as Jones, as snappy as Tillis or as robust as Charles. Nelson's like a chameleon who blends in with his surroundings or a generous actor who accommodates his fellow cast members.

He had both pop and country hits, but he excelled at everything from Broadway and jazz standards to soul, blues and rock. Born down South in the '30s, he attracted some unwanted publicity for his legal problems. But he is more likely to be remembered for his unorthodox singing style: a gravelly purr that implies a life of stoic suffering and resilient spirit matched with phrasing that either pulls back at the beat or

Willie Nelson
***Half Nelson* (Columbia)**
Recorded: 1978-1985
Released: 1985
Willie Compositions: 1/10
Top 40 Singles: "To All the Girls I've Loved Before" (Country #1, Pop #5), "Seven Spanish Angels" (Country #1)
Album Charts: Country #10, Pop #178

Nelson will sing a duet with anyone—even a dead man. He proves as much by adding his vocals to a newly discovered demo of "I Told a Lie to My Heart" by Hank Williams. It's joined by two other unreleased duets (with Leon Russell and George Jones), his hit duet with Merle Haggard on "Pancho & Lefty" and six previously released duets on his partners' 1983-85 albums. The full spectrum of Nelson's duets is on display: from the sublime "Seven Spanish Angels" with Ray Charles to the sappy "To All the Girls I've Loved Before" with Julio Iglesias. Duets with Neil Young, Carlos Santana, Mel Tillis, and Lacy J. Dalton are also represented. **Grade: B**

pushes it forward to make each line distinctively his.

That this description fits both Ray Charles and Willie Nelson indicates just how similar these two giants of American music are. Mutual admirers, they appeared on each other's TV specials and recorded together, most notably on "Seven Spanish Angels," which appeared on Charles's *Friendship* album in 1984 and Nelson's *Half Nelson* in 1985.

The Promiseland

As he had on the *Sugar Moon* session, Nelson brought Haggard's Strangers back to the studio to make an album called *The Promiseland.* He supplemented Haggard's guys with some of his own, including his new electric guitarist, an Arkansas youngster named David Lynn Jones. Jones wrote the title track, a moody tribute to America's potential that also points out how the land's promise has not always been kept. Nelson produced it as a lush anthem with strings without spoiling it.

Even better is Jones's "Here in My Heart," a good impersonation of the bittersweet, post-breakup ballads Nelson used to write. Nelson, in fact, wrote a new one, "I'm Trying Not to Forget You," for this session. The more he insists he's forgetting the woman, the more he remembers her. We've all been there.

Side one is devoted to the slower material, including the album's highlight: a version of Floyd Tillman's "I've Got the Craziest Feeling," which infects the listener with that off-kilter mood, thanks to the way Nelson's voice and Johnny Gimble's fiddle warp the expected rhythms. Side two is devoted to spry, up-tempo swing arrangements, whether the song is Louis Armstrong's "Basin Street Blues" or J. S. Bach's "Minuet in G." Gimble, Jones, Paul Buskirk, the Strangers, and Nelson himself go to town on these.

Partners

In the mythology of Willie Nelson, there's an assumption that RCA was the bad record company that buried him under strings and choirs, while Columbia was the good record company that set him free from all that. But a decade after *Red Headed Stranger*, Columbia got so fed up with their star's defiantly

Willie Nelson
***The Promiseland* (Columbia)**
Recorded: November 1985
Released: March 10, 1986
Willie Compositions: 1/11
Top 40 Singles: "Living in the Promiseland" (Country #1), "I'm Not Trying to Forget You" (Country #21)
Album Chart: Country #1

Produced by Nelson himself at his home recording studio with the Strangers, this album has only one original song and no overarching concept or guest stars—just another eclectic collection of songs from his friends and his childhood. But the more you listen, the more obvious it becomes that this session combines the personal warmth of folk and country music with the highest musical standards of jazz and classical music. Side one is ballads, and side two is up-tempo swing; but the interplay of Nelson's acoustic guitar and Johnny Gimble's fiddle resembles the similar dialogue between Django Reinhardt and Stephane Grappelli.
Grade: B+

Willie Nelson
***Partners* (Columbia)**
Recorded: September 1984
Released: October 6, 1986
Willie Compositions: 1/10
Top 40 Single: "Partners After All" (Country #24)
Album Chart: Country #13

If Nelson seems a bit detached and unusually predictable in his vocals on this album, it may be because he felt alienated by Chips Moman's heavy-handed production that swamped the voice and guitar in violins, female vocals and studio effects. Moman and/or his in-house pianist Bobby Emmons wrote three of the weakest numbers, including the hit single. But even the best songs are sabotaged by the misfit between the singer and the arrangements. **Grade: D**

uncommercial duet and jazz albums with his pals that the label insisted that every second or third album have the glossy production of the era's crossover pop-country.

On *Partners*, producer Chips Moman entombs Nelson's uncomfortable voice in so much echo, strings, and backing vocals that it might as well have been a Chet Atkins production from 1967. Moman even duplicates RCA's sins on a remake of the title track from Nelson's 1969 RCA album, *My Own Peculiar Way*. Promising songs from Neil Young, James Taylor, Johnny Rodriguez, and Ernest Tubb are suffocated on arrival.

I'd Rather Have Jesus

While Nelson was going through the motions on the projects Columbia cooked up for him, he was pouring his heart into projects his sister, Bobbie, wanted to do. Many of them were gospel albums, and one of the best is the overlooked *I'd Rather Have Jesus*. It was as if Willie were willing to do whatever the company asked of him so long as he could also record and release the music he loved.

Willie and Bobbie Nelson
***I'd Rather Have Jesus* (Arrival)**
Recorded: 1986
Released: 1986
Willie Compositions: 0/11
Top 40 Singles: NA
Album Charts: NA

This is one of the Nelson siblings' better small-label gospel projects, if only because Willie and Mickey Raphael bring so many instrumental flourishes to the material, which is mostly public-domain hymns. Bee Spears plays bass and co-produces with Bobbie's son Freddy Fletcher. **Grade: B+**

Island in the Sea

The contrast between the music Nelson wanted to make and the music his record company wanted him to make is illustrated by the next album, *Island in the Sea*. Side one of the original LP includes four Nelson originals and Tom Paxton's folk music classic, "The Last Thing on My Mind," all produced by Nelson with his own band and his preferred sound—stripped down to allow maximum freedom of interpretation and improvisation.

The title track is slight—a valentine to the singer's second home in Hawaii, complete with ersatz Hawaiian motifs. But the other new number, "There Is No Easy Way (But There Is a Way)," offers an unusual twist on Nelson's lifelong exploration of broken marriages in song. Here, at last, the couple tries to get back together, acknowledging that the attempt will be difficult, even painful, while holding out hope that it's worth the effort. Nelson's vocal, egged on by a steel guitar, reflects both the hope and the struggle.

Just as good are two of his earliest and best post-breakup songs: "Wake Me When It's Over" and "Little Things," both from his early Liberty days. They get the sumptuous vocals and jazzy solos that Nelson couldn't have managed in the early '60s. Best of all is the thrilling treatment of the Paxton song, which also benefits from a vocal the composer was never capable of.

But flip the LP over and you find a very different record, a collection of odds and ends left over from Nelson's mid-'80s sessions. "Nobody There but Me" was written by Bruce Hornsby (with jazz legend Charlie Haden), and Nelson sings it with Hornsby and his band—plus Raphael. It works, but it's very different from the first side. Next up is "Cold November Wind," a dying-love ballad that gets a big, melodramatic production from Grady Martin—not bad but different from everything else on the album. The last three songs were produced by Booker T. Jones and co-written by him and Will Jennings. These take the melodrama over the top.

Willie Nelson
***Island in the Sea* (Columbia)**
Recorded: March 1987
Released: June 29, 1987
Willie Compositions: 4/10
Top 40 Single: "Island in the Sea" (Country #27)
Album Chart: Country #14

This schizophrenic album devotes side one to four Nelson originals—two new and two old—and Tom Paxton's "The Last Thing on My Mind." All five are given minimalist arrangements that encourage maximum creativity from Nelson and his band. Side two is devoted to a very different but effective song by and with Bruce Hornsby, a rare production by guitarist Grady Martin, and three overcooked pop numbers produced by Booker T. Jones. **Grade: B**

Opposite: Merle Haggard and Willie appear in support of their *Seashores of Old Mexico* album on August 26, 1988.

Walking the Line

In 1987, Epic Records released two albums featuring collaborations between Nelson and Haggard. The first, *Walking the Line*, was a cobbled-together package of previously released duet and solo tracks by Nelson, Haggard, and/or George Jones. Its only value is collecting in one place Nelson's version of Gregg Allman's "Midnight Rider" (a 1979 single), his duet with Jones on "I Gotta Get Drunk," and the Haggard/Jones duet on "Yesterday's Wine."

Willie Nelson, George Jones, and Merle Haggard
***Walking the Line* (Epic)**
Recorded: 1978–1982
Released: June 16, 1987
Willie Compositions: 4/10
Top 40 Singles: NA
Album Charts: NA

This is a compilation of previously released duet and solo tracks by the three singers in various combinations. It pulls together some scattered, worthy tracks but adds nothing to them. **Grade: C**

Above: Johnny Cash, Kris Kristofferson, Willie, and Waylon Jennings in a promotional still from the 1986 movie *Stagecoach*. Opposite: Standing next to Kris Kristofferson and Waylon Jennings, Willie accepts his induction into the Country Music Hall of Fame at the Grand Ole Opry House in Nashville on September 29, 1993.

Seashores of Old Mexico

More ambitious was *Seashores of Old Mexico*, an attempt to replicate the artistic and commercial success of Nelson and Haggard's 1983 duet album, *Pancho & Lefty*. It didn't come close on either count, but it is not without its pleasures. Haggard's five compositions include two old ones (the slight but amusing title song and the masterful farewell song, "Silver Wings"). "Shotgun and a Pistol" is a kind of sequel to "Pancho and Lefty," a song about two outlaws who realize that "death is the way of the gun." "Jimmy the Broom" is a skillful portrait of an alcoholic casino janitor and his complicated life that the gamblers never glimpsed.

The album's one dud is a version of the Beatles' "Yesterday," which Haggard sabotages with a half-hearted, disdainful vocal, even though it was a highlight of Nelson's only RCA live album. The album's triumph is a version of "If I Could Only Fly," the aspirational ballad of a down-and-outer, the best-known song by Austin's immensely gifted but deeply troubled songwriter Blaze Foley.

Nelson's one composition on the album, "Why Do I Have to Choose," benefits greatly from Haggard's duet part, which is far more sensitive than Jennings' on *Take It to the Limit*, where the song first appeared. This time the lyrics receive a minimalist arrangement that allows Nelson to ask in bewildered melancholy why he has to decide between the two women he loves. "The love is not the same," he croons, "but either love is true." On the second verse, Haggard enters to second that emotion.

What's miraculous about this performance is the way it questions the very assumptions of monogamy—a radical proposition in any era, any genre of pop music—in such a laid-back, nonconfrontational, almost regretful way that it allows the listener to think about the issues without getting all riled up first. The song doesn't propose a solution to the conundrum; the track merely acknowledges the dilemma—important in itself. The guitar solos (acoustic, then electric) take the complicated issue into territory where words can't follow—and invites us to come along if we dare.

Willie Nelson and Merle Haggard
***Seashores of Old Mexico* (Epic)**
Recorded: June 1987
Released: October 13, 1987
Willie Compositions: 1/10
Top 40 Singles: NA
Album Chart: Country #31

Nelson is basically a guest on this album dominated by Haggard's vocals, Haggard's compositions, Haggard's band, and Haggard's late-'80s slow, slow tempos on Haggard's label. The title track is a throwaway adventure story, and the spiritless version of the Beatles' "Yesterday" is a missed opportunity. But the ballad versions of Blaze Foley's "If I Could Only Fly," Nelson's monogamy-challenging "Why Do I Have to Choose," and Haggard's character study of "Jimmy the Broom" are brilliant. **Grade: B+**

What a Wonderful World

In the '80s, Nelson seemed to be working three dif ferent kinds of record-making: tribute/duet albums, solo albums of newish material, and solo albums of vintage material. In 1988, it was time to do another vintage project, this time with one duet to bait record buyers and a Chips Moman neo-country politan production.

The problematic results on *What a Wonderful World*, are epitomized by the title track, best known as a Louis Armstrong single. With his bubbly, infectious optimism, Armstrong could get away with singing lines as trite as "the colors of the rainbow, so pretty in the sky," but those words sound wooden in the mouth of a heartbreak master like Nelson. It doesn't help that Moman ups the sugar content by piling on synths and a choir.

The fairy-tale sentiments of Rodgers & Hammerstein's "Some Enchanted Evening" sound stiff and uncomfortable sung by the man who wrote "Night Life." The high-glucose duet with Julio Iglesias on "Spanish Eyes" is further still from Nelson's usual mixed feelings about relationships. Even "Moon River," a moody, unsettled song well matched to Nelson's personality, has its fine vocal and harmonica part sabotaged by synths and singers.

When musical elements are massed together on predictable paths like this, all sense of individual choice evaporates—and with it, any whiff of personality. We listeners are confronted not by human beings revealing themselves in their musical decisions but by a preprogrammed machine that runs over us.

Lincoln "Chips" Moman produced more than a dozen albums for Willie.

Willie Nelson
***What a Wonderful World* (Columbia)**
Recorded: March 1988
Released: September 20, 1988
Willie Compositions: 0/10
Top 40 Single: "Spanish Eyes" (Country #8)
Album Chart: Country #6

This is the weakest of Nelson's reworking of vintage show tunes and Tin Pan Alley numbers. The material is poorly chosen—its cotton-candy positivity at odds with Nelson's usual conflicted attitude—and the arrangements are overblown. Some elements that sold records in the past—a Julio Iglesias duet, a Chips Moman production, and songs by Harold Arlen, Hoagy Carmichael, and Richard Rodgers—prove ineffectual this time. **Grade: C-**

A Horse Called Music/Born for Trouble

Willie Nelson
A Horse Called Music **(Columbia)**
Recorded: July 1988–March 1989
Released: July 31, 1989
Willie Compositions: 3/10
Top 40 Singles: "Nothing I Can Do about It Now" (Country #1), "There You Are" (Country #8)
Album Chart: Country #2

Nelson and his old Monument Records producer Fred Foster reunite to revisit their 1963 collaboration "I Never Cared for You," two more originals and seven songs from contemporary Nashville songwriters. The aim is to make a mainstream country-radio album, and they do that, creating two hit singles and a modern-sounding blend of pop and country. Sometimes Foster goes overboard with the strings, synths, and singers—and sometimes he shows restraint, allowing a handful of good songs and good performances to be heard. **Grade: B-**

In 1988, Nelson's long marriage to Connie came to an end. They saw less and less of each other as he spent most of his time on the road and on his Texas ranch, while she preferred Colorado and California. They were separated by the time he was working on the 1986 TV movie *Stagecoach*. On the set, Nelson fell in love with his makeup artist, Annie D'Angelo; by 1988, she was pregnant with Nelson's second son, Lukas, and Connie threw in the towel. A third son, Micah, was born in 1990—and Nelson finally married D'Angelo on September 16, 1991.

Three months later, Nelson's first son, Billy Jr., was discovered dead in the barn on the family's old Ridgetop property in Tennessee. After years of being in and out of rehab, in and out of deep debt, he had hung himself. He was 33. He had made a gospel album and had been married and divorced, but he could never seem to carve out a life for himself beyond being a famous man's son.

His father buried his grief by getting back to work. He played the previously scheduled New Year's Eve show in Branson, Missouri. In Patoski's book, Nelson says the biggest disappointment of his life was "losing Billy."

Nelson got back on the road and back in the studio. During his brief stay with Monument Records in 1964, Nelson and label owner Fred Foster collaborated on one of the singer's best singles, "I Never Cared." It was a masterful bit of songwriting—by claiming he never cared about his ex, he reveals how much he did—and it benefited from a minimalist arrangement and a deliberately ambiguous vocal.

The singer and producer took another whack at the song on the 1989 album *A Horse Called Music*. This time Nelson's singing and playing are even stronger, bringing out the Tex-Mex and cowboy flavors in the music and the paradox in the lyrics. Like Moman, Foster adds Nashville strings and backup singers—but he does so more tastefully, keeping them well in the background.

After so many records exploring the past, Nelson clearly wanted to make some contemporary Nashville albums; and he invited Foster to help him on *A Horse Called Music* and its sequel, *Born for Trouble*. Both projects lean on Music Row pickers, strings, and harmony singers to add radio-friendly countrypolitan touches to Nelson's outlaw-country instincts. The twenty songs on the two albums include three by Nelson, five by Nashville writer Beth Nielsen Chapman, two by Nelson's longtime pal Hank Cochran, one by Foster, and nine by other Music Row pros.

Willie Nelson
***Born for Trouble* (Columbia)**
Recorded: December 1989
Released: September 24, 1990
Willie Compositions: 0/10
Top 40 Singles: "Ain't Necessarily So" (Country #17)
Album Chart: Country #31

Nelson and Foster recycle the formula from *A Horse Called Music* with the same musicians and three more songs from Beth Nielsen Chapman. There are none from Nelson but two from his old pal Hank Cochran and one from Foster, who shows more restraint this time around. This results in better art but lower sales. **Grade: B**

Things start out well on *A Horse Called Music*, with Foster exercising restraint on "I Never Cared for You" and two tunes that were clearly crafted for his persona by professional enough writers. Chapman's "Nothing I Can Do about It Now," which became a hit single, finds the singer once again refusing to apologize for all the mistakes he's made. This combination of honest confession and stubborn dignity is the difficult trick that Nelson has modeled for all of us again and again. "The Highway" is a road song with enough picaresque details to carry Nelson's attention and ours.

Things go soft in the middle as Foster goes overboard with his productions and smothers the song. Things perk up at the end with the title track (by Wayne Carson, co-writer of "Always on My Mind") and a remake of "Mr. Record Man," both given stripped-down arrangements that provide room for Nelson's voice and guitar to tell each story. A new original, "Is the Better Part Over," describes a relationship that's running out of steam—or maybe an aging man's life. It's framed by swooping string charts that periodically clear to let the wistfulness come through.

Born for Trouble emphasizes more humor and traditional country instruments such as mandolin, steel, and fiddle. Witty lyrics are reinforced by an up-tempo string band on Chapman's hit single, "Ain't Necessarily So," and by country-swing on Foster's title track. Cochran contributes two examples of the romantic post-mortems that Nelson is so good with. As on its predecessor, this album suffers from Foster's overproduction in the middle but benefits from his better taste early and late.

Highwayman 2

Following the chart-topping success of their debut album, *Highwayman*, the quartet of Nelson, Waylon Jennings, Johnny Cash, and Kris Kristofferson renamed themselves the Highwaymen. Given the press criticism of that first record as a slapdash, impersonal affair, they vowed to do better by bringing more than two original songs to the follow-up, *Highwayman 2*. Unfortunately, these songs weren't very good.

Nelson contributed a pair of new songs, "Texas" and "Two Stories Wide," two of the weakest efforts he ever made public. Over glee-club music, they made the less-than-bold assertions that Texas is swell and there are two sides to every story. Kristofferson recycled one tune each from two of his more forgettable albums, and his singing was even worse than on the first Highwaymen album.

Cash, who wrote the only two originals on the first Highwaymen effort, returns with only "Songs That Made a Difference," a name-dropping list of his songwriting pals from the '60s.

Jennings co-wrote "Angels Love Bad Men," a transparent rewrite of "Ladies Love Outlaws" that's weaker in every respect than the original. Lee Clayton, who wrote "Ladies Love Outlaws" as the title track of Jennings' 1972 album, also wrote the underwhelming "Silver Stallion," the only charting single from *Highwayman 2*.

The Highwaymen
***Highwayman 2* (Columbia)**
Recorded: March 6–9, 1989
Released: February 9, 1990
Willie Compositions: 2/10
Top 40 Single: "Silver Stallion" (Country #25)
Album Chart: Country #4

It was a challenge for four men as talented as Nelson, Waylon Jennings, Johnny Cash, and Kris Kristofferson to make a worse album than their first collaboration, 1985's *Highwayman*, but somehow they managed it. There are six originals this time instead of two, but all of them are tossed-off trifles. To cover up Kristofferson's hoarse croak and Jennings' lack of interest, producer Chips Moman often has the four voices bellowing out in unison like an under-rehearsed college chorus. **Grade: D**

Honky Tonk Heroes

Between the first and second Highwaymen albums, Nelson recorded another supergroup project with three-fourths of the Highwaymen that was far superior musically but went unreleased for 11 years. What happened was, Billy Joe Shaver and his son, Eddy, were laying down tracks at Nelson's Pedernales Recording Studio, searching for the right chemistry. They found it and released a string of brilliant country-rock albums under band name Shaver before Eddy died of a heroin overdose on New Year's Eve 2000 at age 38.

When he wasn't golfing or napping, Nelson would stop by to see how they were doing. He and Billy Joe couldn't resist the temptation to pull out the acoustic guitars and sing some favorite tunes together. Many of the songs were Billy Joe's compositions, and it was so much fun that Nelson invited Jennings and Kristofferson to fly in and add to the party. Eddy and the rhythm section joined in, and the tape rolled. The congenial atmosphere of Nelson's ranch and the low expectations that anything would come of it dispelled the clock-watching, competitive atmosphere of the Highwaymen sessions. Paradoxically, the presence of Eddy's slashing guitar cut away the crust of nostalgia and made these performances as urgent as a heart attack.

Waylon Jennings, Kris Kristofferson, Willie Nelson, and Billy Joe Shaver
***Honky Tonk Heroes* (Free Falls)**
Recorded: 1989
Released: February 15, 2000
Willie Compositions: 0/10
Top 40 Singles: NA
Album Charts: NA

Three-fourths of the Highwaymen gathered at Nelson's Pedernales studio with Billy Joe Shaver to record ten of the latter's best songs. The mix-and-match assortment of solo vocals, duets, and quartets is unified by the relaxed camaraderie, the songwriters' sensibility, and the prodigious rock 'n' roll guitar of Shaver's son, Eddy (the album's co-producer). For all the talk about Nelson and Jennings leaning into country-rock, never did that tag seem as appropriate as on these rip-roaring versions, so surprisingly different from the originals. **Grade: A**

Live at Budokan/ Live at the US Festival/ Live from Austin TX

Of course, the music Nelson made in the '80s wasn't limited to his studio recordings. He spent far more time onstage in front of live audiences than he did in studios in front of producers and engineers. He didn't release a live album during the decade, and his concert performances between 1978's *Willie Nelson and Family Live* and 2004's *Live at Billy Bob's Texas* remained undocumented until the next century.

Beginning in 2006, however, three legal live recordings from the years 1984–90 began to appear. All three featured the classic octet version of the Family: the Nelson siblings (Willie and Bobbie), the English siblings (Paul and Billy), the two electric guitarists (Jody Payne and Grady Martin), and the two tall guys (Mickey Raphael and Bee Spears). All three feature lots of tasteful restraint, inspired improvisation, and extended solos not found on the studio recordings. All three begin with "Whiskey River" and omit the closing version of the same song. The setlists are mostly the same, but a few surprises are added each night. As both a singer and a guitarist, Nelson was at the peak of his powers—and so were his bandmates.

I saw Nelson and the Family almost every year during that period, and I never got tired of them. Though the setlist changed little from night to night—or even year to year—each show was a new experience as the singer and his band altered the solos, the fills, the phrasing, and the accents like the consummate jazz musicians that Nelson, Raphael and Grady Martin were. Ironically, the more they changed things up every night, the better they were able to keep themselves interested in the same songs and thus able to sustain higher standards than they could in the studio.

Like any well-established performer, Nelson must confront the familiarity of his own hits. While most entertainers submit to the predictability of the songs that the audience wants to hear, Nelson tries to find

Willie Nelson
***Live at Budokan* (Legacy)**
Recorded: February 23, 1984
Released: November 18, 2022
Willie Compositions: 4/27
Top 40 Singles: NA
Album Charts: NA

This was Nelson's first-ever performance in Japan, and it was captured in a documentary film that was distributed on laser disc only in Japan. Finally in 2022, it became available as a CD/DVD package in North America. This one has the most songs and the fewest originals, offering instead such live rarities as "Mona Lisa" and "Harbor Lights." The instrumental playing is top-notch but marred by tempos that are sometimes rushed and by less-than-perfect sound.
Grade: B+

Bobbie Nelson (left) and Billy Joe Shaver perform during the Luck Reunion in Spicewood, Texas, on March 16, 2017.

new things in old songs. For the most part, he slowed the tempo, cut down the backing parts, made the beat lighter and more swinging.

By removing the clutter, he opened new spaces in the songs for improvised guitar fills, for blues harmonica shading, and for radically different vocal phrasing. On Kris Kristofferson's "Help Me Make It through the Night," for example, Nelson rushed certain syllables before the beat in his deadpan drawl and sustained others past the beat in his grainy low tenor. This tension between the song's natural route and Nelson's detours made the title plea all the more insistent.

Nelson did this all night as he shifted vocal accents to entirely new words and made it all sound perfectly casual with his serenely confident attitude. Between vocal lines, he and Jody Payne interjected short, telling guitar phrases that extended the possibilities of each chord. Even formerly rabble-rousing songs like "Mamas, Don't Let Your Babies Grow Up to Be Cowboys" took on a languorous, reflective pace as if Nelson hoped to learn something new by replaying it in slow motion.

Every show began with Johnny Bush's "Whiskey River" and ended the same way, a repetition that reinforced the ritual nature of each concert. The audience was so reassured by the familiar architecture that they weren't thrown by the radical revisions within each song. Nelson's vocals would revamp not only the phrasing of the verses but also the actual melodies—flattening the intervals or heightening them, depending on his mood. The solos by Raphael, Martin, Nelson, and his sister were not only longer and more inventive than on the recorded versions, but they would go off on different tangents each evening.

Willie Nelson
Live at the US Festival **(Shout Factory)**
Recorded: June 4, 1984
Released: 2012
Willie Compositions: 10/23
Top 40 Singles: NA
Album Charts: NA

This was the final set of the four-day 1984 US Festival, which had already presented U2, the Clash, Van Halen, David Bowie, and Waylon Jennings. Jennings hung around to sing duets with Nelson on "Good Hearted Woman" and "Mamas, Don't Let Your Babies Grow Up to Be Cowboys." Nelson sang such live rarities as "Why Do I Have to Choose" and "I Can Get Off on You," and the eight-minute, jam-heavy version of "Bloody Mary Morning" is a treat. The outdoor-stage sound is inconsistent, but this may well be Nelson's best live album. The band takes lots of liberties with the songs—liberties that liberate astute listeners as much as the musicians. **Grade: A+**

When they came back to the chorus, though, they would sing and play it close enough to the recorded version that the crowd could sing along. That way, the musicians were happy, the casual fans longing to hear their favorites were happy, and the diehard fans looking for surprises were happy. Everyone was happy. It was some of the most powerful live music I've ever witnessed.

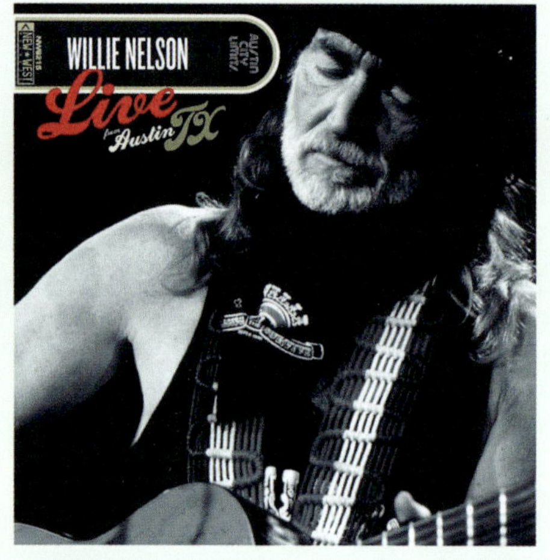

Willie Nelson
***Live from Austin TX* (New West)**
Recorded: September 6, 1990
Released: 2006
Willie Compositions: 8/20
Top 40 Singles: NA
Album Charts: NA

This appearance on the *Austin City Limits* TV show was broadcast live on PBS in 1990 but wasn't released as an album until 2006. The sound is excellent, as are the performances. It contains a rare live recording of his then-recent #1 hit, "Nothing I Can Do about It Now," and the recently written "Still Is Still Moving to Me." The latter and three more songs feature guest vocals by the great Shelby Lynne, most notably on Kokomo Arnold's swaggering "Milk Cow Blues." The extended solos on that song, Lefty Frizzell's "Stay a Little Longer," and "Bloody Mary Morning" from *Phases and Stages* are enough to make this set invaluable. **Grade: A-**

Performing at the Budokan Hall in Tokyo are (from left) Paul English, Willie, and Bee Spears, February 22, 1984.

CHAPTER *6*

Spirit

FOLLOWING HIS MUSE, 1991–2000

"It's just a bump in the road," Nelson told me in 1990.

"Sixteen million dollars is a pretty big bump," I said.

"Not if you say it real fast," he replied.

On a warm November day in 1990, Nelson was lining up a shot on his personal golf course on his sprawling, forty-acre complex in Pedernales, Texas, when a dozen IRS agents suddenly appeared and told the singer he was under arrest for tax violations. It wasn't exactly a surprise; Nelson and the government had been arguing about unpaid back taxes for more than a year. The initial figure was $1.6 million, but with penalties and interest added on, it rose to $16.7 million.

Nelson claimed he didn't have the money, but the IRS didn't believe him. But as the agents combed through the property and his financial records, they changed their minds. He had given away so much, there wasn't much left. Nelson's lawyers wanted him to declare bankruptcy, but he refused to stiff his creditors. He said he was going to solve the problem with "creativity."

Willie tours behind the *Just One Love* album at Amsterdam's Paradiso on April 20, 1996.

Who'll Buy My Memories: The IRS Tapes/The Hungry Years

The problem originated when Neil Reshen, Nelson's manager from 1972 to 1978, put Nelson's excess cash into the same tax shelters that other high earners used. Years later, when the IRS disallowed the shelters, Nelson owed a lot of money in back taxes, money he didn't have on hand because he was so generous to his friends, bandmates, children, and ex-wives.

The "creativity" emerged in Nelson's proposal to the IRS: Why didn't they release the unreleased recordings the government had seized from his Pedernales studio and use the money to pay off his debt? The government, having seen the platinum-album awards they'd seized, was willing to give it a try. They hired a telemarketing company to sell it over the air.

"I live right across the street from my studio," Nelson told me, "so at all hours of day and night I'd go in and record either me by myself or with my band or with whatever musicians were around. The IRS seized all those tapes, so I decided to make an album out of them. I chose the songs and put it together. Some of the songs are old; some have never been out.

"When you call up to order *Who'll Buy My Memories?*, the operator offers you another album. I recorded *The Hungry Years* in 1976 with my band in Bogalusa, Louisiana. But I couldn't get it released because of political problems with record companies, so it has lain there all these years. . . . I thought I had artistic control, but it turned out I didn't. If it wasn't their baby, they don't want to put it out. I think it's one of the best albums I've ever cut with my band."

Maybe they're not the best, but they are certainly valuable additions to his catalog. If Mickey Raphael's "unproduction" on *Naked Willie* revealed the singing and playing beneath the overproduction on the RCA albums, *Who'll Buy My Memories?: The IRS Tapes* could be considered *The Stark Naked Willie*. Re-recording songs from the Pamper demos, Liberty sessions, and RCA sessions from scratch with just voice and acoustic guitar, Nelson reveals not only how strong his early songwriting was but also how much better he was singing and playing in the '80s than in the '60s.

"I really did get frustrated in those years," he told *Goldmine* in 1995, "because I was writing what I felt were good songs. Each time you put out an album that you didn't feel had a chance, there's ten of your children that you feel like didn't get a fair shot.

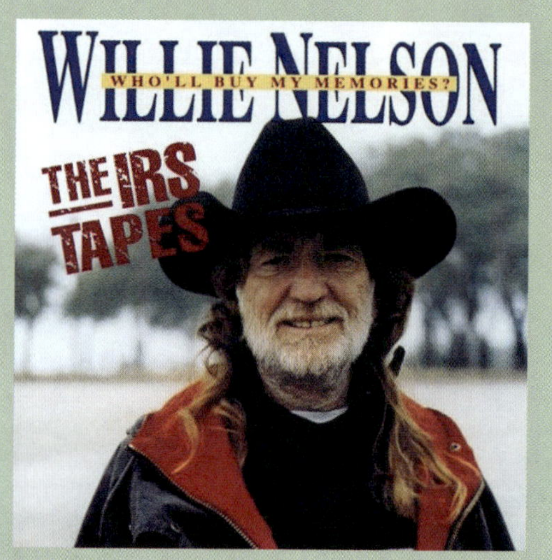

Willie Nelson
***Who'll Buy My Memories?: The IRS Tapes* (Sony)**
Recorded: 1981–1990
Released: June 1991
Willie Compositions: 25/25
Top 40 Singles: NA
Album Charts: NA

These 25 tracks, all Nelson originals from early in his career, were redone from time to time at his home studio over the years. By stripping them down to just his voice and acoustic guitar, he was able to reconsider them and find new surprises in old places. For those who like both the poetry of Nelson's early songwriting and the warmth of his post-*Stardust* singing, this is the best of both worlds, even if the tempos sometimes slow to a crawl. **Grade: B+**

Willie Nelson
The Hungry Years **(Sony)**
Recorded: 1976-1991
Released: 1991
Willie Compositions: 2/15
Top 40 Singles: NA
Album Charts: NA

This shouldn't be confused with a 1982 budget compilation of Pamper demos with the same title. This release, part of Nelson's restitution to the IRS, comes from an unreleased 1976 recording session with the Family in Bogalusa, Louisiana. Mostly these are old country standards by the likes of George Jones, Tommy Collins, and the Wilburn Brothers; but it also includes his first attempts at Rodney Crowell's "Til I Gain Control Again," Tom Paxton's "The Last Thing on My Mind," and Kokomo Arnold's "Milk Cow Blues." Crowell, Ricky Skaggs, and Emmylou Harris recorded overdubs in 1991. **Grade: A-**

Don Was (left), Kris Kristofferson (center), and Willie appear at *Bob Dylan—The 30th Anniversary Concert* at New York City's Madison Square Garden on October 16, 1992.

On the other hand, I also knew that if these songs were as good as I thought they were, they'd always be good and eventually I'd be able to do them again, some way."

"I've always wanted to record an album with just voice and guitar,"' Nelson told me in 1991. "It's a simple and good way to listen to music. You can hear the lyrics, and you can hear the guitar. That's how I learned to play guitar, from Ernest Tubb and Floyd Tillman records. When you hide all that stuff behind all the percussion and the horns, you miss the most important thing, which is the words and melody."

The 1976 recordings on *The Hungry Years* are similar in approach to *The Sound in My Mind*, the album that was actually released that year—and with stronger results. There are no annoying studio effects added, just the sound of a band coming into full possession of its powers. The one new Nelson composition, "Your Memory Won't Die," is a good one. The narrator promises a woman who just left that he'll keep alive her memory if not the marriage. And his warbling, high-tenor duet with Emmylou Harris on the Louvin Brothers ballad "When I Stop Dreaming" is thrilling. He even brings an unexpected depth to two Neil Sedaka songs.

"In the movie *Songwriter*," he told me, "I sing 'Who'll Buy My Memories?' to the little boy who's playing my son. My intention was to follow that movie up with an album with that title. But it was the same thing; the record company didn't want to do it. I had no thought of the IRS when I wrote the song, but now that this whole thing has come up, it's the perfect title. The same thing with *The Hungry Years*. If I'm going for sympathy, I'm going to go all the way."

Clean Shirt

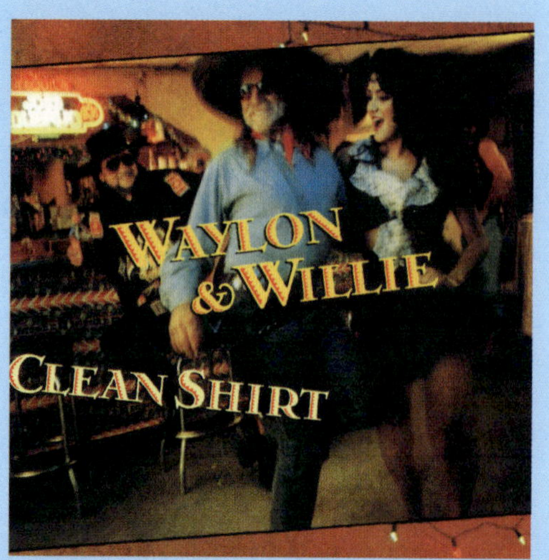

Willie Nelson and Waylon Jennings
***Clean Shirt* (Epic)**
Recorded: March 1991
Released: July 2, 1991
Willie Compositions: 2/10
Top 40 Singles: NA
Album Charts: Country #29, Pop #193

This is a concept album of sorts: two old men named Waylon and Willie sit around boasting of their old, picaresque adventures, each threatening to tell on the other and insisting they could do it all over again if so inclined. Troy Seals co-wrote seven of the ten songs, five of them with Jennings and two of them with Nelson. It's all amusing and congenial, but it doesn't cut very deep. **Grade: B-**

At a June 24, 1991, show in Washington, one might have expected Nelson to change his familiar songs to "Red-Ledgered Cowboy," "Agents Flying Too Close to the Ground," and "Ain't It Funny How Money Slips Away." But, in fact, he never mentioned his IRS problems. Instead, he climaxed the Kennedy Center's Texas Festival by inviting two of its many participants to come onstage and sing with him: Asleep at the Wheel's Ray Benson and Tejano superstar Little Joe Hernandez, who dueted with Nelson on three bilingual Tex-Mex ballads. Here at last was proof of the subtle but perennial Mexican influence on Nelson's music. Here was a wealth of connections that no government agent could take away from him.

"I've always liked to pay my taxes when I'm making money," Nelson told me in 1991. "The IRS was not responsible for what my lawyers did. I don't blame the United States for bad advice I got from my lawyers and accountants. I do think I can negotiate a better deal on the penalties, though. They cut a deal with Chrysler and the Hunt Brothers; they can do the same for me."

In the midst of his IRS troubles, Nelson turned to a reliable moneymaker: another duet album with Jennings. It was the latter's band, the latter's producer, and the latter's label, so Nelson didn't invest a lot in the project: two co-writes, off-the-cuff vocals, and a song by his son Billy (Eddy Shaver, Billy Joe's son, also contributed a song). None of the easily forgettable songs were played onstage or on the radio a year after the album's release, but there was a certain charm to the seeming spontaneity of the session. This was Nelson and Jennings' last duo album (though they did one more Highwaymen recording) and the least successful: modest album sales and no Top 40 singles. This cow had been milked dry.

Across the Borderline

A description of Nelson's next album, *Across the Borderline*, sounds like a recipe for disaster: cover versions of songs by Paul Simon, Peter Gabriel, John Hiatt, Lyle Lovett and Willie Dixon; duets with

Willie and Bob Dylan perform at the Farm Aid concert at the University of Illinois on September 23, 1985.

Bob Dylan, Bonnie Raitt, and Sinead O'Connor; and guest appearances by Simon, Mose Allison, and David Crosby. It sounds like the name-dropping, thrown-together approach that had marked so many of Nelson's recent albums.

Miraculously, though, Nelson imposes his beatific personality on every number, and the album comes together as a showcase for a great singer tackling some great songs. Much of the credit must go to producer Don Was, who had resurrected Raitt's career. Was keeps the song-selection standards high, he makes sure the arrangements remain focused on Nelson's voice, and he induces Nelson to bear down for some of his best singing ever.

For example, on the title song written by Hiatt, Nelson delivers this tale of immigration and disappointment with a desert-dry understatement that removes all the self-pity and leaves just the distilled sadness. On Lovett's "If I Were the Man You Wanted (I Would Not Be the Man I Am)," Nelson adopts a just-the-facts-ma'am storytelling approach that places the title observation beyond dispute. On Dylan's "What Was It You Wanted?" (a song from *Oh Mercy* that Nelson sang on the Dylan tribute TV special), Nelson (and Mickey Raphael's harmonica) gives this romantic cross-examination the sly but relentless attack of an expert prosecutor.

"I enjoy his friendship because he's a great guy," Nelson said of Dylan on the *Fresh Air* radio show in 2006. "He's a little shy and reserved, but, you know, so am I in a lot of ways, so I understand that. We wrote a song together one time . . . , and it was written in a different way, because he sent me a track that he'd already recorded where he just hummed a melody. But the track was great, so I wrote lyrics to his instrumental. And it turned out, I thought, pretty good."

That song, "Heartland," reflects the two men's longtime interest in the plight of American farmers. The song describes the family farm crisis as a kind of biblical plague, a violation of the American dream. The recorded version, though, suffers from the impossible-to-ignore difference between Nelson's effortless croon and Dylan's recently deteriorated voice. A similar gulf separates Nelson and O'Connor on their duet version of Gabriel's "Don't Give Up."

A far more suitable duet partner is Raitt, who nails the mixed feelings of Stephen Bruton's "Getting Over You," though Nelson gets the same effect with many fewer notes. Simon doesn't sing on his two compositions, "Graceland" and "American Tune," but he plays guitar behind Nelson, who gives these splendid tunes a richness of tone and an ease of delivery they've never had before. Nonetheless, the album's best songs are the three Nelson originals. "She's Not You," a 1962 song, and "Valentine," from 1990, are both treated like minimalist pop standards in the style of Nelson's versions of "Stardust" and "Georgia on My Mind." Both the songwriting and singing are good enough to warrant such comparisons.

"Still Is Still Moving to Me" is a Zen koan disguised as a country song. "I can be moving, or I can be still," he sings. "Still is still moving to me." The

Willie Nelson
***Across the Borderline* (Columbia)**
Recorded: October–November 1992
Released: March 23, 1993
Willie Compositions: 4/14
Top 40 Singles: NA
Album Charts: Country #15, Pop #75

Don Was's savvy production keeps the focus on Nelson's voice and draws out some of its best performances ever. John Hiatt's title track brings a clear-eyed realism to the immigration issue. Bob Dylan's "What Was It You Wanted" becomes a skewering romantic cross-examination. A duet with Bonnie Raitt on Stephen Bruton's "Getting Over You" nails the song's mixed feelings. Three Nelson originals are treated like "Stardust." Only the disappointing duets with Dylan (on "Heartland," co-written with Nelson) and Sinead O'Connor mar the record. **Grade: B+**

central guitar figure keeps pushing forward, but the vocal always seems to end up right where it started, as if motion and stillness were two sides of the same coin. And the restless but static music creates a smoky marijuana cloud of meditation where it doesn't matter if you're moving or not. The song became a staple of the live show, and Nelson later recorded a reggae version with Toots & the Maytals.

"The title hit me when I was riding bikes with my wife Annie and my boys Micah and Lukas up in Wisconsin," Nelson writes in *Energy Follows Thought: The Stories Behind My Songs*. "The song had a positive propulsion. When the lyrics came, they were few but felt right. I stated the paradox and just let it hang out there. The music was moving, and that was enough."

Revolutions of Time ... the Journey: 1975–1993

Artistically, *Across the Borderline* was the best solo Nelson release on Columbia in eight years and the highest charting in four. But it was the last one on the current contract, and there was little appetite on either side for signing another. There had been too many arguments about which projects to release and which ones not to. On the other hand, Columbia didn't wait very long to summarize its nineteen years with Nelson in a three-CD, sixty-track compilation. It inevitably leaves out a lot of great music, but it serves a useful function.

Willie Nelson
Revolutions of Time . . . the Journey: 1975–1993
(Columbia)
Recorded: February 9, 1975–November 10, 1992
Released: November 14, 1995
Willie Compositions: 19/60
Top 40 Singles: NA
Album Charts: NA

This three-CD box set documents Nelson's Columbia years with sixty songs on three CDs. The first disc covers the solo recordings from *Red Headed Stranger* in 1975 through *Always on My Mind* in 1982, while the third disc picks up the story from *Tougher than Leather* in 1983 through *Across the Borderline* in 1993. In between is a second disc of twenty duets with everyone from Dolly Parton to Bob Dylan. The compilers reached beyond the obvious hits to dig out overlooked gems such as "Nobody Slides, My Friend" and "In the Jailhouse Now." The thirty-two-page booklet comes with a good essay by John T. Davis and decent discographical info. **Grade: B+**

Opposite: Bob Dylan and Willie share the stage during the *Outlaws & Angels* concert at Los Angeles's Wiltern Theatre on May 5, 2004.

The Highwaymen—Johnny Cash, Willie, Kris Kristofferson, and Waylon Jennings—during rehearsals for *Late Night with David Letterman* in New York City, May 1, 1995.

Moonlight Becomes You/ Nacogdoches Waltz

Two of the best tracks on *Revolutions of Time* were the two from *Stardust*. It wasn't the novelty of a country star singing old show tunes that made that 1978 album a platinum triumph; it was the inspired freshness of Nelson's approach. In contrast to the stiff earnestness of singers like Harry Connick Jr., Michael Feinstein, and Linda Ronstadt, Nelson was the premier standards interpreter of the last third of the twentieth century.

Record companies will never learn, though. Columbia, which had to have its arm twisted to release *Stardust*, declined the chance to release Nelson's superb, early-'90s collection of Tin Pan Alley songs. So *Moonlight Becomes You* was released on the independent Houston label Justice Records.

The project marked a reunion between Nelson and his old Houston buddy Paul Buskirk, who co-produced and played rhythm guitar and mandola. Nelson's spoken introduction to the album, cleverly inserted before the first track so you don't have to listen to it every time, tells the story how Buskirk gave the down-on-his-luck Nelson a job teaching guitar in the '50s and how the two men have been playing standards like these ever since. In fact, one of the album's highlights is Buskirk's most famous song, the irrepressibly bouncy "You Just Can't Play a Sad Song on the Banjo."

Joining Nelson, Buskirk and Buskirk's pal Freddy Powers is Bob Wills' last great fiddler, Johnny Gimble. Nelson grew up on Wills, so swing comes naturally to him. He brings crisply pulsing lead guitar as well as smartly phrased vocals to swing standards such as Johnny Burke and Jimmy Van Heusen's title song. Many of these songs are so obscure that it's a stretch to call them standards, but Nelson makes a good case for them. Nelson broadens the definition of American standards to include songs by such quintessentially country writers as Fred Rose, Buskirk, and Nelson himself.

During the same 1993 sessions at the Pedernales Studio, Nelson, Buskirk, and the same rhythm section cut an all-instrumental album, *Nacogdoches Waltz*, released under Buskirk's name with the tagline "featuring Willie Nelson." Its focus is on the give-and-take between the two soloists.

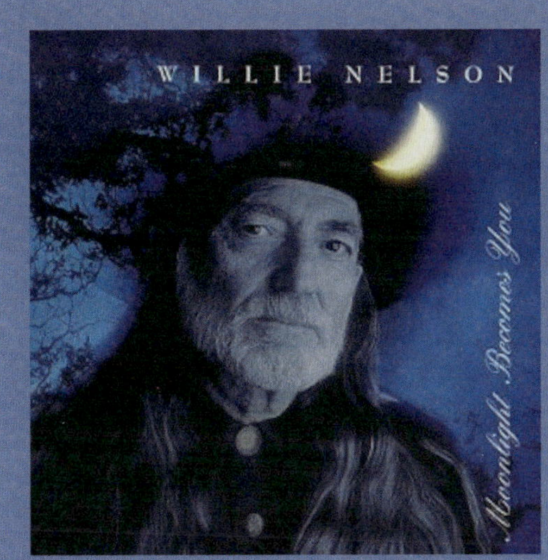

Willie Nelson
***Moonlight Becomes You* (Justice)**
Recorded: Summer 1993
Released: February 15, 1994
Willie Compositions: 2/15
Top 40 Singles: NA
Album Charts: Country #37, Pop #188

Though it made a much smaller splash, this album was nearly as rewarding an exploration of American Songbook standards as *Stardust*. Reuniting with one of his first employers, guitarist Paul Buskirk, Nelson injects a crisp swing into standards like Johnny Burke and Jimmy Van Heusen's title song. And on ballads such as Frank Loesser's "Have I Stayed Away Too Long?" Nelson sounds wistful but never melodramatic. No matter what the source, the self-assurance of Nelson's purring, burnished baritone and his unhurried phrasing is as seductive as ever. **Grade: A-**

Paul Buskirk featuring Willie Nelson
***Nacogdoches Waltz* (Justice)**
Recorded: Summer 1993
Released: 1993
Willie Compositions: 0/10
Top 40 Singles: NA
Album Charts: NA

Buskirk wrote the title tune, co-produced with Nelson and played only the mandola (a tenor mandolin) to contrast with Nelson's acoustic guitar. The material ranges from Ellington to a bouncy ragtime number, from J. S. Bach to the old folk song "Greensleeves." The project is modest, but it does provide a rare glimpse at Nelson's jazz guitar picking. **Grade: B**

Six Hours at Pedernales

Nelson needed another major label contract to feed the payroll of his sprawling empire, but he was in no hurry to sign. He was going to take his time, and meanwhile he could release his pet projects on no-long-term-strings-attached small labels.

"I had so many projects I was working on," he told *Gallery* magazine in 2001, "so many different kinds of music that I had recorded or that I wanted to record, that I needed other outlets, other than the mainstream record labels," he explains. "It's very difficult to get out an instrumental album, for instance, or a jazz album or a blues album on a mainstream label. This way, the music gets circulated and the artist is happy, the record label is happy, and a lot more music can get out there."

Another small Texas label, Step One Records, co-owned by Ray Pennington and Curtis Potter, collaborated with Nelson on an album called *Six Hours at Pedernales*. Pennington, who produced the record and contributed three compositions, overlapped with Nelson at Pamper Music in the mid-'60s, and Potter, who sings duets with Nelson on every track, spent thirteen years in the Texas institution known as Hank Thompson & His Brazos Valley Boys.

Willie Nelson with Special Guest Curtis Potter
Six Hours at Pedernales **(Step One)**
Recorded: Spring 1994
Released: August 2, 1994
Willie Compositions: 4/12
Top 40 Singles: NA
Album Charts: NA

The album's title indicates the quick pace of the recording, which is both a blessing and a curse. The resulting spontaneity gives the songs an unstudied immediacy of a live performance but also encourages predictable, easy-to-learn arrangements. Potter has a purring baritone with an edge and a sure sense of swing, much like Merle Haggard; and this collaboration with Nelson is similar even if it lacks the highest highs or the lowest lows of the Nelson/Haggard partnership. The four Nelson compositions are old Pamper and RCA tracks finally given the Texas dance hall treatment they had on stage but not in the studio back in the '60s. **Grade: B+**

Healing Hands of Time/The Road Goes on Forever

Before he signed a long-term contract with a new label, Nelson released two albums on his original label, Liberty Records, which had been bought and turned into a subsidiary of Capitol. The first album, *Healing Hands of Time*, was a misguided attempt to have Nelson sing older songs (his own and others) over a chamber orchestra. Once again, Nelson is asked to put a new twist on "Night Life," "Crazy," and "Funny How Time Slips Away"—but they'd already been twisted too much.

The one new song, "There Are Worse Things than Being Alone," describes divorce as a "a funeral where nobody dies" and pre-divorce tensions as "a full house and nobody home." It was a song with a lot of potential, and it deserved a better treatment than it got here.

The second Liberty project was the third and final studio album by the Highwaymen, *The Road Goes on Forever*, the quartet's biggest artistic triumph and biggest commercial flop—both by a wide margin. For once, some time and care were put into the song choices and arrangements. The four singers no longer sound like old friends at a reunion trying to remember old songs; they sound like a real, professional ensemble that rehearsed and mastered the material before running tape. Producer Don Was gets credit for herding cats, but the cats delivered once they were pulled together.

Each member contributes one pretty good composition (Nelson's is the old Pamper demo "The End of Understanding"). But the gems are the outside material, chosen not to repay favors but to focus and amplify their strengths rather than indulging their weaknesses. Steve Earle's "The Devil's Right Hand" fuses the temptations and dangers of carrying a gun.

Billy Joe and Eddy Shaver's "Live Forever" captures the inevitability of death in the futile attempt to deny it, and Robert Earl Keen's title track is a Bonnie-and-Clyde story for a new era.

Almost as good as these three classics of Americana music are the two songs from Stephen Bruton and the one from Kevin Welch, two overlooked Texan songwriters with something to say about the challenge of keeping a wild streak going as the years slip behind you. Most importantly, this record sounds like the four men are singing to the listener, not to each other, as if they finally remembered to purpose of popular music.

This photo of the Highwaymen promoted their 1995 album, *The Road Goes on Forever*.

Willie Nelson
***Healing Hands of Time* (Liberty)**
Recorded: Summer 1994
Released: November 1, 1994
Willie Compositions: 6/10
Top 40 Singles: NA
Album Charts: Country #17, Pop #103

It must have seemed a good idea at the time. Nelson had had such good luck with interpreting American Songbook standards with his Texas swing musicians that producer Jimmy Bowen thought maybe it would be interesting to hear them with an actual chamber orchestra. It wasn't. The surprisingly tasteful charts were written and conducted by David Campbell (Beck's father), but Nelson's all-important guitar is missing in action as is his signature syncopation. The four standards are joined by six Nelson compositions, but they all sound embalmed, even the one new Nelson composition, the tantalizingly promising "There Are Worse Things than Being Alone." **Grade: C-**

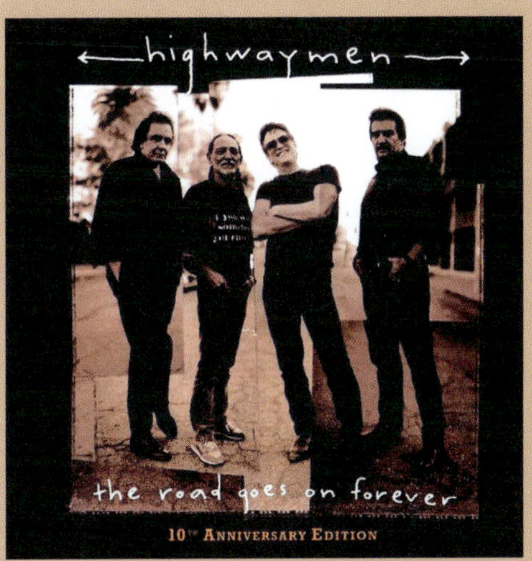

The Highwaymen
***The Road Goes on Forever* (Liberty)**
Recorded: Winter 1994-1995
Released: April 4, 1995
Willie Compositions: 1/11
Top 40 Singles: NA
Album Chart: Country #42

Their first two albums as the Highwaymen were sloppy, thrown-together affairs; but superstar producer Don Was turned this, their third attempt, into the coherent, sparkling showcase they deserved. He realized that the crustiness of these four voices is an asset, not a liability, and chose songs that reflect gruff determination in the face of tough circumstances. Just as importantly, he got them to really learn the material rather than just tossing it off. When the quartet sings Billy Joe Shaver's "Live Forever," they sound as if they're more than halfway there—but you're glad to go along for the ride. **Grade: A-**

Outlaw Country Live from Austin TX

When the Highwaymen tour came to Virginia's George Mason University on June 10, 1995, the four men spent most of their time onstage together, backed by an all-star band featuring Mickey Raphael, Bobby Emmons, Robbie Turner, and Reggie Young. The four leaders shared lead vocals on Guy Clark's "Desperados Waiting for a Train," Hoyt Axton's "Them Downers," and Billy Joe Shaver's "Live Forever."

Kristofferson dedicated "Sunday Morning Coming Down" to Cash, adding, "After he recorded this, I never had to do a lick of work again for the rest of my life." The two men sang it as a duet, while Kristofferson and Jennings dueted on "Help Me Make It through the Night." Cash and Jennings re-created their 1978 duet on "There Ain't No Good Chain Gang," while Cash and Nelson dueted on the old cowboy song, "(Ghost) Riders in the Sky."

Johnny Cash collaborated with Willie not only on *Highwayman* but also on the VH1 *Storytellers* TV special and album.

Various Artists
***Outlaw Country Live from Austin TX* (New West)**
Recorded: September 22, 1996
Released: September 26, 2006
Willie Compositions: 3/14
Top 40 Singles: NA
Album Charts: NA

Recorded for PBS-TV in 1996 but not released as an album until 2006, this summit meeting of Nelson, Jennings, Kristofferson, Kimmie Rhodes, Billy Joe Shaver, Eddy Shaver, and Mickey Raphael is congenial, if not often riveting. Nelson sings on four songs: a duet with Rhodes on her song "Just One Love," a duet with Kristofferson on Nelson's song "We Don't Run," the first unveiling of Nelson's new composition "Too Sick to Pray," and a group sing-along for "On the Road Again." What the proceedings gain in informality, they lose in focus. **Grade: B**

Being on the road together had obviously made the idiosyncratic singers more willing—and more able—to blend the voices than they ever did on their first two albums. Nonetheless, the show's highpoints were Nelson's solo vocals on "Night Life," "I Never Cared for You," and "Angel Flying Too Close to the Ground."

It's worth noting *Outlaw Country from Austin TX Live*, taped in 1996, broadcast nationally the following year on the *Austin City Limits* TV show. Three-fourths of the Highwaymen quartet—Nelson, Jennings, and Kristofferson—sat on wooden chairs in a semicircle at an Austin television studio. Taking Johnny Cash's place were Billy Joe Shaver and Kimmie Rhodes; lurking in the background were Mickey Raphael and guitarist Eddy Shaver.

It was an old-fashioned guitar pull with the cameras rolling; round and round the circle they went until everyone had a chance to sing two or three lead vocals. They tell stories and jokes, join together for a version of "On the Road Again," and they're done.

Just One Love

Justice Records promoted the1995 album *Just One Love* as Nelson's "first country record in over six years," a legitimate boast only if you hold a very narrow definition of the field. Nonetheless, it's a superb, old-fashioned honky-tonk album, featuring ten well-aged standards plus two tunes by the Lubbock-born, Austin-based singer-songwriter Kimmie Rhodes.

Rhodes, who had written cuts for Wynonna Judd and Trisha Yearwood, joined Nelson for vocal duets on her two tender love songs, "I Just Drove By" and the title tune. Singing her enchanting melodies in a breathy soprano, Rhodes almost matches Nelson's taffy-pull phrasing—but no one can liquefy a song line quite like the old Texan. Nelson would repay Rhodes by singing on her best album, 1996's *West Texas Heaven*.

Grady Martin, the album's producer, reinforces that fluidity with a quiet restraint and a slippery swing which seem to echo the leader's vocals. Against this restrained background, the chorus vocals, like the jazz-inflected guitar solos by Martin and Nelson, seem to splash out of the oceanic calm like dolphins. The bulk of *Just One Love* is devoted to old country standards. The best known is Hank Williams' "Cold, Cold Heart," and it receives the same refurbishing as the others. Instead of trying to outsing the original, Nelson illustrates how a relaxed vocal can let the song's bitterness and longing soak into the words and music.

Nelson sings two numbers by his early Texas hero, Floyd Tillman, and captures the romantic longing of "Each Night at Nine" and the marital troubles of "This Cold, Cold War with You." The Cold War wasn't the only military-history term turned into a honky-tonk song in the '50s; Pee Wee King had a hit with "Bonaparte's Retreat," and Nelson reprises it with a lilting bounce. Grandpa Jones, the eighty-one-year-old veteran of a sixty-five-year career as a professional musician, joins Nelson for a spirited duet on Jones's 1946, banjo-powered hit, "Eight More Miles to Louisville."

Willie Nelson
Just One Love **(Justice)**
Recorded: Spring 1995
Released: July 4, 1995
Willie Compositions: 0/12
Top 40 Singles: NA
Album Charts: NA

If in his teens Nelson dreamed of one day becoming a combination of Hank Williams and Frank Sinatra, he achieved it in his sixties. This album contains ten country standards by Floyd Tillman, Hank Williams, and Jim Reeves, plus two new songs by Texas singer-songwriter Kimmie Rhodes, who duets with Nelson on them. He approaches this country music canon as if he were a honky-tonk Buddha who has seen everything and embraces it all in a voice as fluid and mesmerizing as a bubbling creek. There had never been anything like it in country music. **Grade: A-**

The Fred Rose song "It's a Sin" becomes so fatalistic in Nelson's live-and-let-live vocal that the tortured doubts of Eddy Arnold's 1947 original are turned into calm acceptance. Such philosophical acceptance of life's vicissitudes is the key to Nelson's career and never sounded more convincing than in the '90s. He's a role model for us all.

Augusta

Once he aquired his own nine-hole golf course near the recording studio on his property in Spicewood, Texas, Nelson became addicted to the game, often having his engineers jump in a golf cart and bring the latest mixes to him on a fairway. One of his favorite golf buddies was Don Cherry—not Ornette Coleman's trumpeter but the big-band, easy-listening singer who had a #4 pop hit with "Band of Gold" in 1955. Cherry was also a serious golfer; he actually finished ninth at the 1960 US Open behind Arnold Palmer.

Sometimes after a round on the links, Nelson and Cherry would stroll over to the studio and record duet vocals on American Songbook standards over prepared synth-pop tracks. Cherry still had a good voice but sang these songs like every lounge singer in America with a wedding-reception saxophone to match, while Nelson's voice danced all around him.

Spirit

In 1995, Nelson finally signed with another major label: Island Records. As a vocal proponent and conspicuous consumer of marijuana, the country singer felt an affinity with the Jamaican reggae singers who did the same. Because the best of those singers—Bob Marley, Jimmy Cliff, and Toots & the Maytals—made their breakthrough records on Island, Nelson agreed to become the label's first country artist, lured by the promise that Island would help him record an album of reggae arrangements of his old songs—a promise it took nine years to fulfill.

In return for that pledge, Nelson gave Island *Spirit*, his first new album of all-original compositions in nearly five years, his best album of the '90s, and his fifth great concept album, following *Yesterday's Wine*, *Phases and Stages*, *Red Headed Stranger*, and *Tougher than Leather*. The thirteen tracks include five new vocal numbers, four new instrumentals, and four older songs transformed by this new context. Nelson's production is as ambitious as the songwriting—he recorded everything with a drummer-less, bass-less quartet with himself on acoustic guitar, sister Bobbie on piano, Johnny Gimble on fiddle, and Jody Payne on acoustic rhythm guitar.

The chamber-music quality of the instrumentals—given a Spanish tinge on "Matador" and "Mariachi"—

Willie Nelson and Don Cherry
***Augusta* (Sundown) (aka *Duets*)**
Recorded: Early 1993
Released: December 12, 1995
Willie Compositions: 2/13
Top 40 Singles: NA
Album Charts: NA

The title track is a tribute to the Masters Tournament, held every year in Augusta, Georgia, a clue that the glue holding these two singers together is golf, not music. Cherry still has the creamy tenor that made him an easy-listening-pop star in the 1950s, and the cheesy synth-and-sax backing here is a reflection of that. Nelson is a good sport about these duets on old standards, but you don't have to be. This was just the first of three terrible albums the duo made, followed by 2002's *The Eyes of Texas* and 2007's *It's Magic* with diminishing results. **Grade: F**

Willie Nelson
Spirit **(Island)**
Recorded: November 1995
Released: June 4, 1996
Willie Compositions: 13/13
Top 40 Singles: NA
Album Charts: Country #20, Pop #132

No one saw this coming—one of the best albums of Nelson's career. His gifts hadn't disappeared; they were merely hibernating. The thirteen originals not only mark his best songwriting since 1983's *Tougher than Leather*, but they also line up to tell a narrative like his best concept albums. The story of a man falling into despair after his wife leaves him and then climbing out of despair with a reconciliation is further unified by a radical sound that works splendidly. Nelson leads an all-acoustic string band that allows the confessional privacy of the songs to be even more convincing. And everything he's learned from singing jazz standards all these years is applied to his latest compositions with magnificent effect. **Grade: A+**

carries over into the vocal numbers, where the telling pauses in Nelson's delivery can register because there are so few sonic distractions. And it's those pauses as much as the words that tell this story of a man devastated by the sudden departure of his wife. On two songs salvaged from the overlooked album *The Hungry Years*, the narrator sounds stunned to learn that "She Is Gone" and that nonetheless "Your Memory Won't Die." He's so despairing that he's "Too Sick to Pray."

The narrative pivots on two more new songs, where the narrator decides he won't be chased off so easily. Instead of giving up, he's digging in, telling his ex that "I'm Waiting Forever." Why? Because he and she are the kind who don't give up. "We Don't Quit," he sings on the album's closest thing to a mid-tempo song. And that patience pays off in two of the best songs: "I'm Not Trying to Forget You Anymore" and "I Guess I've Come to Live Here in Your Eyes."

These are the exceptions to Nelson's long list of songs about accepting the loss of love. Instead of letting it go, he works hard to bring it back. This is a different take on troubled romance for the songwriter, and the results capture the way a man finally gives into a love he has resisted for so long. Often an arresting acoustic guitar figure creates the tension, and Nelson's vocal releases that stress in one long exhalation of relief.

For all of us who have had a relationship crash and burn, this suite of songs translates that anguish into words and music that we can consider from a distance and get some perspective on. More than that, it offers a path out of that dejection to reconciliation or at least détente. It doesn't matter if this tracks an actual incident in Nelson's own life. What matters is it reflects ours.

How Great Thou Art/ Hill Country Christmas

When Nelson came off the road, he often relaxed by getting together with friends and/or family in his home studio to play some favorite songs. His favorite partner was his sister, Bobbie, who had been playing with him since they were kids in Abbott, Texas, in the 1930s. While Nelson was in between major-label deals in the mid-'90s, he took advantage of the contractual freedom to record two albums with his sister: a gospel record and a Christmas record.

Her piano is out front in the mixes as on no other Willie Nelson album, perhaps because her son was co-producer on the first and sole producer on the second. One can finally hear what she was doing in the background all those years, eschewing single-note runs but slipping melody phrases inside her two-fisted chords as they grab hold of whatever unusual chord her brother throws her way.

Willie and Jody Payne at the Woodstock Music Festival on July 26, 1999.

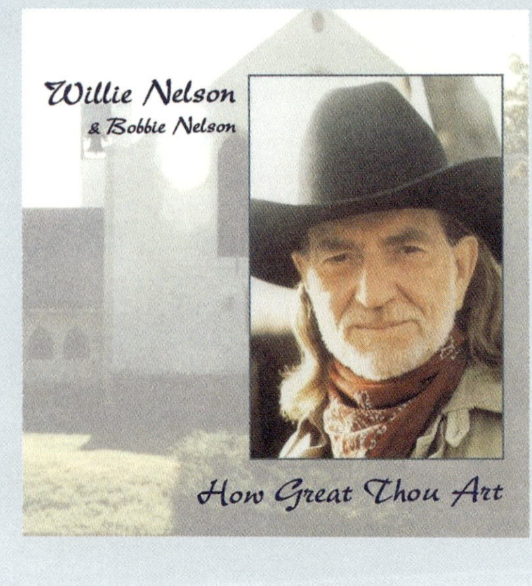

Willie & Bobbie Nelson
***How Great Thou Art* (Finer Arts)**
Recorded: Early '90s
Released: July 1996
Willie Compositions: 1/9
Top 40 Singles: NA
Album Charts: NA

For this session, the Nelson siblings join bassist Jon Blondell to play some old hymns without much rehearsal. The proceedings are as casual and offhanded as a Sunday picnic, but it's fun to eavesdrop on this one. Willie doesn't push the material to get something new out of it, but he does sing one rare original: "Kneel at the Feet of Jesus," a snappy, swinging profession of faith. This album was re-released in 2022 as *Just as I Am: 18 Hymns and Gospel Favorites* with two songs dropped from the original nine and eleven new songs added. It offers more music but no revelations. **Grade: B-**

Willie Nelson with Bobbie Nelson
***Hill Country Christmas* (Finer Arts)**
Recorded: Early '90s
Released: October 14, 1997
Willie Compositions: 3/11
Top 40 Singles: NA
Album Chart: Country #60

The appeal of this holiday album stems from the unfussy arrangements on mostly traditional carols. Willie sings superbly but plays little guitar. His one new song, "El Niño," offers minimalist lyrics about "love is king" but intriguing music that builds ever so patiently over moody piano chords, acoustic guitar fills, ghostly synths, steel, and trumpet from quiet to a big climax. Later it's reprised as an instrumental. On one weird track, Nelson overdubs his voice onto Gene Autry's original single for "Here Comes Santa Claus." **Grade: B-**

VH1 Storytellers: Johnny Cash & Willie Nelson

Nelson and Johnny Cash bonded during their studio sessions and tours with the Highwaymen, and it seemed inevitable that they would record another of Nelson's duet albums. This took the form of a live taping of a show for VH1, a variation on MTV for older audiences. There is only one true duet, but Nelson takes two guitar solos on "Folsom Prison Blues," and the stories on the origins of the songs are interesting. It doesn't offer musical surprises, but it does give us a glimpse into their friendship.

Willie Nelson performs at the State Theatre in Easton, Pennsylvania, on March 19, 1998.

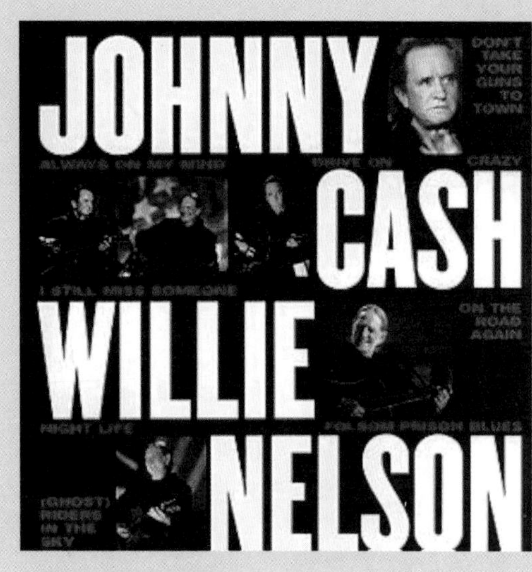

Willie Nelson and Johnny Cash:
VH1 Storytellers: Johnny Cash & Willie Nelson
(American)
Recorded: December 5, 1997
Released: June 9, 1998
Willie Compositions: 6/15
Top 40 Singles: NA
Album Charts: Country #25, Pop #56

"All VH1 wants is two guitars, two stools, and you and Willie," Cash's manager told him. That's what the small TV studio audience and larger TV viewership got in 1997, and that's what was preserved in the CD released seven months later. They sing a true duet on the old cowboy song, "(Ghost) Riders in the Sky," and then trade songs going forward, with Nelson leaning on his best-known numbers and Cash pulling out some rarities. None of these are the best version of a song, but the tale-spinning and joshing between the two friends is disarming. **Grade: B**

Teatro

In the 1990s, when Garth Brooks and Shania Twain were taking over country music, one could well ask, How much can you change the instrumentation, the rhythms, the subject matter, and the attitude and still call it country music? It was a tricky question, because one was testing that tradition as radically as Willie Nelson was on his 1998 album *Teatro.*

The weather-beaten, gray-bearded Texan recorded the project in an abandoned Mexican movie theater in Oxnard, California. Producer Daniel Lanois—best known for his work with U2, Bob Dylan, and the Neville Brothers—framed Nelson's voice with tumbling, shuddering rhythms; dreamy, sustained guitars; and eerie, ethereal echo. The results sound like a Lefty Frizzell show broadcast from a humming silver spaceship in a 1950s sci-fi flick.

For all its otherworldly sound, however, *Teatro* is unmistakably a country album. Six of the fourteen tracks, in fact, come from the 1961–66 period when Nelson was a Nashville songwriter, trying to jump-start his own career. These tales of crumbling marriages are slices of classic honky-tonk, and Nelson's four new compositions, though more hopeful about romance, are in the same vein. When he revives the Pamper demo "I Just Destroyed the World," co-writ-

Harmony singer Emmylou Harris (left), producer Daniel Lanois (center), and lead singer Willie collaborated on the 1998 album *Teatro.*

Willie performs at Denmark's Roskilde Festival on June 30, 2000.

Willie Nelson
***Teatro* (Island)**
Recorded: Late 1997
Released: September 1, 1998
Willie Compositions: 11/14
Top 40 Singles: NA
Album Charts: Country #17, Pop #104

Although it's not credited that way, this is pretty much a duet album with Emmylou Harris. She doesn't sing lead, but her harmony parts are so prominent, so essential to the arrangements that it would be a very different album without her. The way her silky soprano hovers close to Nelson's craggy tenor, but always a small interval up and a split second behind, reinforces the way these songs (six older Nelson compositions, four new ones, and three covers) depict relationships that are close but not quite together. Harris brought not only her voice but also her recent producer, Daniel Lanois, who wraps the music in ghostly echo as if the lyrics were haunted memories. **Grade: A**

ten with Ray Price, he evokes the way a heartbreaker always ends up breaking his own.

"'Destruction' is a heavy word, and *Teatro* is a heavy album," Nelson writes in *Energy Follows Thought*. "Even though you can see that destruction—destroying love, destroying a man, even destroying the life of a woman—as a major theme, *Teatro* was also about reconstruction. What Ray and I had written those many years earlier was renewed in a very different way in that drafty old movie house. A deeply dark song was recast in a new light."

In other words, Nelson remained true to tradition even as he thoroughly refashioned its sound and shape. He pulled it off by aiming his crossover moves at artistic targets rather than commercial ones. He didn't work with drummers from the rock groups Luscious Jackson and the Scott Weiland Band because he thought they'd get his next video on MTV (fat chance) or CMT (even fatter) but because their rolling, rumbling beats captured the way problems develop their own momentum beyond lovers' control. Nelson encouraged Lanois to play his thick-as-cream electric guitar lines not because they were hip but because they evoked the slow-motion quality of a romantic crisis.

Teatro opens with a jazz instrumental by the great Frenchman Django Reinhardt and closes with another jazz instrumental by Nelson himself, who reminds us once again that he is as brilliant as an acoustic guitarist as he is as a singer and songwriter. The breezy, elastic quality of those two swing tunes carries over to the dozen songs in between (ten by Nelson, one by Texas swing legend Chester Odom, and a hymn by Lanois). Joining Nelson, Lanois, and the two rock drummers are jazz keyboardist Brad Mehldau, slide guitarist Brian Griffiths, and two veterans of Nelson's road band—his sister, Bobbie, on Wurlitzer piano and Mickey Raphael on harmonica.

When Nelson sings, "I love you in my own peculiar way," he could be talking about his approach to country. Whether he's singing a creepy murder ballad like "I Just Can't Let You Say Good-bye," the post-breakup lament of "Somebody Pick Up My Pieces," or the transparent fibs of "I Never Cared for You," the arrangements are mighty peculiar indeed—but they deliver the ache and hope that have always been the heart of the music.

Night and Day

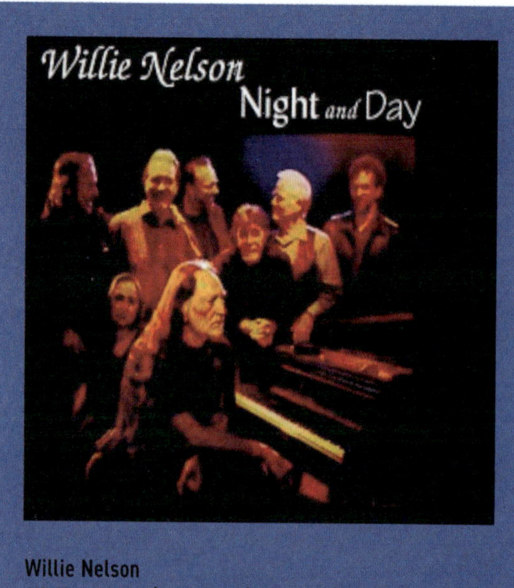

Willie Nelson
Night and Day (Free Falls)
Recorded: Early 1999
Released: July 13, 1999
Willie Compositions: 1/10
Top 40 Singles: NA
Album Charts: NA

These ten instrumentals begin with a pair of Django Reinhardt numbers, relaxes through seven American Songbook classics, and ends with "Bandera," the wordless tune that ended *Red Headed Stranger*. Nelson's impressive guitar themes, fills, and solos are backed by the Family plus fiddler/mandolinist Johnny Gimble. When Nelson and Gimble engage each other in dialogue, the elegance reminds one of the duets between Reinhardt and French fiddler Stephane Grappelli. **Grade: B+**

Nelson is such a good singer-songwriter and interpretive singer that the third leg of the musical stool he stands on is often overlooked. His guitar playing is remarkable, somehow including the harmonic and rhythmic freedom of early jazz with the melodic storytelling of early country music. And by welding these two vintage styles together, he created something modern. And we can all learn something from that trick. To make sure we learned it, he began recording more instrumental tracks after he'd established his economic usefulness to the music biz. But *Night and Day* is his first all-instrumental album under his own name.

Me and the Drummer

One of the songs Nelson sang with Cash on TV was "Me and Paul," a tribute to Nelson's longtime drummer Paul English and a story of the way male friendship can be forged in hard times. But another drummer was also crucial to Nelson's career, and that was Johnny Bush, who began playing with Nelson in 1954, a dozen years before English, and who wrote "Whiskey River," the song that opened and closed Nelson's live show for decades.

And it's Bush who plays the drums on the album called *Me and the Drummer*, joining an all-star band of Texas country-swing musicians. The improvisational interplay among Trigger, fiddler Johnny Gimble, steel guitarist Jimmy Day, and Asleep at the Wheel pianist Floyd Domino is always top-notch and occasionally stunning.

The album's title track was written by Bill McDavid as a kind of sequel to "Me and Paul," though the new lyrics refer to the drummer as the conscience that the narrator marches to. This new album even recycles three songs from the 1985 album *Me and Paul*. All twelve of the originals were written before 1980, and with Joe Gracey, Nelson produced them the way he originally intended them to be heard: with the narrator's assessment of each troubled marriage as ambiguous as the lead vocal's slippery phrasing and the band's melancholy reverie.

Willie Nelson
***Me and the Drummer* (Luck)**
Recorded: Early 2000
Released: June 6, 2000
Willie Compositions: 12/13
Top 40 Singles: NA
Album Charts: NA

The title track, written by Bill McDavid, is a sequel of sorts to Nelson's "Me and Paul," but the other dozen tracks are Nelson originals from the '60s and '70s, songs he wanted to re-record with his own production and hand-picked band. These aren't his best-known early songs but the ones that never got a proper chance the first time around. In a sense, this is the songwriter's opportunity to rewrite history and suggest how effective these titles could be in a different context. And he's right. The songs are brilliant dissections of failed relationships, the singing is superb, and the backing by an all-star band of Texas veterans is sympathetic. **Grade: A-**

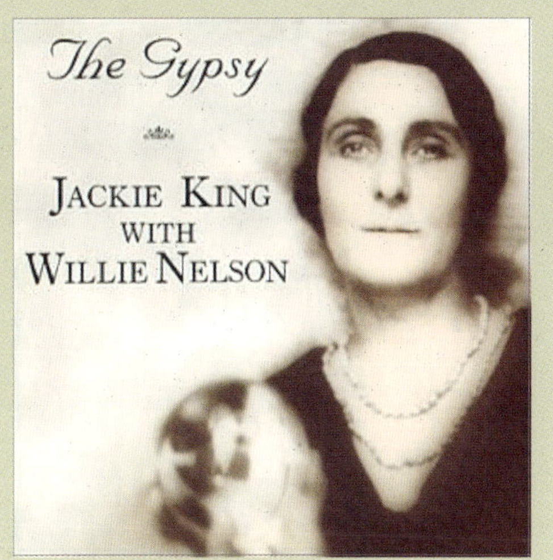

Jackie King with Willie Nelson
***The Gypsy* (Indigo Moon)**
Recorded: 1983–2000
Released: May 8, 2001
Willie Compositions:0/11
Top 40 Singles: NA
Album Charts: NA

In 1984, the album *Angel Eyes* was credited to "Willie Nelson featuring the guitar of Jackie King." This sequel is credited to "Jackie King with Willie Nelson," even though it recycles two tracks from its predecessor and three leftover vocal numbers from those sessions. These are supplemented by five instrumental tracks from a more recent session in San Francisco without Nelson. It sounds like two different albums woven together, but the playing is elegant if old-fashioned, and it's always a treat to hear Nelson in a jazz setting. **Grade: B**

The Gypsy

Nelson put out so many projects on small Texas labels between the late '80s and early 2000s that he decided to put out a sampler album: *Joy*. It featured one track apiece from ten albums by Nelson, his daughter Paula, his golf partner Don Cherry, his jazz buddy Paul Buskirk, and his Highwaymen bandmates Waylon Jennings and Kris Kristofferson. It also included the title track from *The Gypsy*, a 2001 release credited to Jackie King with Willie Nelson.

Milk Cow Blues

Top: Willie plays a solo on Trigger at LA's House of Blues on October 2, 2000.
Mickey Raphael performs with Willie during Kentucky State Fair in Louisville on August 21, 2001.

"Night Life," one of Nelson's earliest triumphs, is a moody, noirish jazz tune in its verses and refrain; but on its bridge it erupts into a blues shout. "Listen to what the blues are saying," he cries. He always did listen, and he soon realized that the notion the blues were a sad, depressed music was at odds with the evidence. The blues are the antidote to sad, depressing situations, and they served as the template for all his songs about staying strong in the wake of romantic disasters. Listeners responded to his songs because

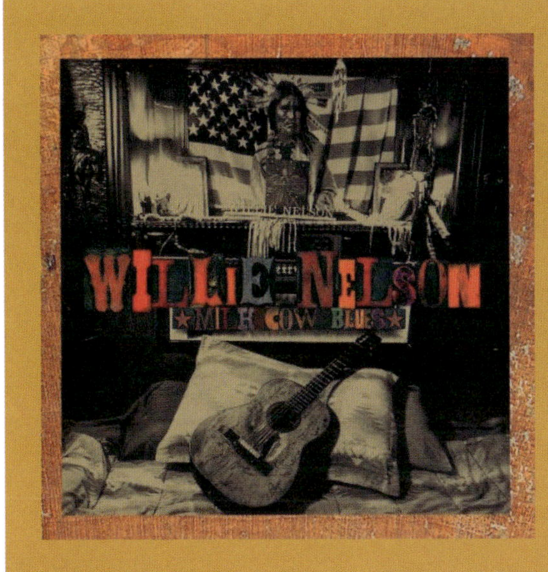

Willie Nelson
***Milk Cow Blues* (Island)**
Recorded: Spring 2000
Released: September 19, 2000
Willie Compositions: 5/15
Top 40 Singles: NA
Album Chart: Pop #83

On this all-blues project, Nelson sings duets with B. B. King, Keb' Mo', Jonny Lang, Susan Tedeschi, and Francine Reed (Lyle Lovett's longtime singer); and the more they bluster, the more Nelson croons in an understatement that betrays the coolest self-confidence in the world. His most compatible partner turns out to be his own guitar; it subtly alters the melody by holding one phrase back and pushing another forward, just as Nelson's vocals do. Dr. John does offer a sly vocal and piano solo on "Black Night." **Grade: B**

he didn't sugarcoat the pain, but neither did he hold back the cure.

Nelson has always sung the blues, if only because his hero Bob Wills did. Texas was filled with blues legends such as Lightnin' Hopkins and T-Bone Walker, and the young Nelson absorbed their influence along with everything else. Wills' kid brother Johnnie Lee had recorded Kokomo Arnold's 1934 blues hit, "Milk Cow Blues," just seven years later—and it was that Western swing version that inspired Elvis Presley to record the song in 1954. And it was Presley's version that prompted Nelson to add the song to his live show, as documented on his album, *Live at the Texas Opry House, 1974*, recorded in 1974 but not released until 2006 as part of *Willie Nelson: The Complete Atlantic Sessions*.

The song became the title track of his first album explicitly dedicated to the tradition. He includes five of the bluesiest songs from his early career—not only "Night Life" but also "Crazy," "Rainy Day Blues," "Wake Me When It's Over," and "Funny How Time Slips Away." To these are added songs associated with Louis Jordan ("Outskirts of Town"), Charles Brown ("Black Night"), B. B. King ("The Thrill Is Gone"), Wilbert Harrison ("Kansas City"), Jimmy Witherspoon ("Ain't Nobody's Business"), and Larry Davis ("Texas Flood"), all recordings that were on the radio in the '40s and '50s when Nelson was still in his teens and twenties.

Nelson is backed by his harmonica whiz Mickey Raphael and by a crackerjack Austin blues band led by co-producer/guitarist Derek O'Brien. All this is well and good, but many of Nelson's under-rehearsed guests pile on the vibrato, melisma, and other embellishments in a way that clashes with Nelson's understatement. He lets the listener hear how coolness under pressure defies wrongdoers more effectively than overreaction.

Rainbow Connection

At the end of 2001, Island transferred Nelson's contract to its new subsidiary label, Lost Highway, designed to serve the audience that overlapped the progressive wing of commercial country and the expanding underground of alternative-country. That relationship will take up much of the next chapter. For his last outing on the Island imprint, Nelson kept a promise to his daughter Amy and threw in a few odds and ends he'd been meaning to record.

Amy had always wanted her dad to make an album of children's songs, like the ones he'd sung to her growing up. She sang two of the lead vocals and co-produced the session with the three musicians who handled almost all the playing: her father, his longtime sidekick David Zettner, and newcomer Matt

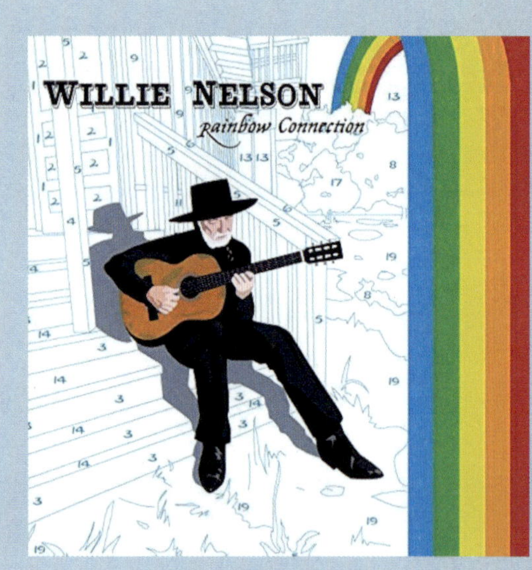

Willie Nelson
***Rainbow Connection* (Island)**
Recorded: December 2000
Released: June 12, 2001
Willie Compositions: 1/13
Top 40 Singles: NA
Album Chart: Country #52

Nelson's final album under the Island imprint was also his first and last children's album, a format he's poorly suited for judging by the first-take-and-leave-it feel of the singing and playing on some pretty corny songs, as if young listeners don't deserve the same musical standards as adults. More interesting are the blues jam and two Mickey Newbury songs at the end. The record does include Nelson's version of the comedy classic, "I'm My Own Grandpa." **Grade: C-**

Hubbard. Unfortunately, the dashed-off, under-rehearsed, under-produced results suggested that no one but Amy was very committed to the project.

More interesting were the three non-children's songs Willie tagged onto the end. Using the same musicians, Nelson did an extended seven-minute version of "Outskirts of Town" from his previous blues album, plus two songs by Mickey Newbury. For these three tracks, the minimalist, acoustic trio format worked. Of course, Nelson had already honored this great Texas songwriter in the single, "Luckenbach, Texas," when he saluted "Hank Williams' pain songs and Newbury's train songs."

While the quality of his studio sessions in the '90s varied greatly, the quality of his live shows was astonishingly consistent. That doesn't mean they all sounded the same, even though they often contained the same repertoire. At an August 25, 1994, show at the Wolf Trap Performing Arts Center in Virginia, for example, he tackled Kristofferson's "Me and Bobby McGee" for the umpteenth time.

This time, though, the sixty-one-year-old Nelson changed the rhythm from a two-step to a shuffle and completely altered the melody as if he were singing a harmony to the original, unheard melody. The result created a brilliant tension between the listeners' memory of the song and Nelson's transformation of it. He did the same thing to songs by himself, Bob Wills, Leon Russell, and Irving Berlin.

When he came to the chorus, however, he would sing close enough to the recording that the audience would recognize it with pleasure. Then he'd be off on another tangent through severely syncopated patterns, harmonically stretched solos, and melodically altered vocals. Thus, he was able to hold the attention of the casual fan and the hipster fan as well as the musicians in his band, the Family.

It helped that Nelson's low-key charisma kept the crowd on his side no matter how far he strayed from the tried and true. With his shoulder-length hair falling from his red-bandana headband, his bristly white beard, and his beaming smile, he seemed more like a kindly, eccentric uncle than the musical revolutionary he actually was.

The decade of the '90s began with a protracted battle with the IRS, his fourth marriage, and his final Top 30 country single, all in 1991. His finances took a hit, but his creativity seemed undiminished. Out of the glare of country radio, he released some of his finest albums: *The Hungry Years*, *Across the Borderline*, *Spirit*, *Teatro*, *Night and Day*, *Moonlight Becomes You*, *Just One Love*. Of course, he also made some of his worst—*Clean Shirt*, *Augusta*, and *Rainbow Connection*—as well as many in between. The question for him moving forward—and for the listeners looking to him for clues—was whether he could keep up the artistry as the business declined.

Willie and Kermit the Frog attend the Songwriters Hall of Fame induction ceremony at New York City's Sheraton Hotel on June 14, 2001.

CHAPTER 7

You Don't Know Me

THE DECLINE & ALL THAT JAZZ, 2001–2011

When Universal Music reassigned Nelson from the conglomerate's Island imprint to its Lost Highway venture, it seemed like a good idea. Then again, the idea of pairing Nelson and producer Chet Atkins at RCA in the '60s had also seemed like a good idea at first. In both cases, Nelson's singing was too often buried beneath clumsy production gambits, which in turn eventually led to frustrated, disengaged vocals from the singer himself.

In the 2000s, these problems were exacerbated by Nelson's weakened voice, his low productivity as a songwriter, and his reluctance to spend any more time in a recording studio than absolutely necessary. In many ways, this became as much a lost decade for the artist as the '60s. In both decades, however, he released overlooked gems that suggested that his talent was not dead, merely on vacation. In both cases, that gift would flourish in the subsequent decade.

During its twelve-year run, Lost Highway put out memorable records by Lyle Lovett, Lucinda Williams, Mary Gauthier, Hayes Carll, Ryan Adams, and Shelby Lynne. Their most crucial release was the movie soundtrack *O Brother, Where Art Thou?*, which triggered an old-time string-band renaissance. The record sold more than eight million copies and won the Album of the Year at both the Grammys and the CMA Awards.

"This whole *O Brother, Where Art Thou?* soundtrack brought everybody back to square one," Nelson told *Performing Songwriter* in 2002. "That's country music in its rawest form. And, occasionally, we have a tendency to get a little too far away from that—trying to go pop, you know, when the best way to go pop is to go country. . . . The problem is, with a lot of these radio formats, it has to be this way or you don't get played. It'd be hard for Hank Williams to come back now and get any airplay."

Willie plays a show at the Mountain Winery in Saratoga, California, on September 30, 2003.

LUCK

But the spellbinding simplicity of *O Brother* eluded Nelson during his years at the label. Part of it was his own fault. He turned 70 on April 29, 2003, and he was understandably inclined to take it easy. It didn't take much effort to show up and run through some old songs with his friends in the studio; it took even less time if it was a one-time-only concert. Lots of famous artists were eager to sing with Nelson, and their names helped him sell records. No songwriting was required and little rehearsal.

Maybe this approach worked for the singer, but it didn't work for us, the listeners. We respond to Nelson's best recordings because they illustrate how one can face up to life's defeats with a mixture of honesty and fortitude. Whether the song was written by Nelson himself or the Gershwin brothers, each mini-drama was cathartic. But what could we make of these tossed-off performances? How to amuse oneself with other famous people? How is that useful to our lives?

Such celebrity get-togethers always sound tantalizing to the consumer, but they rarely deliver as much as they promise. Everyone's busy, and no one wants to spend time working out arrangements. Everything's done on the fly, and the first try is often the last. Eager to make an impression on Nelson and on the audience, the guests often overstate their vocals and fail to connect with a band of strangers. The constant shifting from one artist's style to the next can create whiplash and destroy any sense of a unified album.

The Great Divide

The partnership between Nelson and Lost Highway got off to an unfortunate start with the 2002 album *The Great Divide*, whose guest-star format had enough commercial success to set a bad example. Three years earlier, Clive Davis at Arista Records had resurrected Carlos Santana's career with *Supernatural*, an album that paired the aging legend with younger, hotter artists, most notably Matchbox Twenty leader Rob Thomas. Thomas sang and co-wrote the album's hit single, "Smooth," overseen by his regular producer Matt Serletic. Lost Highway thought that team could do the same for Nelson.

Willie Nelson
***The Great Divide* (Lost Highway)**
Recorded: Summer 2001
Released: January 15, 2002
Willie Compositions: 1/12
Top 40 Single: "Mendocino County Line" (Country #22)
Album Charts: Country #5, Pop #43

Matchbox Twenty singer Rob Thomas wrote three songs and sang on one of them; and his producer, Matt Serletic, wrote four more, two with Elton John's lyricist, Bernie Taupin. Thomas writes great pop-rock hooks, and Serletic makes great-sounding alt-rock singles—but neither seems to understand the elastic swing of Nelson's rhythms nor the low-key minimalism of his music. They steamroller the subtleties of Nelson's still-marvelous voice with heavy-handed 4/4 rhythms and overblown strings, choirs, and synths. Nelson lets it all roll off his back and still manages some nice moments—especially on the title track, the one song he co-wrote, and in his duet with Bonnie Raitt on "You Remain." But this is one of his lesser releases. **Grade: C-**

But Serletic's streamlined, high-tech production proved a poor fit for Nelson's loose and earthy instincts. He sang duets with Thomas and everyone from rap-metal growler Kid Rock to soul crooner Brian McKnight, from adult-contemporary purrer Sheryl Crow to trad-country twanger Lee Ann Womack. The duet with Womack, "Mendocino County Line," was a respectable, modest hit. But for the most part, these under-rehearsed, tentative duets sound as if they were set up for commercial rather than musical reasons. In some cases, Nelson wasn't even in the same room with his duet partner—never a good approach.

"I was always concerned about overproducing," Nelson told *Texas Music* magazine in 2003. "I always thought the vocals should be out front. 'Cause if you don't listen to my lyrics, I'm lost. It's important that the lyrics be heard, and a lot of times, in an effort to go commercial—whatever that means—you get too many overproduced records."

Willie at the Westwood in Los Angeles on February 9, 2002.

The Essential Willie Nelson

"Mendocino County Line," one of the few bright spots on *The Great Divide*, is the final track on *The Essential Willie Nelson*, a career retrospective. The first track is the 1961 Paul Buskirk version of "Night Life," followed by singles and album tracks from Liberty, Monument, RCA, Columbia, Island, and Geffen, including a rare track with U2 and an unreleased track with Aerosmith.

Willie Nelson
***The Essential Willie Nelson* (Legacy)**
Recorded: 1961-2001
Released: April 1, 2003
Willie Compositions: 11/22
Top 40 Singles: NA
Album Charts: Country #24, Pop #179

This is the second album with this title. The earlier, single-disc release was limited to eight years on one label (RCA), but this two-CD, forty-one-track compilation draws from thirty-two years and multiple labels. Most of the hit singles and classic songs are here, plus some late-career rarities, making this a valuable introduction for the uninitiated. **Grade: B+**

Stars & Guitars/ Songs

The commercial success of *The Great Divide* convinced Lost Highway to push the formula further by adding more guest stars, more producers, more synths, and more backup singers in a one-night-only live concert at Nashville's Ryman Auditorium. The resulting album, *Stars & Guitars*, is a predictable disaster. Three of the duets from the studio album are re-created onstage in even weaker versions, thanks to the rushed tempos, the heavy-handed backbeat, and the competitive over-singing. How are these overblown arrangements any less egregious than what RCA did to Nelson in the '60s?

Willie Nelson & Friends
***Stars & Guitars* (Lost Highway)**
Recorded: May 27, 2002
Released: November 5, 2002
Willie Compositions: 4/18
Top 40 Singles: NA
Album Charts: Country #18, Pop #133

Not one of these eighteen songs is improved by these live performances at this extravaganza where guest stars shuffled on- and offstage like customers at Starbucks. Nelson doesn't seem to have much connection to his vocal partners nor to the band that pushes through the songs like a snowplow shoving nuances aside. The best moments—ballad vocals by Aaron Neville, Patty Griffin, and Vince Gill—involved scant participation by Nelson, who sounded detached all night. **Grade: C-**

Willie Nelson
***Songs* (Lost Highway)**
Recorded: 1961-2002
Released: February 15, 2005
Willie Compositions: 11/20
Top 40 Singles: NA
Album Charts: Country #13, Pop #64

This single-CD anthology of previously released recordings covers Nelson's career from the original 1961 Pamper demo of "Crazy" to the RCA version of "Good Times," from the Francine Reed duet on "Funny How Time Slips Away" to the 2002 *Stars & Guitars* live treatment of "On the Road Again." These are great songs, but not the best versions—and that's true of much of this project. If you want a compilation of Nelson's finest performances, this is not the place to find them. **Grade: B-**

Run That by Me One More Time

Ray Price reprised his version of Nelson's "Night Life" one more time on *Stars & Guitars*, but he's in friendlier territory on his second duet album with his old employee, *Run That by Me One More Time*. Though it was released by Lost Highway, it was recorded with the Justice Records house band—guitars, fiddle, steel, and rhythm section—before the new contract was signed. As such, it boasts the no-nonsense basics of a classic honky-tonk session—free from major-label expectations—and that brings out the best in both singers.

"I can't remember which lyrics or notes were written by me and which by Ray," Nelson says of "I've Just Destroyed the World" in his book *Energy Follows Thought: The Stories Behind My Songs*. "All I can recall is talking about how men have a say of screwing up relationships with women. I can still hear Ray saying, 'You got that right, Willie. But maybe rather than talk about it, we'd do better to sing about it.'"

Willie at the 1995 installment of his Fourth of July Picnic, Luckenbach, Texas.

Willie Nelson and Ray Price
***Run That by Me One More Time* (Lost Highway)**
Recorded: Circa 1995
Released: July 1, 2003
Willie Compositions: 4/11
Top 40 Singles: NA
Album Chart: Country #62

If the first Nelson/Price duet album, 1980's *San Antonio Rose*, focused on songs that had been hits for Price and his '50s/'60s peers, this one digs into the vaults for songs unknown to most listeners. Two of them, "The Cold War with You" and "Deep Water," are recycled from the earlier disc; and four others are from Nelson's extensive, pre-*Red Headed Stranger* catalog, including "I'm So Ashamed," sung with contrarian confidence, and "I've Just Destroyed the World I'm Living In," a Pamper demo co-written by the two men back in the day. As always, the give-and-take between Price's silky precision and Nelson's rumpled looseness is pure pleasure. **Grade: A-**

Live and Kickin'/Live at Billy Bob's Texas/Outlaws and Angels/Songs for Tsunami Relief: Austin to South Asia

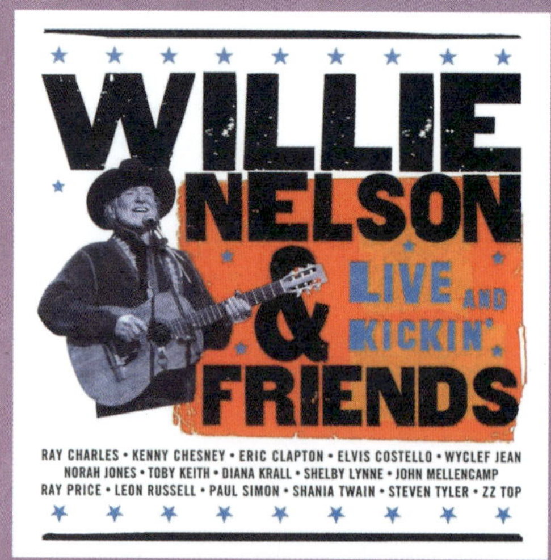

Willie Nelson
Live and Kickin' **(Lost Highway)**
Recorded: April 9, 2003
Released: June 24, 2003
Willie Compositions: 3/15
Top 40 Singles: NA
Album Charts: Country #4, Pop #42

This sequel to *Stars & Guitars* boasts bigger stars and a better band. But instead of the guests paying tribute to Nelson's songwriting, he seems to be paying tribute to theirs. The duets with Paul Simon, Diana Krall, Elvis Costello, Leon Russell, Ray Charles, and Toby Keith come off well; but the others sound like the perfunctory, off-the-cuff jams they are. **Grade: C+**

Willie Nelson
Live at Billy Bob's Texas **(Smith Music)**
Recorded: October 11, 2003
Released: May 4, 2004
Willie Compositions: 9/28
Top 40 Singles: NA
Album Charts: Country #27, Pop #168

No guest stars this time—just Willie and the Family doing a typical early-2000s show at the massive entertainment complex that inspired the mechanical bull scenes in the movie *Urban Cowboy*. There were twenty songs on the original one-CD release, then it was repackaged with a DVD that included the same twenty plus eight more and some backstage interviews. Bobbie's piano is buried in the mix, and Willie's voice is not as strong as it once was. But he takes enormous, revelatory liberties with the original melodies in both his vocals and guitar solos. Here's some of his wildest picking ever. **Grade: A-**

Various Artists
***Songs for Tsunami Relief: Austin to South Asia* (Texas Roadhouse)**
Recorded: January 9, 2005
Released: April 12, 2005
Willie Compositions: 3/7
Top 40 Singles: NA
Album Chart: Country #57

This show was a benefit for the victims of the December 24, 2004, tsunami in Indonesia that killed 228,000 people. The diverse Austin music scene teamed up for this quick-turnaround concert. Instead of performing with unprepared guests, Nelson lets them do their own mini-sets—and Natalie Maines, Patty Griffin, Alejandros Escovedo, Spoon, and Kelly Willis turn in terrific work. Nelson takes over for the sparkling, final seven numbers and emphasizes his guitar solos in jams with the band at brisk tempos. Here's the best released version of the song "The Great Divide." Bruce Robison and Mickey Raphael perform Robison's "What Would Willie Do?" the best song ever written *about* Nelson. **Grade: B+**

Ray Price and Willie perform during the *Live and Kickin'* concert at New York's Beacon Theatre on April 9, 2003.

Willie Nelson
***Outlaws and Angels* (Lost Highway)**
Recorded: May 5, 2004
Released: September 21, 2004
Willie Compositions: 3/19
Top 40 Singles: NA
Album Charts: Country #10, Pop #69

This cable-TV special, a tribute concert for Nelson, was staged at L.A.'s The Wiltern. James Caan obnoxiously announces each guest, sometimes in the middle of a song, and his hype goads vocalists who should know better to over-sing or miss their entrances. Several of the old-timers sound froggy; everyone sounds under-rehearsed. The talent—Nelson, Merle Haggard, Al Green, Carole King, Toots Hibbert, Lucinda Williams, Keith Richards, Jerry Lee Lewis—is impressive but squandered in this embarrassment. **Grade: D**

It was so easy the first time, so why not do it again? Nelson returns to the formula of *Stars & Guitars* for *Live and Kickin'*, another live album from a one-night-only show with guest stars. James Stroud is the producer again, but the locale is New York this time—and the names are bigger. The batting average of successful musical encounters is higher this time, but not high enough to make this an essential Willie Nelson album. The worst of these lazy live albums with guests was the barely listenable *Outlaws and Angels*.

Nelson was much better off without all the celebrities and hoopla with a straightforward documentation of another night "On the Road Again" with Willie Nelson and Family. That was the case with the excellent *Live at Billy Bob's Texas*, recorded in 2003. Almost as good was the heartfelt mini-set Nelson contributed to the benefit concert memorialized as the 2005 album *Songs for Tsunami Relief: Austin to South Asia*.

Keith Richards and Willie onstage during the *Outlaws & Angels* concert at the Wiltern Theatre in Los Angeles on May 5, 2004.

It Always Will Be

Nelson could still rouse himself to great performances when he was onstage with his own band, but when he got in the studio, especially when surrounded by players or singers he didn't know that well, he seemed to tune out. That dynamic made this decade as frustrating for Nelson fans as the '60s.

In the midst of this string of underwhelming albums, Nelson wrote the most pointed political song of his career. On Christmas Day, 2003, disheartened by a war in Iraq based on false claims and faulty reasoning (Saddam Hussein didn't possess nuclear weapons, and 9/11 was launched from Afghanistan, not Iraq), Nelson penned "Whatever Happened to Peace on Earth?," which asked discomfiting questions such as "How much oil is one life worth?" and "How much is a liar's word worth?"

He recorded a simple, hymn-like arrangement with piano and released it on something he called the Peace DVD with two related tracks: an earlier recording of his 1968 anti-war song, "Jimmy's Road," plus a new recording of Mark Twain's "The War Prayer." He lent the new song to the Dennis Kucinich campaign, but he refused to put the new song on an album.

Willie Nelson tours in support of *The Great Divide* at Amsterdam's Paradiso on May 23, 2002.

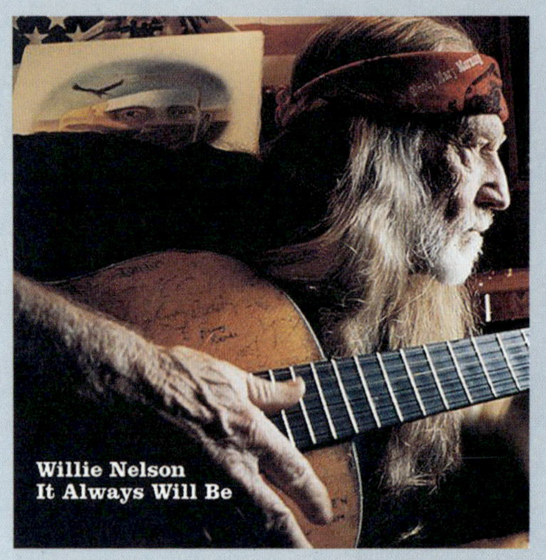

Willie Nelson
***It Always Will Be* (Lost Highway)**
Recorded: 2004
Released: October 26, 2004
Willie Compositions: 3/14
Top 40 Singles: NA
Album Charts: Country #12, Pop #75

This studio album (recorded catch as catch can at five different studios) isn't all that different from Nelson's triumphant comeback projects of the 2010s: a handful of originals, some Music Row numbers, some contributions from his kids, a left-field cover (Tom Waits' "Picture in a Frame"), and a few duets. It's not quite as good because the tempos drag, the originals are weak, and the sound changes from track to track. On the other hand, the Norah Jones duet, the Toby Keith-penned workingman's blues, and the hard-swinging "I Didn't Come Here (And I Ain't Leavin'") are terrific. **Grade: B-**

Norah Jones and Willie perform during the *Live and Kickin'* concert at the Beacon Theatre in New York City on April 9, 2003.

"I don't want any money out of it," he told *No Depression* in 2004, "but I still believe everything that's out there. I don't care about airplay. I knew it wouldn't get airplay because there's hundreds of channels out there who are on the other side. They might play it and ridicule it a little bit. . . . I knew there was a couple of lines that might piss off a few folks. But if I didn't do that, I'd have failed in what I was trying to do, which was to get the message across that what we're doing and the direction we're going is not right."

But like his friend Merle Haggard's, Nelson's politics are often hard to pin down. On the one hand, his outspoken support for family farmers and marijuana legislation has marked him as a liberal, as has his public support for such liberal political candidates as Kucinich, Anne Richards, and Beto O'Rourke. On the other hand, he's supported such non-liberal libertarians as Ross Perot and Kinky Friedman and has often collaborated with Toby Keith, a right-wing warrior who had publicly feuded with the left-leaning Dixie Chicks over President Bush.

"Toby is a great singer and writer," Nelson told me in 2020. "I don't care who you like politically, all I care is, 'Can you sing and write? And do you want to do a song with me?' If you do, I'm all for it."

Unlike someone such as Lee Greenwood, whose music is as one-dimensional as his politics are conservative, Keith is an immensely gifted singer and songwriter despite his sometimes-abrasive views. Early in 2022, Keith invited Nelson to sing a duet on a new song, "Beer for My Horses," a troubling celebration of lynching. Despite its vicious message, it had a rousing chorus, as a posse chief shouts out in a tavern, "Whiskey for my men, beer for my horses."

By contrast, Keith's "Tired," which Nelson recorded compellingly on *It Always Will Be*, is the lament of a factory worker and his wife who've played by the rules and been cheated of their reward by an unfair system. In Nelson's version more than Keith's, there's a fire smoldering under the weariness—a hint that he's not accepting his fate.

Countryman

In 2005, a movie called *Brokeback Mountain*, directed by Ang Lee from a Larry McMurtry screenplay, told the story of two working cowboys in Wyoming who have a sexual affair in the midst of a violently anti-gay culture. It was a well-made, old-fashioned Western about an extremely unconventional topic. Nelson, who has compared the gay rights movement to the Civil Rights movement, contributed his version of "He Was a Friend of Mine," an early Bob Dylan rewrite of a folk song, to the movie's soundtrack.

The film became a cause célèbre that year, and Nelson was inspired to record a 1981 Ned Sublette song, "Cowboys Are Frequently Secretly Fond of Each Other," a humorous approach to the situation the movie had taken quite seriously. It was released as a single and even inspired an answer song, "Ain't Going Down on Brokeback Mountain," which mocked male-heterosexual panic at the intrusion of gays in hypermasculine arenas. Both of these gay-cowboy songs and "Beer for My Horses" wouldn't show up on a Willie Nelson album until the 2009 anthology, *Lost Highway*.

It made sense that Nelson had long wanted to make a reggae album, for his advocacy of marijuana's healing properties was matched only by the Rastafarian musicians from Jamaica. He had even inserted the reggae hymn "By the Rivers of Babylon," made famous by Jamaica's Melodians, into a 1980 album of Protestant church music, *Family Bible*.

Opposite: Willie performs on the NBC TV show, *Apollo at 70: A Hot Night in Harlem*, on June 19, 2004

"These reggae guys told me that how they first started playing reggae was by listening to a country station out of Miami or somewhere late at night," Nelson told *New Country* in 1996. "They could hear

Willie Nelson
***Countryman* (Lost Highway)**
Recorded: 1995–2004
Released: August 2, 2005
Willie Compositions: 9/12
Top 40 Singles: NA
Album Charts: Country #6, Pop #46

There's a reason they call albums like this "brave artistic risks." It's because there's a real chance for failure, and Nelson's attempt to make a reggae record is a fiasco. You have to salute him for trying it—but the cheesy arrangements; the half-hearted transformations of Nelson, Johnny Cash, and Jimmy Cliff songs; the stiff approximations of a reggae beat; and the uneasy mix of musicians from Jamaica, Texas, and producer Don Was's Michigan make this one barely listenable. **Grade: F**

the voices, and they could hear the melody, but they couldn't hear the bottom; they couldn't hear the bass. So, they started putting their own rhythms to these country melodies, which is what these guys told me reggae came from. So, it's not surprising that you can take any country song and do it reggae style."

With Don Was, producer of Bonnie Raitt's breakthrough albums and future president of Blue Note Records, at the controls, Nelson worked on and off on a reggae album for nine years but could never get it right. He sang a duet with Toots Hibbert (justly dubbed the "Jamaican Otis Redding") on Johnny Cash's "I'm a Worried Man," but they sounded as if they were at different recording sessions. He tried to adapt eight of his '60s songs and a new one to the reggae beat, arriving at an uneasy compromise that did justice to neither. Finally, he threw up his hands and allowed Lost Highway to put it out as it was.

You Don't Know Me: The Songs of Cindy Walker

Strangely enough, Nelson followed up one of his worst albums with one of his best. Over the course of his career, he would devote a whole album to each of these songwriters: Lefty Frizzell, Kris Kristofferson, Roger Miller, Hank Williams, Cindy Walker, George Gershwin, and Harlan Howard. All of them are good, but the Kristofferson and Walker projects are the ultimate example of great songs finding a great singer—or perhaps, a great singer finding great songs.

Walker was a better singer than Kristofferson, but she soon realized her songwriting was the better talent. As a teenager, for example, she had composed "Dusty Skies," a song that evoked the recent Dust Bowl storms. It was recorded by Bob Wills and again by Nelson on his 2006 album, *You Don't Know Me: The Songs of Cindy Walker*. Nelson was himself a teenager when he heard Wills and the Texas Playboys knocking out such Walker numbers as "Dusty Skies," "Miss Molly," and "Cherokee Maiden." Before long, Nelson was playing the songs onstage.

"I was doing 'Miss Molly' and 'Bubbles in My Beer' and 'I Was Just Walkin' out the Door' when I was a teenager," he says in the 2006 album liner notes. "Wills was a big hero of mine," Nelson told the *New York Times* in 2006, "and Cindy is from Mexia, Texas, which is only a few miles from Abbott, where I was born and grew up. I didn't know her personally in those days, but I was well familiar with her writing. I told her years ago I wanted to do an album of her songs; she'd probably given up on me."

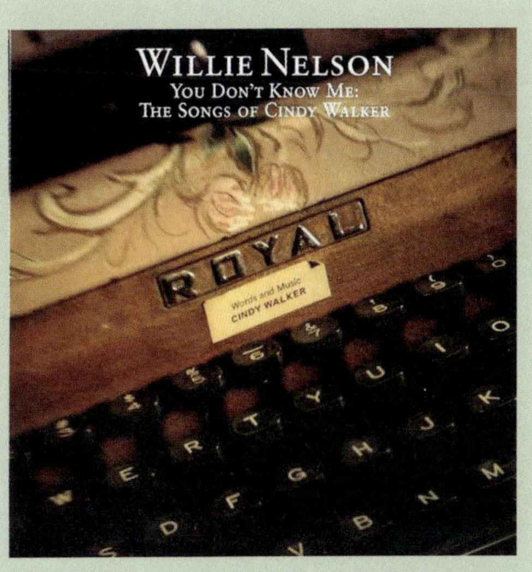

Willie Nelson
You Don't Know Me: The Songs of Cindy Walker
(Lost Highway)
Recorded: Late 2005
Released: March 16, 2006
Willie Compositions: 0/13
Top 40 Singles: NA
Album Charts: Country #24, Pop #114

Walker, who wrote more than fifty songs that Bob Wills recorded as well as hits for Eddy Arnold, Ernest Tubb, Hank Snow, Webb Pierce, and Gene Autry, is one of country music's greatest songwriters. But seldom have her works been recorded as sympathetically as they are here by her fellow Texan Nelson and an all-star Nashville band featuring Buddy Emmons, Charlie McCoy, and Brent Mason. Whether as funny as "It's All Your Fault" or as poignant as "I Don't Care," these numbers are brilliantly crafted by Walker and gracefully understated by Nelson. **Grade: A+**

As on the Kristofferson album, you can hear how Nelson's supple singing brings out the sheer elegance of Walker's words and music. This is true whether the number is as poignant as Walker's most famous song, "You Don't Know Me," the confession of a love that never spoke up for itself, or as bouncy and witty as "Don't Be Ashamed of Your Age," a celebration of senior citizen hijinks.

On the latter number, Nelson demonstrates his freedom from all the expectations of one's seventh decade not by fighting against them but by shrugging them off dismissively and cruising into town on a Saturday night in a musical hot rod driven by Trigger, Johnny Gimble's fiddle, Buddy Emmons' steel, and harmonica from Mickey Raphael's role model, Charlie McCoy. On the album's title tune, Nelson manages to convey the paradoxical yearning and shyness as powerfully as Walker's words do.

Unlike Kristofferson, Walker was not just a songwriter Nelson admired but also one that greatly influenced him. Nowhere is this more obvious than on Walker's song, "Not That I Care," a hit for her co-writer, Webb Pierce. The narrator asks a friend about an ex-lover, pressing for more and more details, all the while insisting, "not that I care." The resemblance to Nelson's "I Never Cared for You" is bolstered not just by the title but also by the storytelling device: revealing the narrator's true feelings by having him claim the opposite.

Walker could always push her lyrics one step further. For her, it wasn't enough to describe a heartbroken drunk watching the bubbles in his beer; she had him peering into the emptiness inside each bubble, a vacancy that resembled the drinker's dreams, which had all burst, just as the bubbles were about to. Such details made her characters more than just faceless stereotypes; each was a distinct character that a singer/actor as talented as Nelson could readily inhabit.

Texas songwriter Cindy Walker is the subject of Willie's 2006 tribute album, *You Don't Know Me*.

In her 2006 *Los Angeles Times* obituary, Walker is quoted as saying that the best tunes "are songs with a face. You recognize them. You know them. It's like a person. They have a face that's outstanding. Other songs don't have a face; you just hear them, that's all. The really good ones are few and far between."

Even at age 87 in 2005, Walker was still pitching songs with hard-to-forget faces. In fact, it was a pitch to Nelson and his producer Fred Foster that led to the idea of devoting a whole album to her music. When it was released on March 16, 2006, she got to hear it, declaring it was her favorite recording of her compositions. Seven days later, she died.

"She was a very good friend," Nelson told the *Fresh Air* radio show in 2006. "We had talked about doing an album of her songs for years, but I just hadn't got into the studio to do it, you know, for one reason or another. I'm glad I did it when I did, because Cindy's health was deteriorating pretty well at that time. And I was just hoping that I could get the album completed and out while she was still here to listen to it. And as it happened, she did get to hear it before she died. And she loved it. She called me up and told me, you know, a lot of great things about how she enjoyed it. And she really made me feel good about getting it done."

Remember Me, Vol. 1

When producer James Stroud was working with Nelson in 2004–2005 on studio albums such as *It Always Will Be* and live albums such as *Live and Kickin'*, he helped Nelson record *Remember Me, Vol. 1*, an album of favorite old country songs with a band of Stroud's favorite Nashville pickers. Buried in the credits is one for Cindy Walker on background vocals, shortly before Nelson's tribute to her and her subsequent death.

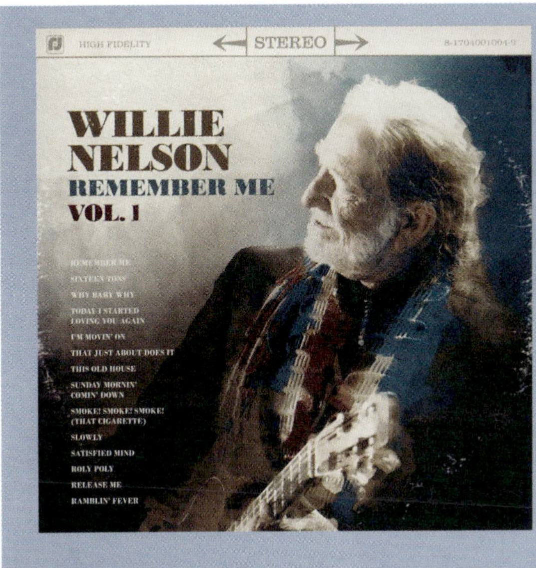

Willie Nelson
Remember Me, Vol. 1 **(R&J)**
Recorded: Circa 2004–2005
Released: November 22, 2011
Willie Compositions: 0/14
Top 40 Singles: NA
Album Chart: Country #40

Nearly half the albums in Nelson's catalog could justifiably carry this title, as if Nelson could hear the favorite songs of his childhood calling out to be remembered—whether country, Western swing, or American Songbook numbers. All but one of this album's fourteen songs were written before his 1975 breakthrough with *Red Headed Stranger*. Producer James Stroud doesn't try to modernize anything, so Nelson and an all-star band can relive the past on songs by Haggard, Merle Travis, George Jones, Hank Snow, and more. It was such exemplary country music that no Nashville label would release it until six years after it was made. **Grade: B+**

Willie and Toby Keith appear together at the Academy of Country Music Awards at the Mandalay Bay in Las Vegas on May 21, 2003.

Willie Nelson
***Songbird* (Lost Highway)**
Recorded: Early 2006
Released: October 31, 2006
Willie Compositions: 4/11
Top 40 Singles: NA
Album Charts: Country #19, Pop #87

In 2006, a pre-scandal Ryan Adams offered to produce an album for his labelmate Nelson, with Adams' band, the Cardinals. Among the oddball song choices are tunes from the Grateful Dead, Fleetwood Mac, Leonard Cohen, and Adams himself. This all works better than you'd think. Adam's eccentricity and noisy guitar nudge Nelson out of his old habits, and Nelson's understated delivery and Zen-like aura tempers Adams' nervous energy and worst impulses. The result is an inspired collaboration—and the best-ever version of Cohen's "Hallelujah." **Grade: B+**

Songbird

If the partnership between Nelson and Lost Highway was meant to connect the aging singer to the Americana movement he helped inspire, the results thus far were pretty meager. The celebrity-studded live albums were disappointments; the terrific Cindy Walker tribute and the terrible reggae album had nothing to do with the contemporary alt-country scene. But the connection finally clicked on Nelson's next album, *Songbird*.

Americana star Ryan Adams had been recording for Lost Highway since 2001, both as a solo artist and as leader of the bands Whiskeytown and the Cardinals. He was undeniably talented as a singer, songwriter, and stage performer—but there was always something jittery about him, as if he had to overdo everything to compensate for his insecurity. When he teamed up with Nelson, however, he finally met the Zen calm he'd been missing his whole career. Adams responded with the best work of his life.

Nelson is backed by Adams and the Cardinals plus Mickey Raphael and Ollabelle keyboardist Glenn Patscha, with the steel guitar of the Cardinals' Jeff Graboff pushed way up in the mix. Nelson brought along three old songs and one new one; Adams wrote one and pushed Nelson to tackle songs by Jerry Garcia, Gram Parsons, Leonard Cohen, and Christine McVie. It turns out that these are all good ideas, not only because Nelson is a much better singer than Garcia or Cohen but also because he's a much steadier presence than Parsons or Adams.

On Cohen's much-covered "Hallelujah," for example, Nelson deflates the pomposity much as he did on "Bridge over Troubled Water" and turns an over-the-top anthem into a personal reflection, more conversational and more rewarding as a result. His one new song, "Back to Earth," is a similar anthem with religious overtones also made more dramatic by a reduced effort. Adams counters Nelson's minimalist singing with maximalist rock 'n' roll guitar, but the two factors find a fruitful balance.

Last of the Breed

The Walker tribute and the Adams collaboration would prove to be the high points of Nelson's tenure with Lost Highway. After those two experiments, Nelson's life settled back into a comfortable routine. He played approximately 150 live dates a year,

Willie on *The Late Show with David Letterman* at the Ed Sullivan Theatre in New York City on March 28, 2006.

including a Fourth of July Picnic and a Farm Aid Benefit. In 2005, for example, the Picnic was held at Billy Bob's Texas in Fort Worth with Bob Dylan and the Doobie Brothers. Two months later, Farm Aid celebrated its twentieth anniversary with a September show in the Chicago suburbs with such regular stalwarts as Nelson, Neil Young, John Mellencamp, and Dave Matthews.

Nelson was so comfortable in his tour bus, still nicknamed "Honeysuckle Rose," that he would often sleep in his bunk there, even if he had a room at a fancy hotel nearby. When he got off the road, he would spend time with the family in Malibu, California, or Maui, Hawaii. But he kept gravitating back to Texas, to the house he bought in his hometown of Abbott or the house on the Spicewood property he'd reclaimed from the IRS.

The latter had the advantage of a golf course, where he often played thirty-six holes in a day, and a recording studio where he could hang out after the sun went down at "golf-thirty." With the tape machines running, he could play whatever he wanted with whoever was handy, whether it be his own band, admirers as different as Aerosmith and Asleep at the Wheel, or his old friends from the days before *Red Headed Stranger*. Sometimes Nelson would even travel to Nashville, New York, or Los Angeles to record some music.

In the fall of 2006, he traveled to Franklin, Tennessee, forty minutes south of Nashville, for a get-together with Ray Price, Merle Haggard, Kris Kristofferson, Vince Gill, and producer Fred Foster to sing some old songs in an old-fashioned way. A newish Nelson composition, "Back to Earth," done as mystic duet with steel guitarist Jon Graboff on *Songbird*, was now done as a traditional country hymn with tinkling piano and lonesome harmonica on an album called *Last of the Breed*. In another echo of his 2006 highlights, Nelson sang two more Cindy Walker songs as duets with Price.

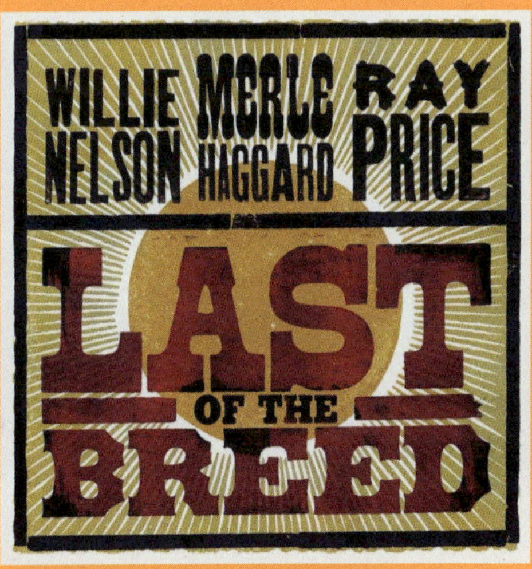

Willie Nelson, Merle Haggard, and Ray Price
***Last of the Breed* (Lost Highway)**
Recorded: Fall 2006
Released: March 20, 2007
Willie Compositions: 1/22
Top 40 Singles: NA
Album Charts: Country #7, Pop #64

Though this album is credited to a trio, the three singers appear together on only half of the twenty-two tracks. There are five Nelson/Haggard duets, three Nelson/Price duets, a Haggard solo number, a Nelson/Price/Kris Kristofferson trio, and a Price/Vince Gill duet. Despite the hodgepodge nature of the project, you can tell these old warriors are enjoying themselves immensely on these old hillbilly standards—and the enjoyment proves contagious. **Grade: B**

Haggard contributed two compositions, and Kristofferson one—but eighteen of the twenty-two songs were vintage country numbers associated with Bob Wills, Lefty Frizzell, Buck Owens, Floyd Tillman, Gene Autry, and Hank Williams. None of the vocalists overexerted himself, but they'd been singing these songs all their lives—and they hadn't grown tired of them yet. Foster kept everything simple, and the relaxed vibe was adopted by everyone involved.

The three men enjoyed themselves so much that they went out on a short tour together in September. It was one of the very few instances that Nelson toured with a duet partner who wasn't named Jennings. When the *Last of the Breed* tour stopped at Maryland's Merriweather Post Pavilion on the sixth, Haggard and his band, the Strangers, did a full set, with Nelson joining them on Haggard's "Okie from Muskogee," Townes Van Zandt's "Pancho and Lefty," and Floyd Tillman's "I'll Keep on Loving You."

Then Nelson and his Family band did a full set of their own, with Haggard playing guitar on the first six songs and Price singing with Nelson on "Crazy" and "Night Life." Maybe there could have been more collaborations, but the men were determined to maintain their individual identities. That's what made the collaborations so interesting, because they brought such different personas to the music. A sampling from that tour was released as a DVD, *Last of the Breed Live in Concert*, but not as an audio recording.

Moment of Forever

A Nelson fan could get whiplash in these years, as the singer went from a jangly country-rock project with Adams to a retro-country flashback with Haggard and Price to a synth-laden project with bro-country star Kenny Chesney. An amiable, handsome fellow with a friendly voice, Chesney had become a superstar with a series of easy-to-like, easy-to-forget singles that managed to combine the crowd-pleasing aspects of Garth Brooks and Jimmy Buffett. At this point in his career, however, he wanted to do something more ambitious and prestigious.

Rather than risk his winning streak, he did this not on a Kenny Chesney album but on a Willie Nelson album. The album would be called *Moment of Forever* and would be co-produced by Chesney and Buddy Cannon. Cannon was a Nashville veteran who'd written hits for Mel Tillis, Vern Gosdin, and George Strait and who'd been Chesney's producer of choice since 1997. This was Cannon's first time working with Nelson, and they would hit it off so well that they'd become a tight, productive songwriting/producing team in the 2010s and 2020s.

On this first collaboration, however, Chesney and Cannon gave Nelson the state-of-the-art, ready-for-radio treatment with synths, compressed drums, and layered guitars. This approach had been disastrous when tried by Matt Serletic on *The Great Divide* or by James Stroud on *Stars & Guitars*, but counterintuitively it works on *Moment of Forever*.

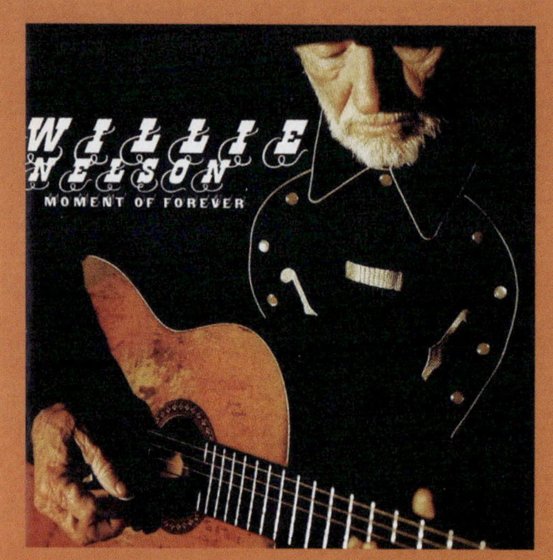

Willie Nelson
***Moment of Forever* (Lost Highway)**
Recorded: Late 2007
Released: January 29, 2008
Willie Compositions: 3/13
Top 40 Singles: NA
Album Charts: Country #8, Pop #56

This shouldn't have worked. Pop-country star Kenny Chesney and his longtime producer Buddy Cannon co-produce this album by surrounding Nelson's voice with synths, loud drums, and slick guitars. But Nelson's reinvigorated voice rises above the flavor-of-the-month production to sing convincingly on three impressive new compositions plus strong material from Kris Kristofferson, Randy Newman, Bob Dylan, and Guy Clark. Assisted by Mickey Raphael's ghostly harmonica, Cannon's savvy mix allows Nelson to dominate his surroundings. **Grade: B+**

Maybe it was because Cannon, a former bassist, understood the crucial role of syncopation on Nelson's records. Maybe it was because Cannon knew to bring Nelson's voice and guitar and Raphael's harmonica up in the mix. Maybe it was because Chesney picked such good songs by Guy Clark, Randy Newman, Kris Kristofferson, and Bob Dylan. Maybe it was just because Nelson was feeling reinspired after his 2006–2007 recording triumphs and put more of himself into the writing and the singing.

The album starts with "Over You Again," co-written by Nelson with his sons Luke and Micah. It's a return to the father's primary songwriting obsession: looking back at a failed relationship to try to understand what went wrong. This time, the narrator is going through it a second time with the same woman, wondering why he didn't learn his lesson the first time. It's a question we've all asked ourselves. In the same vein is another new Nelson composition, "You Don't Think I'm Funny Anymore." The more the narrator complains that his wife is tired of his jokes, the funnier the song becomes.

Along the same lines, Kristofferson's title tune allows Nelson to acknowledge that the shortest relationships sometimes create the longest memories. All these problems can disappear, however, if you stay focused on the present (as he sings on his own "It's Always Now") or if you take one more puff of marijuana (as he sings hilariously on Clark's "Worry B Gone").

Lost Highway

Moment of Forever would be Nelson's last album of new material for Lost Highway, and it capped off a four-album winning streak after his relationship with the label had begun so disappointingly. Part of the problem early on was the label's reliance on gimmicks to restore the singer's commercial profile by matching him with guest stars and guest producers both onstage and in the studio. Nelson went along with the plan uncomplainingly, and the results were better-than-average sales and worse-than-average music.

But part of the problem was his obviously less-than-total investment in the projects. He sang respectably but without the emotional punch of his best records. That seemed to change in 2006 when he got to do his dream project of a tribute to Cindy Walker and a reunion with Merle Haggard and Ray Price. Fired up by those encounters, he responded enthusiastically to unlikely collaborations with Ryan Adams and Kenny Chesney. By the time the two parties figured out how to work together, it was over.

Willie Nelson
Lost Highway (Lost Highway)
Recorded: 2001-2009
Released: August 11, 2009
Willie Compositions: 5/17
Top 40 Singles: NA
Album Charts: Country #29, Pop #173

Nelson released a dozen albums for Lost Highway Records between 2002 and 2008, ranging from one of his best ever, *You Don't Know Me*, to one of his worst, *Countryman*. After he left the label, this compilation album was released to collect some of the more memorable—if not the best—moments. Included are duets with Rob Thomas, Lee Ann Womack, Ray Price, Shania Twain, Lucinda Williams, Diana Krall, and Elvis Costello. Released for the first time on a Nelson album were his Toby Keith duet "Beer for My Horses," two outtakes from his sessions with producer Chips Moman, his controversial single "Cowboys Are Frequently Secretly Fond of Each Other," and the answer song, "Ain't Going Down on Brokeback Mountain." **Grade: B**

Willie Nelson plays the Stagecoach Country Music Festival at the Empire Polo Field in Indio, California, on May 5, 2007.

Two Men with the Blues

A lot of people didn't hear the jazz element in Nelson's music, but Wynton Marsalis heard it. The celebrated jazz trumpeter recognized the elastic sense of rhythm, the improvisatory spirit, and the roots in African-American blues. As the head of Manhattan's Jazz at Lincoln Center, Marsalis was in a position to showcase this side of Nelson's work in a concert that resulted in the album *Two Men with the Blues*.

Neither man is comfortable with cutting-edge modernity; both are at their best when squeezing new juice out of the pre-Beatles music of the '30s, '40s, and '50s. Nelson's first love was the Western swing of Bob Wills, and Marsalis's was the hard-bop of Art Blakey. But the two men found common ground in the mid-century show tunes and blues hits that became standards in black clubs and white clubs alike in those years.

The two shows at Lincoln Center featured a septet—Nelson, Raphael, and Marsalis's current quintet—and repertoire that emphasized the blues: two by Nelson, two by Hoagy Carmichael, others by Jimmy Reed, Louis Jordan, and Merle Travis. Nelson, Raphael, Marsalis, saxophonist Walter Blanding, and pianist Dan Nimmer all get plenty of room to solo, pushing six of the songs past the five-minute mark.

When they tackle Carmichael's "Stardust" and "Georgia on My Mind," the tempos are slower, the vocals are more conversational, and the dramatic pauses are longer than on the singer's 1978 chart-toppers. This time, each tune opens with a long, lyrical piano solo; and the horns take their time to enter. But when they do, they use Nelson's phrasing as a template for fills and solos that lead the melody into bluer notes and oilier rhythms.

Nelson had never really worked with trumpets and saxophones before—except for the hard-to-find *Sugar Moon* session in the mid-'80s and as background padding in Nashville—and it's fascinating how the

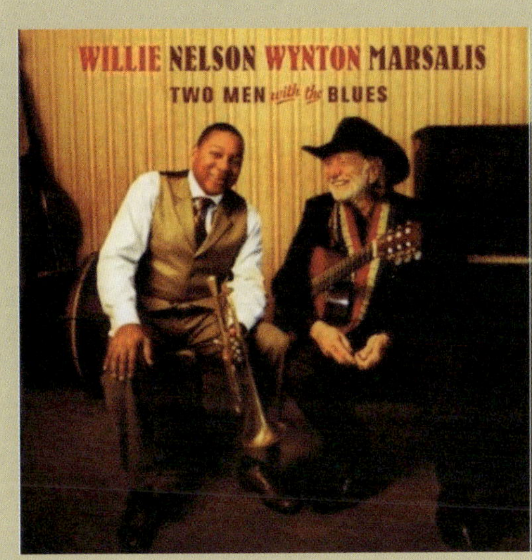

Willie Nelson and Wynton Marsalis
***Two Men with the Blues* (Blue Note)**
Recorded: January 12-13, 2007
Released: July 8, 2008
Willie Compositions: 2/10
Top 40 Singles: NA
Album Chart: Pop #20
Nelson's jazz tendencies had never been as obvious as on this live-concert collaboration at New York's Jazz at Lincoln Center. Nelson and Mickey Raphael join one of the most successful jazz combos of the day, the Wynton Marsalis Quintet, finding common ground in the blues. Nelson doesn't dig into the more melancholy, complex side of his songwriting nor the boundary-pushing innovation of modern jazz, but he sounds like he's having a ball on these old blues vehicles, matching the jazz virtuosos phrase for phrase. **Grade: B+**

vocal qualities of the horns mirror his own voice. Of course, Raphael's harmonica is sort of a horn, and he demonstrates to the others how to complement Nelson's tenor and guitar with echoes and responses.

"These songs, heard this way with this group—that's never been done before," Nelson claims in the Blue Note press release. "Whatever I'm doing, if you put Wynton and these guys around it, that brings it up to a different level." In the same release, Marsalis adds, "We're like the big city meets the country. Mickey is the sound of the train . . . and we're like the car horns."

Willie enjoys a toke on the *Honeysuckle Rose* tour bus in Austin in 2007.

Willie and the Wheel

More vintage blues and show tunes were on tap for Nelson's next project, *Willie and the Wheel*, a collaboration with Asleep at the Wheel produced by the band's Ray Benson and executive produced by Jerry Wexler. Wexler had wanted to record a Nelson tribute to Bob Wills in 1974 but had been foiled by Atlantic's decision to close its country division. Given a second chance, Wexler helped pick out the songs, including five so old that the songwriter credits are listed as "Traditional."

Asleep at the Wheel had been backing up Nelson, Haggard, and Price on the *Last of the Breed* tour and were primed to follow Nelson wherever he went. And Nelson was comfortable with this Western swing revival band; he'd already added guest vocals to Asleep at the Wheel albums in 1985, 1988, 1993, 1994, 1997, 1999, 2001, and 2007. He would do so again in 2008, 2010, 2015, and 2021. These included four Wills tribute albums and two Christmas records.

The Wheel's bassist, Kevin Smith, would soon join Nelson's Family, when Bee Spears died in 2011. Pianist Floyd Domino, a founding member of the Wheel who had left to play with Waylon Jennings,

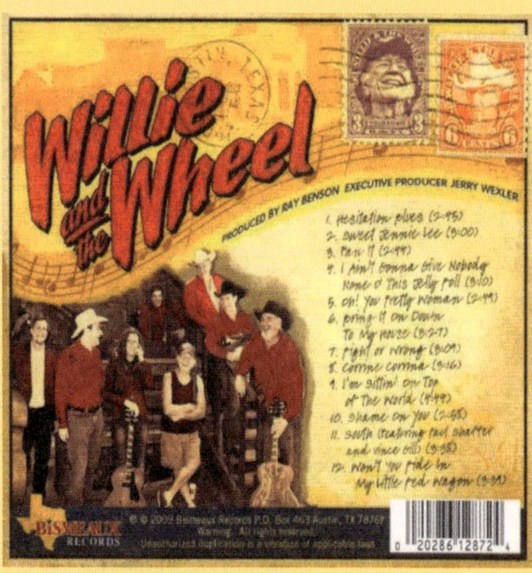

Willie Nelson and Asleep at the Wheel
Willie and the Wheel **(Bismeaux)**
Recorded: November–December 2007
Released: February 3, 2009
Willie Compositions: 0/13
Top 40 Singles: NA
Album Charts: Country #13, Pop #90

As he got older, Nelson allowed his swing rhythms to become more and more relaxed. This allowed plenty of room for his elegant phrasing, but it often became too much of a good thing. Asleep at the Wheel takes Nelson back to the Texas dance halls of his youth and puts a lively bounce back in his swing on a set of vintage Gulf Coast dance numbers. The horn section emphasizes the Dixieland roots of so much Bob Wills music, and the band's soloists are in top form. Ray Benson provides the Wills shout-outs, while Nelson provides the Tommy Duncan crooning. **Grade: A-**

was back in the band on an emeritus basis and lit up these new tracks. Trumpeter Dave Alexander, trombonist Mike Mordecai, and clarinetist Jonathan Doyle furthered Nelson's explorations with horn soloists. All in all, the connections between Asleep at the Wheel, Nelson, Haggard, and Jennings are often underappreciated, proving that Western swing had more influence on the outlaw country movement than most people know.

Orville Peck and Willie perform during the Austin City Limits Music Festival at Zilker Park on October 13, 2024.

American Classic

Nelson's new label, Blue Note Records, was founded in 1939 as a home for trad-jazz New Orleans artists such as Sidney Bechet and George Lewis before embracing such '50s modernists as Miles Davis, Thelonious Monk, Sonny Rollins, and Horace Silver. Nelson had more affinity for the earlier jazz, but he used his tenure at the label as an opportunity to scratch his jazz itch as never before.

For listeners, it was a chance to hear how popular song's examination of romantic relations can be deepened by adding the uncertainty principle of jazz, for what's more uncertain than a love affair? It was also a chance to hear how jazz's virtuosity gained in meaning when tethered to lyrics that actually grapple with the paradoxical union of desire, delight, and disappointment.

If we include the collaboration with Asleep at the Wheel (released on the band's own Bismeaux label), Nelson created a tetralogy of albums exploring the borderland between jazz and country. The third album in this series was *American Classic*, which found Nelson backed by such contemporary jazz stars as the Crusaders' keyboardist Joe Sample (who'd worked with Joni Mitchell), bassist Christian McBride (who'd worked with Joshua Redman and Chick Corea), singer-pianist Diana Krall, and her guitarist Anthony Wilson.

Willie Nelson
***American Classic* (Blue Note)**
Recorded: Early 2009
Released: August 25, 2009
Willie Compositions: 0/12
Top 40 Singles: NA
Album Charts: Country #14, Pop #43

It's not that there's anything wrong with this album of jazz standards; it's just that there's nothing right about it either. Nelson and some of the decade's top jazz musicians play with such hushed politeness that it has a narcotic effect on the listener. It seems to have had the same effect on the participants, who never seem to push themselves, the tempos, or the harmonies very hard. It's symptomatic of the ennui that Nelson's disruptive guitar licks are heard on only one song. **Grade: C+**

The producer was Tommy LiPuma, best known for working with Krall, Natalie Cole, and Barbra Streisand. In contrast to Benson's lively production of *Willie and the Wheel*, LiPuma encourages Nelson's laid-back minimalism with an emphasis on patient tempos, drum brushes, tinkling piano, understated bass, and background strings. It's all very tasteful—so tasteful, in fact, that it grows sleepy. This is the weakest album in the tetralogy.

Willie performs with Ray Benson and Asleep at the Wheel for a CBS TV broadcast on March 5, 1988.

Here We Go Again: Celebrating the Genius of Ray Charles

Nelson finished up his run of four country-jazz albums by reuniting with the Wynton Marsalis Quintet for *Here We Go Again: Celebrating the Genius of Ray Charles*. The first live-concert collaboration between Nelson and Marsalis (recorded in 2007 and released on CD in 2008) was so successful that this follow-up (recorded in 2009 and released in 2011) was inevitable. The same seven musicians from the first show are on hand plus singer Norah Jones, who had sung one duet with Nelson on *American Classic*. This time she sings four more duets with the Texan plus two lead vocals of her own.

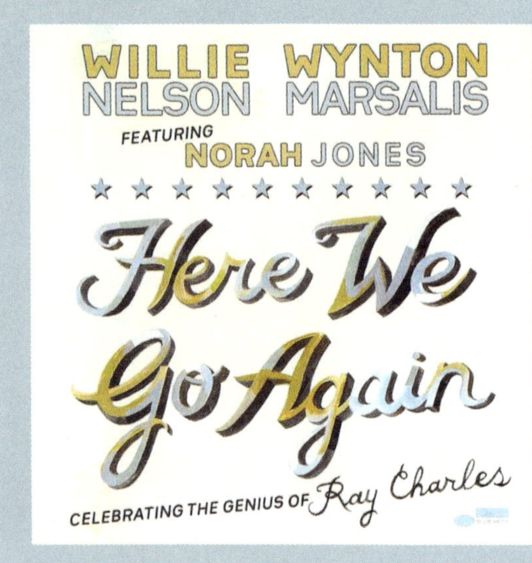

Willie Nelson, Wynton Marsalis, and Norah Jones
Here We Go Again: Celebrating the Genius of Ray Charles
(Blue Note)
Recorded: February 9-10, 2009
Released: March 29, 2011
Willie Compositions: 0/12
Top 40 Singles: NA
Album Charts: NA

The concept seemed a natural: Have Nelson pay tribute to his good friend and like-minded musician with the help of a top jazz band. But its occasional successes on the blues and jazz standards are overshadowed by the failures. Rock 'n' roll songs need to rock, even when they incorporate jazz flourishes; and country songs need to be conversational. Jones has a lovely voice, but she has trouble matching her duet parts to Nelson's phrasing. **Grade: B-**

This show was devoted to a dozen songs recorded by Charles—Nelson's sometime duet partner. This should have been a slam-dunk success, for it's hard to think of two artists more similar than Nelson and Charles—nor soloists as gifted as Raphael and the Marsalis Quintet. But somehow it misfires. The Marsalis combo excels on the jazz standards: "Come Rain, Come Shine" and "Makin' Whoopee," both sung by Jones alone.

But they falter on rock 'n' roll numbers such as "Hallelujah, I Love Her So," "Hit the Road, Jack," and "What'd I Say," going for subtlety when the songs require a funky groove to work. Those songs can accommodate hip jazz parts, but only if those improvisations respond to the groove rather than trying to replace it. The four songs from Charles's early-'60s explorations of country are fine, but both Jones and the rhythm section have trouble adjusting to Nelson's unconventional phrasing.

Country Music

Nelson had signed with Lost Highway in 2001 in part beca/use he so admired its soundtrack for the movie *O Brother, Where Art Thou?* That T-Bone Burnett–produced CD went multiplatinum with its back-to-basics approach to hillbilly music, much as *Red Headed Stranger* had a quarter-century earlier. Somehow Nelson never got to make a similar record for Lost Highway, but in 2010 he finally did it with Burnett on the album *Country Music* for Rounder Records.

The backing band was an all-acoustic, drummer-less string band but for Buddy Miller's driving, brooding electric guitar. But the biggest challenge for Nelson was not the backing band but the repertoire of gospel, train, and coal-mining songs from Appalachia. These Anglo-Celtic songs, with their lilting phrasing and high, lonesome vocals, represent a kind of country music very different from the Western swing and honky-tonk dance music that Nelson had grown up on in Texas. If Eastern country music grew out of the Carter Family, Western country music grew out of Jimmie Rodgers.

Moving from one to the other requires more modification than outsiders might guess. Over the course of this album, you can hear Nelson adjusting to this terra incognita, sounding most comfortable on the gospel and boogie numbers and responding respectably to the others. One wishes, however, that there'd been a sequel to this project, for it was clear that the singer had more to give this tradition than he was ready for on the first attempt.

"I said at one point we should call it *Country Music, In Case You Forgot*," he told *Uncut* magazine in 2010. "Because country music as most people have known it over the years has gone through a lot of changes—a bigger sound, people trying to go pop, and trying to make it something other than what, in my opinion, it's really supposed to be. Which is fiddles, guitars, steel guitars, mandolins, and people singing. . . . Simplicity is the hardest thing to come up with."

Nelson played just one song from *Country Music* in his 2010 concert at Baltimore's Pier Six Pavilion, but "Nobody's Fault but Mine" was delivered in a moody, drummer-less arrangement that reflected T-Bone Burnett's studio production. And the album's theme of revisiting and reinterpreting songs from country music's past was reflected throughout the evening.

Neil Young and Willie appear together during the Farm Aid concert at Miller Park in Milwaukee, Wisconsin, on October 2, 2010.

Willie Nelson
***Country Music* (Rounder)**
Recorded: Late 2009
Released: April 20, 2010
Willie Compositions: 1/15
Top 40 Singles: NA
Album Charts: Country #4, Pop #20

This could have been called *O Willie, Where Art Thou?* Producer T-Bone Burnett creates a sequel to his *O Brother, Where Art Thou?* by assembling an ensemble of bluegrass pickers from the Del McCoury Band and the Nashville Bluegrass Band alongside Americana stalwarts Buddy Miller and Jim Lauderdale. Miller's low-register electric guitar motorizes Doc Watson's "Freight Train Boogie," and the drummer-less band encourages Nelson's startlingly confessional vocals on such hymns as "Satan Your Kingdom Must Come Down" and "House of Gold." Nelson does fairly well with this out-of-his-comfort-zone material, but he should have gotten another shot at it. **Grade: B**

Nelson sang not only such live staples as Johnny Bush's "Whiskey River," Kris Kristofferson's "Help Me Make It through the Night," and Elvis Presley's "Always on My Mind"; but he also added such surprises as Tom T. Hall's "Shoeshine Boy" and his own seldom-played numbers "Superman" and "Healing Hands of Time." Nelson attacked each number with a strange mixture of genuine affection and reckless irreverence, reshaping the melody as if he were a jazz singer and guitarist—which he is.

It is seldom remarked that Nelson is one of the most inventive guitarists in American music, altering time and tune with fast phrases and forceful chops on an acoustic guitar so worn that it bears a gaping hole where his pick has repeatedly scraped the wood. He enjoys the perfect foil in harmonica virtuoso Mickey Raphael, and the two men filled Nelson's classic composition "Night Life" with dizzying solos that left enough of the familiar song to satisfy the audience but changed it enough to keep the band interested after playing it several thousand times.

"A lot of seventy-five-year-olds already decided to hang it up a long time ago," Nelson told *Rolling Stone* in 2009. "I would never be in that mindset, because I enjoy what I'm doing. As long as I'm healthy, I'll never leave the road—well, if people stopped showing up, that might be a reason to quit it. But I'm watching people like B. B. King or Ernest Tubb, who toured until he died. I'm not ready to quit. I'm not ready to die either."

CHAPTER 8

Last Man Standing

THE COMEBACK, 2012–2025

On the title track of his 2018 album *Last Man Standing*, Willie Nelson sang, "One thing I learned about running the road is 'forever' don't apply to life. Waylon and Ray and Merle and old Harlan lived just as fast as me." This, of course, was a reference to Waylon Jennings, Ray Price, Merle Haggard, and Howard Harlan. "I still got a lotta good friends left, and I wonder who the next will be."

During two terrible weeks in the fall of 2021, he learned who the next ones would be. Between October 16 and 28, Johnny Bush, Jerry Jeff Walker, and Billy Joe Shaver died in quick succession. And then Charley Pride died on December 12, a month and a day after he received the Willie Nelson Lifetime Achievement Award at the CMA Awards.

Walker had migrated to Austin around 1970 because he had heard that Nelson was uniting folk-rock hippies and honky-tonk rednecks into one audience. Walker came from the former group, but he embraced the fusion and became the face of the scene almost as much as Nelson himself. They remained friends ever after.

"I talked to Jerry Jeff in the hospital a few months ago when he was sick," Nelson told me in 2021. He paused and added, "I once heard Jerry Jeff say the funniest thing I ever heard anyone say onstage. He said, 'The only difference between Hank Williams and me is that Hank went backstage to throw up.'" Nelson adds, "Johnny Bush and I were great buddies. We started out making music at the same time in San Antonio. I was his first manager."

Nelson and Bush were twentysomething nobodies when they joined Ray Price & the Cherokee Cowboys in the early '60s as a bassist and drummer, respectively. Nelson financed Bush's debut album in 1967, and in 1972, Bush had a Top 15 country hit with "Whiskey River," a song he'd written himself. Nelson admired the song so much that he began to open and close his every concert with the number. Bush lived off the royalties for years.

Willie Nelson at Pinewood Performing Arts in Lincoln, Nebraska, on May 15, 2024.

Willie

Now they were gone, and the COVID pandemic had locked the nation down, depriving Nelson of not only his main source of income but also his connection to an audience that inspires him as much as he inspires them.

"What's discouraging right now is you can't go and play to your crowd," Nelson told me that year. "How do I cope with it? I cuss a lot. I'm lucky; I count my blessings. I'm glad I don't have that fucking virus. So many people are getting sick and dying. I'm just trying to stay out of the way and stay healthy so I can get back to playing again."

But Nelson is not one to give up easily. He might have died when he lay down on a snowy street in 1960, when his house burned down in 1970, or when his lung collapsed in 1981. His career seemed to die when he turned forty without a Top 5 record of his own, when his first three record labels gave up on him, and when his fourth released him after he fell off the country radio playlists. But in every case, he picked up his guitar, his trusty Trigger, and got back at it.

In "Last Man Standing," the narrator indulges in some understandable grieving: "It's getting hard to watch my pals check out, cuts like a wore-out knife." But in the end, he refuses to let it get him down. "I don't wanna be the last man standing," he sings, then adds with a wink, "On second thought, maybe I do. Yeah, maybe I do."

If Nelson was the last man standing, at least he was standing tall. By 2021, he was well into a late-career resurgence that few had expected after an early-2000s slump and a seventy-fifth birthday. But since 2012, Nelson was writing more than he had since the early-'70s and making consistently better records, too. The catalysts for this change were a new label and a new collaborator.

The label was Legacy Records, a subsidiary of Columbia, the company that had let Nelson go in 1993, on the heels of releasing one of his finest albums, *Across the Borderline*, believing the singer had run out of gas. Nineteen years later, they changed their minds, acknowledging that Nelson had a reserve tank no one had known about. Legacy had started to handle the reissues of Columbia's old catalog; now its mission was expanded to handle the label's older artists.

The collaborator was Nashville producer/songwriter Buddy Cannon, previously awarded for his work with George Strait and Kenny Chesney. When Chesney was invited to produce a Willie Nelson album, the younger star asked Cannon to co-produce the sessions that yielded *Moment of Forever*. Nelson was so impressed that he invited Cannon to produce the singer's first release on Legacy, 2012's *Heroes*.

Heroes

This was a clearing-the-throat project, a getting-used-to-each-other session for Nelson and Cannon. To make things easier, it's mostly a series of duets with guest stars both familiar (Merle Haggard, Ray Price) and new (Sheryl Crow, Coldplay). But mostly, it's a showcase for Willie's son Lukas, who sings on nine of the fourteen songs, including three that he wrote himself. He comes across as a young man with more promise than accomplishment.

His father contributed three new compositions of his own, two of them co-written with his new partner, Cannon, who acquits himself well both as songwriter and producer. "Come on Back, Jesus" is an unconventional prayer that asks the Messiah to come back to a "world done gone crazy" and to pick up a brawling John Wayne on his way.

"Hero" takes a more skeptical attitude toward a messianic musical "hero," who was once "king of the bars" but now sings on the street and sleeps in his car. It's funny with a serious undercurrent. You can hear Nelson questioning the value of his own stardom—of our own reputations. "Roll Me Up" meditates on mortality with a chuckle, sung with help from Kristofferson, Snoop Dogg, and Jamey Johnson. The lyrics are Nelson's funeral instructions set to a bouncy, cheerful sing-along: Just mix his ashes with some high-grade marijuana, twist it up in rolling papers, light it up, and pass it around.

It was the first of many humorous rebuttals to death that would continue with "Still Dead," "Bad Breath," "Heaven Is Closed," "One More Song To

Willie and Lukas Nelson at Farm Aid in Burgettstown, Pennsylvania, on September 16, 2017.

Write," and "Last Man Standing." This was a fertile new territory for Nelson's songwriting. Just as he had spent most of his career telling us in song that romantic heartbreak should hurt but not cripple us, that we should accept it as part of life and carry on, now he was singing the same message about death.

"We're all going to die," he told *Rolling Stone* in 2014. "Who was it—Seneca the thinker—that said you should look at death and comedy with the same expression of countenance? You can't be afraid of living or dying. You live and you die; that's just what happens, so you can't be afraid of either."

Willie Nelson
***Heroes* (Legacy)**
Recorded: Winter 2011/2012
Released: May 15, 2012
Willie Compositions: 3/14
Top 40 Singles: NA
Album Charts: Country #4, Pop #18

This album is mostly a showcase for Willie's son Lukas as he sings with his dad on Texas honky-tonk standards, tunes by Tom Waits and Pearl Jam, and three originals by Lukas himself. The album is fleshed out by more duets with Merle Haggard, Jamey Johnson, Ray Price, and Sheryl Crow; a remake of Coldplay's "The Scientist"; an anti-hero title track; and Nelson's death-defying anthem, "Roll Me Up (And Smoke Me When I Die)," the inevitable result of Nelson's twin fascinations with marijuana and mortality. **Grade: B**

Let's Face the Music and Dance

The two albums Nelson released in 2013 were familiar formats for him: American Songbook standards and duets with famous guests. But with Cannon in charge, these sessions had a different feel from Nelson's earlier takes on these templates. The producer kept the arrangements understated and relaxed so the singer could celebrate his eightieth birthday year in a setting conducive to his less muscular and more nuanced singing and picking at that age.

The standards album, *Let's Face the Music and Dance*, was recorded at Nelson's home studio with the Family. The one Nelson original, "Is the Better Part Over?" written in the late-'80s when his marriage to Connie was ending, is one of his classic romantic postmortems about what happens "when the raging river turns into a stream." It's one of his best, with some of the jazziest chord changes of his late-career compositions.

What's interesting is the way he picks standards that articulate the earlier, more hopeful phase of a love affair, a subject he seldom tackled in his own writing. The album's title track, by Irving Berlin, is a resolution to make the most of that phase, to love while the music's still playing, "before the fiddlers have fled, before they ask us to pay the bill." There "may be trouble ahead," Berlin writes; but such trouble is material for a Willie Nelson song. In the meantime, let's enjoy this delightful Berlin melody and the amorous feelings it reflects.

That romantic optimism takes on a more carnal aspect on old tunes such as "Walking My Baby Back Home" and Berlin's "Marie (The Dawn Is Breaking)." And the inspiration for the plentiful guitar fills and solos can be found in the two Django Reinhardt instrumentals, "Nuages" and "Vous et Moi." He had recorded the two tunes more aggressively on 1999's *Night and Day*, but this time they boast an easy grace. That's what we listeners want from our artists—to reflect the age they are rather than the age they wish they were.

Willie Nelson
***Let's Face the Music and Dance* (Legacy)**
Recorded: Late 2012
Released: April 16, 2013
Willie Compositions: 1/14
Top 40 Singles: NA
Album Charts: Country #16, Pop #49

On his latest album of mid-twentieth-century standards, the dominant mood is relaxed swing, unusually sunny singing, and lots of buoyant give-and-take between Bobbie's piano and Willie's guitar. Sometimes things get too relaxed for their own good—and it could have benefited from more change-of-pace numbers as Carl Perkins' jumpy blues "Matchbox" or Spade Cooley's snappy Western swing "Shame on You." But the understated grace of the performances is hard to gainsay. **Grade: B+**

To All the Girls . . .

Only three musicians from *Let's Face the Music* carry over to the Nashville sessions for the duets album, *To All the Girls . . .*: Willie, Raphael, and B-3 organist Jim "Moose" Brown. Brown gives both projects those buttery, bottom-heavy chords that bluesify the arrangements. The title, *To All the Girls . . .*, is borrowed from the hit duet with Julio Iglesias—but Iglesias is not involved this time. Instead, the title refers to the album concept: eighteen duets with eighteen different women.

Once again, Cannon keeps the proceedings restrained—both vocally and instrumentally—so the focus remains on the songs and not on the personalities. By using the same band and the same sound on every selection, he makes this far more cohesive than most celebrity-guest albums. And that allows him and Nelson to finesse the stumbling blocks of such projects: the jarring shifts from track to track and the tendency to show off.

Cannon's daughter Melonie sings Nelson's "Back to Earth," and Nelson's daughter Paula sings John Fogerty's "Have You Ever Seen the Rain," the album's single. Dolly Parton contributes a recent composition, "From Here to the Moon and Back," and gives it a giddy, romantic duet vocal. Nelson contributes a new composition, "It Won't Be Very Long," a bouncy memory of childhood music-making, sung with the Secret Sisters.

Especially powerful are the duets on Kristofferson's "Don't Tell Me How the Story Ends" (with Rosanne Cash), Jennings' "She Was No Good for

Willie performs in a concert for the Intrepid Fallen Heroes Fund at New York City's Four Seasons Restaurant on June 5, 2013.

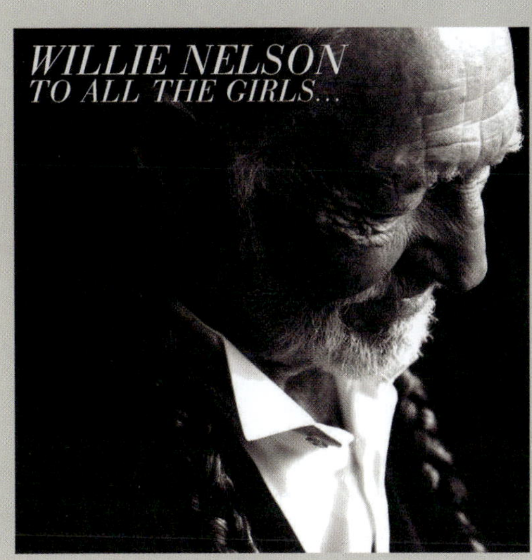

Willie Nelson
***To All the Girls . . .* (Legacy)**
Recorded: Early 2013
Released: October 15, 2013
Willie Compositions: 5/18
Top 40 Single: "Have You Ever Seen the Rain" (Country #36)
Album Charts: Country #2, Pop #9

There's a difference between singing with understatement and just singing quietly. Nelson does the former, maintaining a dramatic tension even as he lowers the volume. On this collection of duets with female singers, some of the guests match the host's understatement; and some just sing quietly. The best moments come from Miranda Lambert, Rosanne Cash, Mavis Staples, Alison Krauss, Shelby Lynne, and Emmylou Harris. **Grade: B+**

Me" (with Miranda Lambert), Bill Withers' "Grandma's Hands" (with Mavis Staples), Bruce Springsteen's "Dry Lightning" (with Emmylou Harris), the vintage swing standard "Till the End of the World" (with Shelby Lynne), and the Mexican-flavored "No Mas Amor" (with Alison Krauss). All are contemplations of endings—romantic or mortal—and the theme is more personal to Nelson than ever.

Band of Brothers

The first three Legacy albums proved that Cannon was an effective producer for Nelson's music. But the producer made an even bigger contribution when he reawakened the singer's muse by forging an effective songwriting partnership.

"Roger Miller once told me, 'When the well runs dry, you have to let it alone for a while and let it fill up again,'" Nelson said in our 2021 interview. "And that's what I did. You know it's full again when the ideas start bubbling up inside you again. You don't have control over it; you have to wait for it to happen. I just write down what I'm thinking, and that's pretty much it. If you're a songwriter, you're going to write songs."

Cannon helped Nelson prime the well by coming up with an unusual co-writing methodology. The singer texts his producer with a stanza or a handful of lines, and the producer texts back with some rewritten and/or additional lines. After some more back-and-forth texts, when they've reached a critical mass of words, Nelson will email a sound file with some musical ideas.

"Buddy is a great producer; he knows great musicians and cuts great records in Nashville," Nelson told me in 2021. "I'll write a verse and text it to him. Then he'll write a verse and text it back. Then I'll send him a bit of melody attached to an email, and he'll send it back after he's messed with it. We go back and forth, and pretty soon we have a song. He's up there in Nashville, and I'm usually in Texas when I'm not on the road, so we have to do it

Willie and Pete Seeger perform during the Farm Aid concert in Saratoga Springs, New York, on September 21, 2013.

that way. I don't know why it works so well. I just accept it and be thankful for it."

Nelson liked this approach because he could stick to his pre-pandemic schedule of touring on the road and relaxing at home. More importantly, he didn't have to endure those awkward pauses in a co-writing session where each writer is wincing, trying so hard to think of the next line that they seem to need a laxative. This way, he could wait for the next line to come when it wanted to. Suddenly the songs came pouring out of him as they hadn't since the mid-'90s when he did *Spirit* and *Teatro*.

Cannon ups the humor quotient in Nelson's songwriting. It had always been there, but it was usually overshadowed by the serious songs about troubled relationships. But now the comedy is on an even par with the tragedy. It's as if Nelson were telling us that stoic dignity in the face of romantic disaster is admirable, but laughter is more liberating.

Sometimes this attitude is subtle, as on "I Thought I Left You," which Nelson sings to an

Willie, President Barack Obama, and John Fogerty share the stage on the South Lawn of the White House on November 6, 2014.

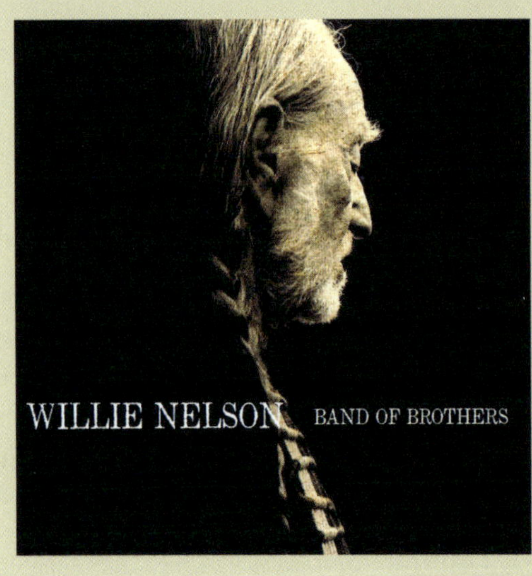

Willie Nelson: *Band of Brothers* (Legacy)
Recorded: Early 2014
Released: June 17, 2014
Willie Compositions: 9/14
Top 40 Singles: NA
Album Charts: Country #1, Pop #5

With his new songwriting partner, producer Buddy Cannon, Nelson brings out the funny side of his music as never before. Sometimes humor is the best way to make a serious point, as on songs such as "Bring It On," "I Thought I Left You," and "Used to Her." The duo co-wrote nine of the fourteen songs here, and it's a measure of their success that the best hold their own against the two comic/tragic songs written by Billy Joe Shaver, "Hard to Be an Outlaw" and "The Git Go," the latter a duet by Nelson and Jamey Johnson. **Grade: A-**

ex-lover as if it were the most serious song in the world. But the lyrics are less sober than the vocal, and when he sings, "You're like the measles, you're like the whooping cough; I've already had you, so why in heaven's name can't you just get lost?" it's funnier without the wink than it would have been with it. Sometimes the humor is blatant, as in the bouncy "Wives and Girlfriends," which has Nelson merrily wishing that the two teams never meet.

"Do you remember when *Reader's Digest* had several pages of jokes in an issue, and they called the section 'Laughter Is the Best Medicine'?" he asked me in 2021. "I think that's true. It just works. When you laugh, you feel better about your problems than you do when you cry. Roger Miller and I were really good friends, and no one's funnier than Roger. We were riding down the I-35 south in Texas one time. The sun was going down over the hills; it was just beautiful, and Roger said, 'Just think what God could have done if He had some real money.'"

There are serious songs too, like "Guitar in the Corner," which allows that wooden box to represent the love songs written for an ex and allows the singer to wonder if it has any songs left for someone else. He asks another ex to "Send Me a Picture" so he can understand why their love once seemed so promising. But the most memorable numbers are the funny ones, such as "The Wall," which seems to admit that old people do "hit a wall" at a certain point and then adding that if you hit it hard enough, the wall comes "crashing down."

In 2006, Nelson explained his late-life songwriting methodology on the *Fresh Air* radio show. "If there's a guitar or piano around, I will use it; but I can usually write it all in my head. And then I'll get a guitar when I find one and go over the lyrics and the melodies and probably wind up changing it several times before I finally decide this is the way I want it. . . . I used to have this theory that, well, if you don't remember it, it ain't worth remembering. But later on in life, I figured out, well, maybe I should jot down this one because I don't want to forget it."

December Day: Willie's Stash, Vol. 1

The next release, *December Day: Willie's Stash, Vol. 1*, credited to Willie Nelson and Sister Bobbie, grew out of countless impromptu jam sessions between the two siblings on the tour bus in the 2000s. They would while away the hours, playing standards from their childhoods and overlooked Willie compositions from over the decades. They finally recorded their favorites in 2010 with a lightly swinging rhythm

Willie Nelson and Sister Bobbie
***December Day: Willie's Stash, Vol. 1* (Legacy)**
Recorded: 2010
Released: December 2, 2014
Willie Compositions: 13/20
Top 40 Singles: NA
Album Chart: Country #26

The thirteen originals include three new songs and ten relative obscurities given fresh life. The seven covers were all written before 1950, the year Willie turned seventeen and Bobbie nineteen. It's a ballad-heavy collection, and producer Cannon's intimate minimalism reveals some of Willie's finest late-career singing, especially on his own "Who'll Buy My Memories" and "Walkin'" as well as Nat King Cole's "Mona Lisa." The album, finally released in 2014 from Nelson's "stash" of home recordings, comes in a handsome package with Raphael's liner notes and photos of the co-leaders' hometown: "Abbot City Limit, Pop. 356." **Grade: A-**

section behind the extended solos by Willie, Bobbie, and Mickey Raphael.

The three new songs are three of Willie's weirdest. "I Don't Know Where I Am Today" and "Amnesia" tackled uncertainty with some of the largest, least likely melodic intervals of his career. "Laws of Nature" presents a philosophical system as if it were an elementary school science lesson.

Willie Nelson at the Library of Congress in Washington on November 17, 2015.

Willie and the Boys: Willie's Stash, Vol. 2

The word "stash" usually refers to a supply of marijuana "stashed away" out of sight of the law and saved for a rainy day. But the pleasure Nelson got from smoking a good one was much the same as the pleasure he got from recording old songs with his sister, his sons, or his Family band in his studio by the Pedernales River. He never knew if or when he would release those tapes, but the pleasure made it worthwhile whatever the music's fate. And he took to calling the growing pile of tapes in his studio his other "stash."

The second release in the Willie's Stash series was *Willie and the Boys*, recorded with Lukas, Micah, and producer Cannon's favorite players. The repertoire is heavy on the Hanks: Williams, Cochran,

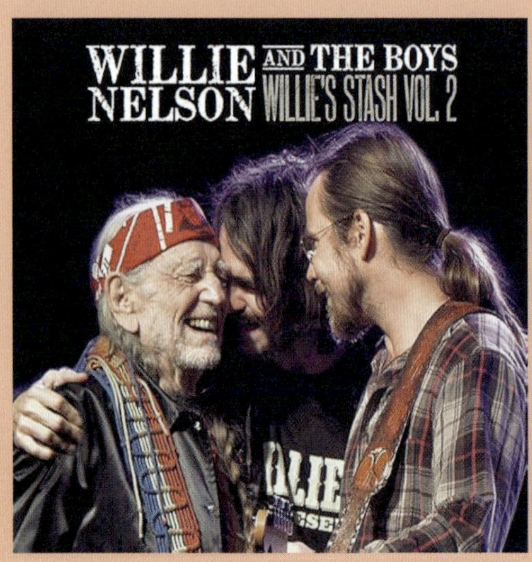

Willie Nelson with Lukas Nelson and Micah Nelson
***Willie and the Boys: Willie's Stash, Vol. 2* (Legacy)**
Recorded: 2011-2017
Released: October 20, 2017
Willie Compositions: 1/12
Top 40 Singles: NA
Album Charts: Country #19, Pop #134

In 2011, Willie Nelson and his son Lukas went into their home studio with little preparation to jam on some country standards with a crackerjack band. Seven of the eleven songs were by Hank Williams Sr., Willie's vocals were terrific, Lukas's vocals were pretty good, and the band was loose and spirited. Producer Buddy Cannon overdubbed vocals by Lukas and his brother Micah to every track, added a twelfth song, and released the results in 2017. **Grade: B**

Willie has recorded jazz compositions by both the French guitarist Django Reinhardt (left) and the American pianist Duke Ellington (right).

Locklin, and Snow. Just as Johnny Cash once gave his daughter Rosanne "The List" of essential country songs to know, Willie is giving Lukas and Micah his own "List," demonstrating how the tunes should be done and inviting them to follow along. This album allows us to see tradition handed down from one generation to the next in real time.

"When Lukas and Micah were growing up," Nelson told *Mojo* in 2013, "I just sort of left instruments lying around, not really trying to push it on them. One day we just started playing the guitar and piano, and next thing Micah was over playing the drums and the guitar, so they just sort of got into it naturally."

Django and Jimmie

For *Django and Jimmie*, their fourth full album together, Nelson and Merle Haggard sing not as everyman surrogates for the audience, addressing lovers and running buddies that any of us might be talking to. Instead, they sing about themselves and their own

Willie Nelson with Merle Haggard
***Django and Jimmie* (Legacy)**
Recorded: Early 2015
Released: June 2, 2015
Willie Compositions: 5/14
Top 40 Singles: NA
Album Charts: Country #1, Pop #7

This album allows Nelson and Haggard to have fun with their own legends. They acknowledge their greatest influences: not only Django Reinhardt and Jimmie Rodgers but also marijuana and "The Family Bible." They pay tribute to a dead colleague on "Missing Ol' Johnny Cash" and admit they never expected to "Live This Long." Haggard wrote four songs, and Nelson five, four of them with Cannon, who produced. **Grade: B+**

An autographed postcard of Jimmie Rodgers, "The Father of Country Music," circa 1930.

larger-than-life mythologies. This can limit our identification with the narrators in the songs, but for those of us who have invested enough time in following these two singers, it's a treat to hear them discourse on their biggest influences, their favorite drugs, their departed friends, and their advancing years.

Some of the most personal songs were written by others. The title track, for example, was penned by Jimmy Melton and Jeff Prince; but it rings true as Nelson sings about his artistic debt to France's "jazz-playing gypsy" Django Reinhardt and Haggard sings his debt to Mississippi's "singing brakeman" Jimmie Rodgers. When they join voices on the refrain, "Might not have been a Merle or a Willie if not for a Django and Jimmie," they sound like they mean it.

They explain their preference for marijuana over whiskey and pills on "It's All Going to Pot," a song written by Jamey Johnson (who shares the lead vocals) and Cannon, who produced the album. When they confess their surprise at having lasted so many years, they rely on a song, "Live This Long," written by Shawn Camp and Marv Green. The lyrics evoke the many decades of "kicking out the foot lights" and "living the night life," a nod to Haggard's and Nelson's signature songs, before adding the funny but rousing refrain: "We would've taken much better care of ourselves if we would have known we was gonna live this long." Haggard wrote "The Only Man Wilder Than Me," which allows each singer to salute the other.

Summertime: Willie Nelson Sings Gershwin

Nelson combined the Songwriter Tribute format he'd used on the Kris Kristofferson and Cindy Walker albums with the American Songbook format he'd used on *Stardust* for his next album, *Summertime: Willie Nelson Sings Gershwin*. The Booker T. Jones role of producer/keyboardist was now split between Cannon and pianist/arranger Matt Rollings, who demonstrated a deft touch for keeping things in the no-man's-land between vintage pop and traditional country.

The songs represent mid-twentieth-century pop at its best, while the musicians—two-thirds of the Family plus a handful of Nashville and L.A. ringers—represent country at its most sophisticated. As a result, these are unlike almost any Gershwin interpretation you've heard and unlike almost any country record you've heard. And that aura of novelty allows him to make these old songs sound new and thus open a new doorway for Nelson to deliver these meditations on life and love to his listeners.

Willie Nelson
***Summertime: Willie Nelson Sings Gershwin* (Legacy)**
Recorded: Late 2015
Released: February 26, 2016
Willie Compositions: 0/11
Top 40 Singles: NA
Album Chart: Pop #40

This is the first of Nelson's American Songbook collaborations with keyboardist/arranger/co-producer Matt Rollings. It's also the best, thanks to the higher quality of songwriting and the relaxed authority of the singing. No strings or horns this time—just the transparency of a small, tight band backing Nelson on some of the best songs of the mid-twentieth century. Steel guitarist Paul Franklin and harmonica whiz Mickey Raphael really shine—duet singers Cyndi Lauper and Sheryl Crow less so. **Grade: B+**

Willie performs on *Austin City Limits* in Texas on December 31, 2015.

For the Good Times: A Tribute to Ray Price

Nelson usually saluted his biggest influences by singing duets with them or by recording their compositions. He had already recorded two duet albums with Ray Price (1980's *San Antonio Rose* and 2003's *Run That by Me One Last Time*) and a trio album with Price and Haggard (2007's *Last of the Breed*). Now he was going to record a tribute to Price—who had died at the end of 2013—not by recording the latter's compositions but by recording songs made famous by him.

Willie Nelson
***For the Good Times: A Tribute to Ray Price* (Legacy)**
Recorded: Early 2016
Released: September 19, 2016
Willie Compositions: 2/12
Top 40 Singles: NA
Album Charts: Country #5, Pop #84

The album includes only one song written by Price and no duets with anyone—just Nelson singing songs from every phase of Price's long career in arrangements close to the originals, revealing not only how close he could get to his mentor but also the crucial differences. Vince Gill adds prominent harmony vocals on the six tracks featuring the Time Jumpers, the Nashville-based Western swing band led by Gill and steel guitarist Paul Franklin. Producer Fred Foster and arranger Bergen White, who'd both worked on Price's final album, work with Nelson here—even the strings are helpful. You can tell Nelson's heart is in this one. **Grade: B+**

God's Problem Child/Last Man Standing

A story that's often told about Nelson is that he made all his crucial creative breakthroughs and reached all his artistic peaks in the 1970s. That's when he made his three concept-album masterpieces (*Yesterday's Wine*, *Phases and Stages*, and *Red Headed Stranger*), his defining American Songbook album (*Stardust*), his defining duet album (*Waylon & Willie*), his defining tribute album (*Willie Nelson Sings Kristofferson*), his defining gospel album (*The Troublemaker*), and his defining live album (*Willie and Family Live*). The prevailing view has been that everything after that decade was nothing but admirable variations on those themes and proof of his prodigious longevity.

But this book has already argued that that's a distortion of what actually happened. Starting in 1984, he dove into jazz—with Jackie King, Wynton Marsalis, and Asleep at the Wheel—as never before. He began singing more often about death and more often with humor—sometimes simultaneously. *Who'll Buy My Memories?: The IRS Tapes* was the first and best venture into unaccompanied solo recordings. Albums such as *Me and Paul*, *Always on My Mind*, *Across the Borderline*, *Teatro*, *Just One Love*, *Band of Brothers*, and *You Don't Know Me: The Songs of Cindy Walker* stand up well against the '70s.

And his trio of *Yesterday's Wine*, *Phases and Stages*, and *Red Headed Stranger* were not his only concept albums. Both 1983's *Tougher than Leather*

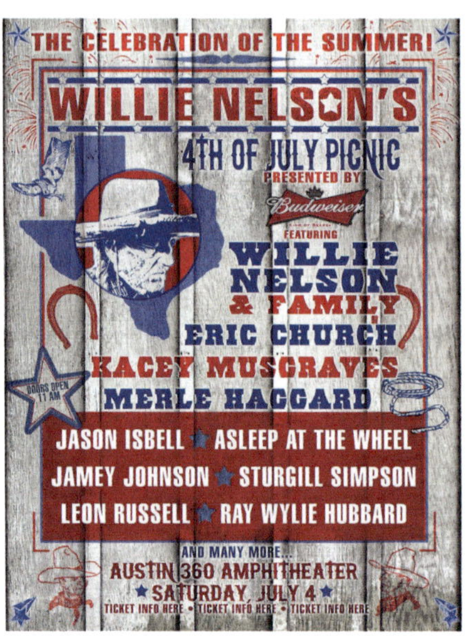

Willie Nelson
Last Man Standing (Legacy)
Recorded: Late 2017
Released: April 27, 2018
Willie Compositions: 11/11
Top 40 Singles: NA
Album Charts: Country #3, Pop #14

Nelson and producer Buddy Cannon co-wrote all eleven of these songs, and this is the peak of their songwriting partnership. The words are as funny ("Bad breath is better than no breath at all") and edgy ("It goes like this 'cause I wrote the song") as ever, but the music is more powerful than before. A muscular rhythm section keeps the up-tempo songs jumping, while the harmonica, organ, and steel flesh out the slow ones. And in these songs about old age and death, the musicians help Nelson reach the best singing of his—or anyone's—post-eighty-year-old career. The Cracker Barrel deluxe edition adds three bonus tracks. **Grade: A+**

Willie Nelson
God's Problem Child **(Legacy)**
Recorded: Late 2016
Released: April 28, 2017
Willie Compositions: 7/13
Top 40 Singles: NA
Album Charts: Country #1, Pop #10

Nelson and producer Buddy Cannon co-wrote seven of these thirteen songs, most of them responses to growing old, watching friends die, and knowing you're headed in the same direction. Some of the reactions are funny, such as the live-show staple, "Still Not Dead"; a value-of-forgetting number, "Delete and Fast Forward"; and the comic confessional, "I Made a Mistake." More serious are Nelson/Cannon's reflection on old age, "It Gets Easier"; Donnie Fritts' "Old Timer"; and Gary Nicholson's "He Won't Ever Be Gone," an elegy for Merle Haggard. **Grade: A**

and 1996's *Spirit* were just as cohesive and just as powerful. And I'll argue that his next two albums with Buddy Cannon, 2017's *God's Problem Child* and 2018's *Last Man Standing*, are two volumes of a single, splendid concept album on growing old and facing up to looming death. Though they don't have a narrative thread (always the weakest factor in the earlier efforts anyway,) they are unified by the same producer, the same musicians, the same songwriters, the same subject matter, and the same attitude.

At the top of this chapter, we talked about the song "Last Man Standing," and how its willingness to joke about death allows the narrator to shrug off the threat and move forward. This two-volume concept album offers more Nelson-Cannon songs in the same vein: "Still Not Dead" (a Mark Twain–like declaration that reports of his death have been greatly exaggerated), "Delete and Fast Forward" (a technological metaphor for getting over the past and moving on to the future), "Bad Breath" ("Bad breath is better than no breath at all"), and "Heaven Is Closed" ("Heaven is closed, and hell's overcrowded; I think I'll just stay where I am").

Humor is healthy unless it becomes a defense mechanism to deny the reality and finality of death. The power of this two-volume concept album is the way it balances the wisecracking refutations of death with the sobering acknowledgments of its destructive power and growing closeness. Nelson and Cannon wrote eighteen of the twenty-four songs in this two-album project, but some of the best serious songs come from outsiders.

Donnie Fritts' heartbreaking "Old Timer," for example, warns against self-delusion. "You think you're still a young bull rider," the narrator warns a longtime friend over a slow, piano-and-harmonica hymn, "till you look in the mirror and see an old timer." Jamey Johnson and Tony Joe White wrote "God's Problem Child" and sing it with Nelson and Leon Russell. Over a patient, swamp-funk groove, the words tell of a long life that tested God's patience but never broke it. And Gary Nicholson's "He Won't Ever Be Gone" is an elegy for a recently deceased Merle Haggard, ar-

guing that he will always be with us in a way, because he "left us a lifetime of song."

But the song that cuts deepest was written by Nelson and Cannon. "Something You Get Through" is a jazz-flavored ballad that might be about losing someone to the breakup of an affair. But in the context of these albums, it means more if heard as losing someone to the Grim Reaper. So, when Nelson sings over the bittersweet chord changes, "It's not something you get over," the deeper hurt of death sets up the line, "it's something you get through."

For decades, Nelson had been telling us that when love breaks down, you've got to face up to it. You can't back away from it; you can't deny it; you can't get stuck in it. You've got to struggle with the pain, the anger, and the loss, because only then can you get *through* it and emerge on the other side ready for more. Now that he's making up story songs about death, that same message means more than ever.

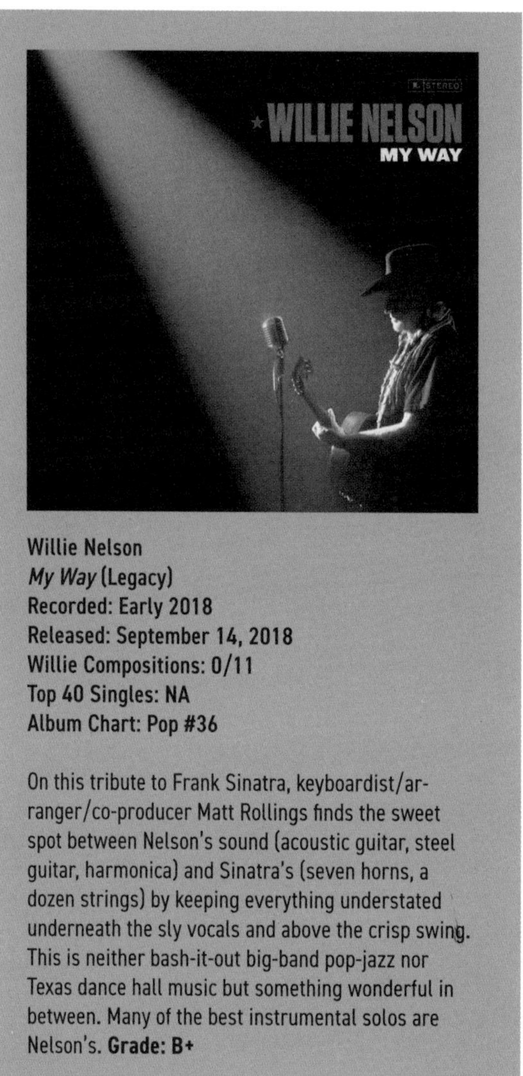

Willie Nelson
***My Way* (Legacy)**
Recorded: Early 2018
Released: September 14, 2018
Willie Compositions: 0/11
Top 40 Singles: NA
Album Chart: Pop #36

On this tribute to Frank Sinatra, keyboardist/arranger/co-producer Matt Rollings finds the sweet spot between Nelson's sound (acoustic guitar, steel guitar, harmonica) and Sinatra's (seven horns, a dozen strings) by keeping everything understated underneath the sly vocals and above the crisp swing. This is neither bash-it-out big-band pop-jazz nor Texas dance hall music but something wonderful in between. Many of the best instrumental solos are Nelson's. **Grade: B+**

My Way/ That's Life

Nelson was so happy with his Gershwin album *Summertime* that he asked the same producers (Buddy Cannon and Matt Rollings) and the same core band (Mickey Raphael, steel guitarist Paul Franklin, drummer Jay Bellerose, bassist David Piltch, and guitarist Dean Parks) to help the singer realize another dream project: a tribute to his favorite singer, Frank Sinatra. This would be even more ambitious, for it would involve string and horn arrangements by Rollings. The first session, released in 2018 as *My Way*, was so successful that they did a second session, released in 2021 as *That's Life*.

"I don't try to mimic Frank's phrasing," Nelson told me in 2021, "because I knew that's how he felt it. I phrase each song the way I feel it. I probably phrase it differently every time I sing it because I don't remember how I did it before. It would be boring as hell to do it on the beat the same way every time. And I don't like to be bored."

Each album includes eleven songs closely identified with Sinatra; each album boasts one duet with a female singer (a good Norah Jones on *My Way*, a better Diana Krall on *That's Life*). In both cases, the octogenarian Nelson has less lung power than in his *Stardust* days but even better phrasing instincts. Rollings' arrangements are tasteful, always supporting, never obscuring the vocal. The three folkloric instruments (acoustic guitar, harmonica, and steel guitar) lend a rural flavor that Sinatra's originals never had.

The young Sinatra had the lung power to belt out the choruses with a triumphant swagger. It was impressive, but it sometimes tempted him into pure bombast. The old Nelson can't belt it out anymore, but neither does he fall into self-aggrandizing strutting. On the two albums' title songs, the ultimate bragging vehicles, Nelson deflates the machismo. When he purrs, "I did it my way," he doesn't sound defiant; he sounds as if he's glad he followed his own path and he's glad you followed yours. When he

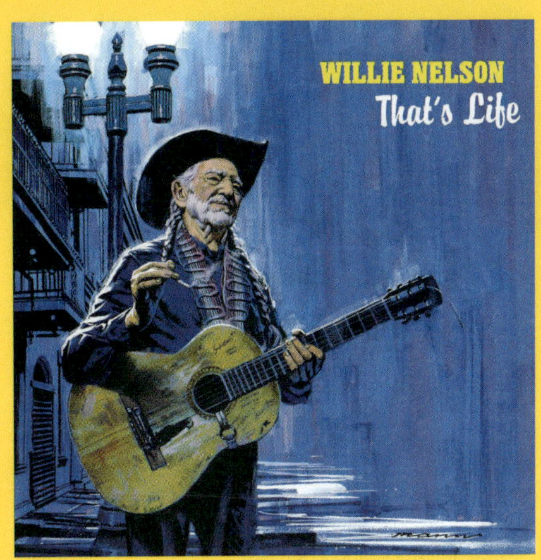

Willie Nelson
***That's Life* (Legacy)**
Recorded: Late 2020
Released: February 26, 2021
Willie Compositions: 0/11
Top 40 Singles: NA
Album Chart: Pop #58

This sequel to 2018's *My Way* finds keyboardist/arranger Matt Rollings and many of the same musicians once again helping Nelson refashion his favorite Frank Sinatra numbers. The song selections are less predictable and more interesting, but the vocals and arrangements are less burnished. **Grade: B+**

croons, "That's life . . . , you're riding high in April, shot down in May," he accepts his fate as a marijuana-mellowed stoic, not as a whiskey-soaked brawler.

"I knew Frank, and I liked him," he added in 2021. "We did a couple of shows together, recorded a few songs together. We were pretty close. I worked with him in Vegas. One of my biggest regrets was he once invited me to his place, and I couldn't do it because I had to leave in a hurry to be somewhere else. I wish I could have gone."

Frank Sinatra, seen here in London in 1950, has often been described by Willie as his favorite singer.

Ride Me Back Home

Nelson had been trying to make a movie based on his 1975 breakthrough album *Red Headed Stranger* ever since the album came out. Robert Redford had optioned the script by Bill Witliff, but nothing ever seemed to happen. So, Nelson bought back the rights and shot the picture on his own property in Spicewood, where he built an Old West town complete with jail, chapel, saloon, and pharmacy. The 1985 movie that resulted was underwhelming, but Nelson kept the set in decent repair and named it Luck, perhaps a shortened version of Luckenbach. A sign in the town informed visitors, "When you're here, you're in Luck. When you're not, you're out of Luck."

Sometimes he held his Fourth of July picnic there. In the 2010s and 2020s, he hosted the Luck Reunion in March, to coincide with the South by Southwest Music Conference in nearby Austin. Most of the time, he had it to himself to entertain friends and to indulge his fantasy that he was a nineteenth-century cowboy outlaw.

Sepia photos of Luck illustrated his 2019 album *Ride Me Back Home*. The title track, written by Sonny Throckmorton, finds an old cowboy asking his beloved horse to carry him back to hills that resemble those around Luck, where there's still some green grass and room for roaming. That valedictory spirit is also evident in "One More Song to Write," written by Nelson and producer Cannon. Over a relaxed, mid-tempo country lope, Nelson sings he's got one more bridge to burn, one more lesson to learn, as Trigger and Raphael's harmonica wave goodbye to the past.

The album's highlight, though, is "Nobody's Listening," one of the few songs Bee Spears wrote before dying in 2011. This one, however, was a keeper, perhaps the best song about the family-farm crisis that Nelson had been working to alleviate since the first Farm Aid concert in 1985. The lyrics tell of a Louisiana farmer wiped out by a hurricane, but the main message is not that the farmer's in trouble but that no one hears his cries for help. Nelson sings it slowly but implacably over the funereal piano and piercing steel. The listener is left with the realization that mere awareness is not enough if help never arrives.

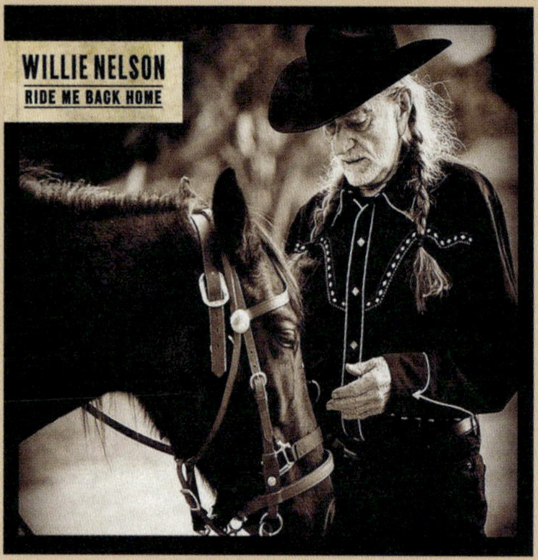

Willie Nelson
Ride Me Back Home **(Legacy)**
Recorded: Winter 2018/2019
Released: June 21, 2019
Willie Compositions: 4/11
Top 40 Singles: NA
Album Charts: Country #2, Pop #18

Nelson wrote just four of these eleven songs—three with producer Buddy Cannon and one by himself from 1971—but his fascinating wrestling match with remorseless time continues. "The more I reject it," he purrs over a lively country shuffle, "the more that it kicks in." There are two terrific songs by Guy Clark, including a powerful elegy for a dead spouse, and one from Bee Spears about a foreclosed farmer. Not every song is that good, but the best are compensation enough. **Grade: B+**

First Rose of Spring

For his next album, *First Rose of Spring*, Nelson mostly dropped the wisecracking and let the hurt of passing time seep into his songs. He and producer Cannon wrote only two of them, but the nine obscure country songs they picked to supplement the mood do the job superbly. The title track, for example, was a recent number from second-tier country star Randy Houser. It remembers a lover as "the first rose of spring" when first they met. Now that she has died, only that memory remains. It could easily have descended into maudlin sentimentality, but Nelson sings with such reserve that he reveals the deep sorrow without losing his essential dignity. That's true of the whole album.

Charles Aznavour's "Yesterday When I Was Young," a #9 country hit for Roy Clark in 1969, reminds us that we never believe our youth will end while we're in it—but it always does. "Love Just Laughed," by Nelson and Cannon, reminds us that we may think we're deciding whether a love affair will continue or end; but usually the feeling will overrule us. This is one of the final additions to Nelson's stock of troubled romance songs, and it's one of the best. "I'll Break Out Again," a 1974 album cut for Merle Haggard, and "The Only Hell My Mama Ever Raised," a #8 country hit for Johnny Paycheck, both imply that old age is a kind of prison that one can try to escape—but not for long.

Nelson sang harmony on Billy Joe Shaver's original recording of "We Are the Cowboys," and he sings the lead vocal on the version for *First Rose of Spring*. Nelson leans into a definition of cowboys that includes "Texicans, Mexicans, black men, and Jews." Back in 1967, Nelson had been the first country star to take

Opposite: Willie at the annual Luck Reunion in Luck, Texas on March 13, 2019.

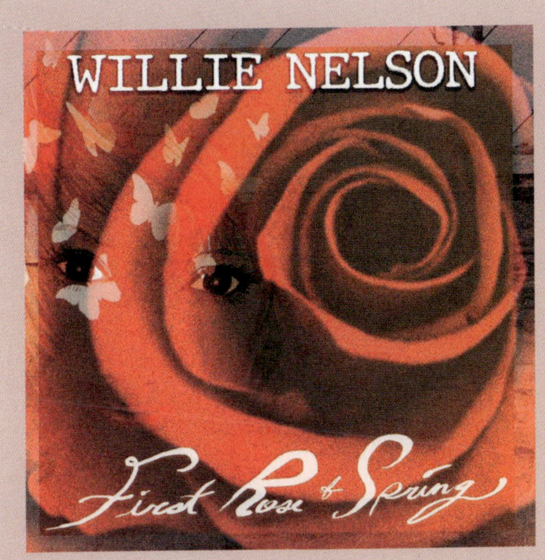

Willie Nelson
First Rose of Spring **(Legacy)**
Recorded: Winter 2019–2020
Released: July 3, 2020
Willie Compositions: 2/11
Top 40 Singles: NA
Album Charts: Country #5, Pop #49

Nelson has long been known for his relaxed approach to music, but he has never sounded more relaxed than on this album. Whether he's singing a romantic ballad like the title track or the lazily swinging remake of the 1952 Jimmy Dean hit "Just Bummin' Around," Nelson's voice and guitar ease into every phrase with sumptuous tone and infinite patience. Chad Cromwell's drum brushes, Mike Johnson's steel guitar, and Mickey Raphael's harmonica all reinforce the mood. Toby Keith, Randy Houser, Billy Joe Shaver, Chris Stapleton, and Nelson himself all contribute strong songs.
Grade: A-

the groundbreaking African-American singer Charley Pride on tour—Nelson even went so far as to regularly kiss Pride onstage. And a few years later, Nelson hired the Jewish harmonica player Mickey Raphael.

In the song, Shaver implies that cowboys are as likely to round up words for a song as they are cattle for a sale. "We are the cowboys, the true sons of freedom," Nelson sings. "We are the men who will get the job done. We're picking our words, so we won't have to eat them. We're rounding them up and then driving them home."

"Billy Joe wrote a lot of great songs," Nelson told me in 2021. "I was honored that he wrote one about me, 'Willie the Wandering Gypsy.' One of his last songs was 'We Are the Cowboys,' and that pretty much sums up who Billy Joe was. He knew where he was going and how he was going to get there. I loved everything about him, especially the way he wrote. He's an old Texas boy, he knows what he wants to say, so he says it straight out, and he says it well. We always say, 'You can always tell a Texan, but you can't tell him much.'"

Willie Nelson: American Outlaw/ Long Story Short: Willie Nelson 90 at the Hollywood Bowl

Nelson's astonishing run of strong studio albums was twice interrupted by one of his team's favorite gambits: a live concert with lots of famous guest stars that could then be packaged as a two-CD, one-DVD box set. The first, *Willie Nelson: American Outlaw*, was held at Nashville's Bridgestone Arena on January 12, 2019, and released in 2020. The second, *Long Story Short: Willie Nelson 90 at the Hollywood Bowl*, was held in L.A. on April 29–30, 2023. Don Was, his producer on *Across the Borderline* and *Countryman*, acted as musical director on both projects. Both proved diverting but inessential recordings.

Willie Nelson tours in support of the *Ride Me Back Home* album at the Los Angeles Convention Center on February 8, 2019. Opposite: Chris Stapleton and Willie play the Rock & Roll Hall of Fame induction ceremony at New York City's Barclays Center on Friday, November 3, 2023.

Various Artists
Willie Nelson: American Outlaw (Blackbird)
Recorded: January 12, 2019
Released: December 11, 2020
Willie Compositions: 15/32
Top 40 Singles: NA
Album Charts: NA

In early 2019, a host of country stars—past, present, and alternative—gathered at Nashville's Bridgestone Arena to pay tribute to Nelson. The first two-thirds of the show were devoted to singers on their own tackling songs associated with Nelson (though not necessarily written by him) and the last third to Nelson himself singing duets with various guests. The show was broadcast on A&E and then released as a two-CD, one-DVD package, with a few songs appearing in one format but not the other. As often happens at these tribute shows, some singers—most notably Lee Ann Womack, Margo Price, Steve Earle, Jamey Johnson, Emmylou Harris, and George Strait—rose to the occasion, and some didn't. **Grade: B**

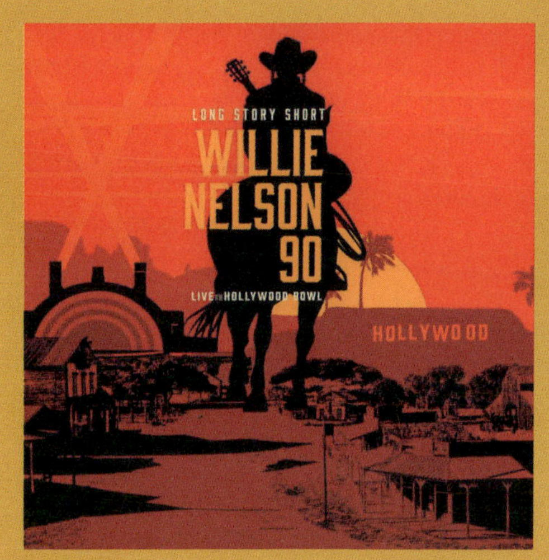

Various Artists
Long Story Short: Willie Nelson 90 at the Hollywood Bowl (Legacy)
Recorded: April 29–30, 2023
Released: December 15, 2023
Willie Compositions: 14/39
Top 40 Singles: NA
Album Charts: NA

This ninetieth birthday party celebration closely followed the format of its predecessor, *American Outlaw*, albeit with bigger guest stars: Keith Richards, Neil Young, Beck, and Dwight Yoakam. Some of the best singing, however, came from the singers with lower profiles: Charley Crockett, Lyle Lovett, and Rosanne Cash. **Grade: B**

The Willie Nelson Family

After making so many albums with Cannon's handpicked band, Nelson wanted to record with his road band again. The onstage Family was now a septet, with Lukas Nelson replacing Jody Payne and Kevin Smith replacing Bee Spears. For this album, *The Willie Nelson Family*, the definition was expanded to include biological as well as musical family members; and the onstage septet was supplemented by three more of Willie's kids: Micah, Paula, and Amy.

And the paterfamilias decided that the one thing they all had in common—ever since he and Bobbie had sat on the same piano bench in Abbott—was gospel music.

Of course, Nelson has a broad-minded view of what qualifies as a gospel song. After all, he included the reggae classic "By the Rivers of Babylon" on 1980's *Family Bible*. This time he includes George Harrison's Eastern-mysticism anthem "All Things Must Pass" and Nelson's own "Heaven and Hell," which compared those afterlife destinations to the ups and downs of marriage on *Phases and Stages*. On Nelson's "Too Sick to Pray," the narrator brings along a doctor's note as he asks God's pardon.

Willie Nelson
***The Willie Nelson Family* (Legacy)**
Recorded: Early 2021
Released: November 19, 2021
Willie Compositions: 7/12
Top 40 Singles: NA
Album Charts: NA

The title refers to both Nelson's musical family and his genealogical family (his sister, Bobbie; sons Lukas and Micah; and daughters Paula and Amy). Both groups are represented on this selection of gospel hymns, from both the standard Protestant hymnal and the bohemian catalogs of Nelson, Kristofferson, and the Beatles. They're recorded casually, perhaps too casually. The two older siblings, Willie and Bobbie, provide the highlights, while the youngsters fumble attempts at George Harrison's "All Things Must Pass" and the Carter Family's "Keep It on the Sunny Side." Willie produced with Steve Chadie. **Grade: C+**

Sam Bush, Willie, and Keith Richards perform during the concert *Sing Me Back Home: The Music of Merle Haggard* at Nashville's Bridgestone Arena on April 6, 2017.

A Beautiful Time

Cannon is back on board for the next album, *A Beautiful Time*, which opens with the Rodney Crowell/Chris Stapleton co-write, "I'll Love You Till the Day I Die," and Nelson makes it clear that that day is not far off. He responds to this by declaring, "I Don't Go to Funerals," adding, "and I won't go to mine." Maybe not, but this album can be heard as a compilation of musical speeches he might make at his own funeral.

For instance, the title track, penned by Shawn Camp, is a more wistful, more thoughtful rewrite of "On the Road Again" as a slow waltz. Nelson once again celebrates life on the road, but he can see the final exit up ahead. "When the last song's been played," he sings over a dreamy steel guitar, "I'll look back and say, 'I sure had a beautiful time.'"

Like Crowell, Jack Wesley Routh is an ex-son-in-law of Johnny Cash; and Routh's "Dreamin' Again" asks, "What's a gift to the giver [when] there's nobody there to receive?" It's not only the dead who lose in an encounter with death; the living left behind do as well. In the meantime, however, the best connections are often the oldest—for friendship can improve like vintage guitars and "Dusty Bottles."

The album also includes "Energy Follows Thought," the closest Nelson has ever come to explaining his philosophy of songwriting. Over a ghostly, *Teatro*-like soundscape, he urges would-

Willie Nelson
***A Beautiful Time* (Legacy)**
Recorded: Late 2021
Released: April 29, 2022
Willie Compositions: 5/14
Top 40 Singles: NA
Album Charts: Country #13, Pop #100

Nelson and Cannon co-wrote five of these songs, and Cannon produced all of them with his Nashville band and Raphael. The arrangements are patient and minimalist, and Nelson's voice is thinner than ever. But he turns these handicaps to his advantage by sharing his considered thoughts about a long life and its approaching end in an avuncular, confiding tone. Even the non-originals by Rodney Crowell, Leonard Cohen, Chris Stapleton, Shawn Camp, and the Beatles further the mission. **Grade: A-**

be songwriters to get the minds working—both the conscious and subconscious parts—and then follow where it leads, even if it's to a story you hadn't expected. "Imagine what you want," he half-sings, half-speaks, "then get out of the way." The song provided the title for a book about songwriting he wrote with David Ritz and Mickey Raphael in 2023.

I Don't Know a Thing about Love

Having recorded tribute albums to Kris Kristofferson, Hank Williams, Roger Miller, Cindy Walker, and George Gershwin, Nelson dedicated a similar project, *I Don't Know a Thing about Love*, to another giant of twentieth-century songwriting: Harlan Howard. Much as Texas's Nelson himself did, Michigan's Howard established himself in Nashville in the years of 1959–61 with covers by Ray Price and Patsy Cline that became big hits. Unlike Nelson, however, Howard didn't pursue a performing career. Instead, he focused on songwriting and wrote some four thousand songs, including one hundred Top 10 country hits as well as a few pop and R&B hits before he died in 2002.

Nelson handpicked ten of those songs, nine of them big hits for the likes of Buck Owens, Waylon Jennings, Bobby Bare, Johnny Cash, and Charlie Rich. The tenth, "Beautiful Annabel Lee," is an odd condensation of an Edgar Allan Poe poem into a hillbilly reverie. Nelson doesn't radically rearrange anything, preferring merely to expand the pauses in the phrasing and to nudge them in the direction of the Western swing he grew up on. At this stage of his career, Nelson can't outpower the younger men who had the hits back in the '60s and '70s—but he can out-phrase them.

(From left) Micah Nelson, Lukas Nelson, Amy Nelson, Willie, and Annie D'Angelo at New York City's Hard Rock Café on June 6, 2013.

Willie Nelson
***I Don't Know a Thing About Love* (Legacy)**
Recorded: 2022
Released: March 3, 2023
Willie Compositions: 0/10
Top 40 Singles: NA
Album Charts: NA

Nelson's tribute to songwriter Harlan Howard combines the cream of the country hitmaker's four thousand songs with Nelson's late-career sly understatement and producer Cannon's tasteful all-star band. Highlights include "Tiger by the Tail" (a hit for Buck Owens), "Life Turned Her That Way" (a hit for Mel Tillis and Ricky Van Shelton), "She Called Me Baby" (a hit for Patsy Cline, Charlie Rich, and Candi Staton), and "Busted" (a hit for Johnny Cash, Ray Charles, and John Conlee). **Grade: B+**

Bluegrass

Producer T-Bone Burnett recorded Nelson with a drummer-less band of bluegrass all-stars for the 2010 album *Country Music*. It was a worthy experiment, but it didn't quite work, because the singer was trying to accommodate the music's unfamiliar vocabulary of classic bluegrass: high, lonesome vocals and a high-octane mandolin chop. His efforts were valiant but sounded studied rather than instinctive. In 2023, producer Buddy Cannon tried the fusion again with better results.

The pickers were different but came from the same top tier of bluegrass pickers—including three-fifths of Alison Krauss's Union Station. But the repertoire was different; instead of one Nelson original, he wrote all dozen tracks, nine of them before 1972. And this time, Nelson wasn't trying to sound like Carter Stanley or Lester Flatt. Instead, he sang like himself and allowed the all-acoustic band to fill in around him as best they could.

Songs as familiar—and as well crafted—as "Bloody Mary Morning," "Sad Songs and Waltzes," "Yesterday's Wine," and "Still Is Still Moving to Me" sound new again thanks to the lighter, more translucent backing. That makes us listeners reconsider them and appreciate a different angle on the stories they tell.

Willie Nelson
***Bluegrass* (Legacy)**
Recorded: Early 2023
Released: September 15, 2023
Willie Compositions: 12/12
Top 40 Singles: NA
Album Charts: NA

This album should have been called *Country Music*, and the 2010 album *Country Music* should have been called *Bluegrass*. Both albums feature Nelson singing with a drummer-less string band of bluegrass all-stars, but the 2023 record finds Nelson singing a dozen of his favorite and bluesiest originals with a relaxed confidence that allows his backing band—and his listeners—to relax and enjoy an Appalachian front-porch slant on East Texas tavern songs. **Grade: B+**

Jody Payne plays guitar with Willie at Austin's Star of Texas Fair and Rodeo on March 4, 2008.

The Border

Nelson turned ninety on April 29, 2023, and suddenly the wear and tear on his voice became too obvious to ignore. Ever since he'd turned seventy, his voice was noticeably thinner and less powerful. For most of those twenty years, he was able to finesse the problem by singing more softly and carefully. On most of his Legacy releases, he may have lost his oomph—but he still had that plummy tone that made his vocals so comforting, so inviting. But in 2023, that tone was growing raspy and ragged around the edges.

Instead of trying to ignore the change, the wily Nelson turned it to his advantage. On his final three studio albums before this book's publishing deadline, he used his fraying tone as a signifier of an old man's hard-won wisdom and reluctantly lost vitality. For *The Border* and *Last Leaf on the Tree*, both released in 2024, he either wrote songs or found songs that could use that vocal scratch to enhance the drama of the monologues.

The Border opens with its title track, written by Rodney Crowell and Allen Shamblin. This acoustic guitar corrido is the weary lament of an aging US border patrolman caught between American vigilantes and Mexican human traffickers in Texas's Big Bend. You can hear in Nelson's grating vocal the toll that all those years have taken on the narrator and his Latino wife. The modest melody doesn't demand much of the singer, but the eleven stanzas of a complicated story do.

Crowell wrote "Many a Long and Lonesome Highway" in 1989 as a kind of sequel to his "'Til I Gain Control Again," which Nelson recorded several times. The earlier song spoke of "Out on the road that lies before me now, there are some turns where I will spin." The newer song speaks of "Many a long and lonesome highway lies before us as we go . . . , look for me where the four winds blow." The lyrics mention a father's dying words, and Nelson's hoarse vocal implies he's rehearsing his own.

Willie Nelson
***The Border* (Legacy)**
Recorded: Winter 2023-2024
Released: May 31, 2024
Willie Compositions: 4/10
Top 40 Singles: NA
Album Chart: Country #50

Five songs by Buddy Cannon (four co-written by Nelson), two by Rodney Crowell, and one apiece from Shawn Camp, Mike Reid, and Larry Cordle supply the old-man characters that Nelson and his roughened voice can inhabit. This they do quite effectively, whether pretending to be a border patrolman, a long-married husband, or Hank Williams' guitar.
Grade: B+

Last Leaf on the Tree/ Oh What a Beautiful World

On *Last Leaf on the Tree*, Nelson turns his frail voice into an asset. Many (though not all) of the songs reflect on aging and looming mortality, and the translucent quality of his thinned but still agile voice creates the ghostly sound that fits these lyrics.

The album ends with "The Ghost," a tune he wrote in 1962 about an old love affair, a memory that makes the silence "unusually loud tonight." Now it sounds as if that ghost is the personification of his own long past stretching out behind him. Nelson uses his trademark, mid-line pauses to acknowledge his reluctance to confront the specter, and the song ends with the apparition laughing as it bids its final farewell.

The record begins with the title track, a Tom Waits song about the final leaf on an autumn tree, missing all his friends now gone and bracing himself for the inevitable descent. The slight tremble in the vocal only heightens the effect. Maybe Nelson can't punch out the notes as firmly as before, but he still knows exactly where to land them.

Willie contributed only one new song to the album, but it's a good one. Co-written with his youngest son, Micah, "Color of Sound" opens with the mind-tickling question: "If silence is golden, what color is sound?" Over the graveyard breezes of Sam Grendel's bass recorder, Willie's tired voice finds beauty in the end of the journey. "Every road that leads nowhere, every road that's homebound," he sings, "every wind that's blowing breathes the color of sound."

The album was produced by Micah, who chose two songs by Neil Young (Micah's longtime employer), two by Waits, and one apiece from the Flaming Lips, Beck, Keith Richards, Warren Zevon, and Nina Simone, supporting them with an eerie, art-rock soundscape behind his father's voice and guitar. The liner notes' long list of instruments played by Micah includes dulcimer, charango, surdo, dead leaves, coins, and cicadas. These sounds reinforce the noir feel of the project.

Willie's first album of 2025 found him reuniting with producer Buddy Cannon to record another of the singer's tribute albums to one of his favorite song-

Willie Nelson
***Last Leaf on the Tree* (Legacy)**
Recorded: Early 2024
Released: November 1, 2024
Willie Compositions: 2/13

The production by Nelson's youngest son Micah echoes the eerie, late-night feel of Daniel Lanois' production of Nelson's *Teatro.* Lanois plays pedal steel, and Micah supplements that with unusual instruments to create a spare, art-rock backdrop to his father's voice and acoustic guitar on songs by Tom Waits, Neil Young, Beck, and the like. But as soon as Willie opens his mouth it all resembles a backroom East Texas picking party, circa 1959—no matter who wrote the songs and who plays behind them. The frailty of the lead vocals only reinforces the powerful mood of looming mortality. **Grade: A-**

writers. His previous projects saluted the older generation (Lefty Frizzell, George Gershwin, Cindy Walker) or his own generation (Kris Kristofferson, Roger Miller), but *Oh What a Beautiful World* nodded to a younger songwriter: Rodney Crowell. Of course, Crowell was seventy-four by the time Willie released this album four days before his ninety-second birthday. But it's significant that Willie was now celebrating younger artists (his kids, Crowell, Chris Stapleton), as if he wanted to make sure his life's work would carry on.

Willie Nelson
Oh What a Beautiful World (Legacy)
Recorded: Late 2024
Released: April 25, 2025
Willie Compositions: 0/12

Willie sings a dozen songs written or co-written by Rodney Crowell, a gifted Texan songwriter himself. Willie's ninety-one-year-old voice is a frail husk of its former self, but his genius for phrasing is intact, and his half-spoken, half-sung vocals are perfect for the wistful looks backward at childhood and marriage that dominate the track list—a mood reinforced by Bobby Terry's steel guitar and Mickey Raphael's harmonica. Crowell's 2014 album *Tarpaper Sky*, probably his best, provides three songs, including the title track, a duet between Willie and the songwriter. The tune's celebration of simple pleasures is echoed on the numbers plucked from all stages of Crowell's career, including songs recorded by Jerry Jeff Walker, Keith Urban, Tim McGraw, and Guy Clark. **Grade: B+**

Willie recorded his first Crowell song in 1976 ("Til I Gain Control Again' on *The Hungry Years*) and then waited until the years 2022–2025 to record fifteen more. If Willie was a key figure in the "Outlaw Country" movement, Crowell was a linchpin of what became known as "In-Law Country," the progressive-country movement of the late '70s and '80s that included Crowell's employer Emmylou Harris, his then-wife Rosanne Cash, and his mentor Guy Clark. They were less likely to write about the loner in "On the Road Again" and more likely to write about a married couple staying home and "Making Memories of Us," even if that past was hard-fought and hard-won. It's a different approach to country music—more Carter Family than Jimmie Rodgers—and it's a treat to hear Willie tackle this subject matter at the end of his career.

Willie Nelson was eighty-two when he came to the Merriweather Post Pavilion on August 19, 2015. The skin hung loosely from his thin arms, but even so, he was younger than his drummer, eighty-three-year-old Paul English, and his eighty-four-year-old sister Bobbie Nelson, who needed assistance to get to the piano bench. In recent years, the band had some youth with the presence of Willie's sons Lukas and Micah, but that summer those two were off playing with Neil Young. Willie no longer had the vocal power and tone he enjoyed in the last century, but he still had the best phrasing of any living American singer and as radical an imagination as one will find in any musician.

And he still insisted on playing any kind of music he felt like. After devoting the first dozen songs to his familiar country classics, he took a left turn into seemingly disconnected songs by Hank Williams, Hoagy Carmichael, Billy Joe Shaver, and Django Reinhardt. He connected them all with the sheer force of his personality and wrapped up the show with two funny marijuana songs: "It's All Going to Pot" and "Roll Me Up and Smoke Me (When I Die)."

It's tempting to see Nelson as a bastion of tradition amid the metastasizing changes of commercial country-pop. But perhaps it's more accurate to see him as a bastion of weirdness in a realm of formula. Few country artists were making records in the twenty-first century as adventurous as the ones Nelson has made since he turned sixty-seven—records full of harmonica solos, waltzes, jazz chords, swing phrasing, jokes about death, and chronicles of irresponsible behavior. Maybe it's most accurate to say that weirdness is the tradition that Nelson best represents.

Epilogue

"Merle Haggard and those guys can sing circles around me as far as being country singers," Nelson told *GRAMMY Magazine* in 1994, "but I enjoy singing country music, and I can do it. George Jones is, as far as I'm concerned, the best country singer that ever lived. I know all the songs, and I can play them all on the guitar. But I also enjoy hearing jazz, and I enjoy blues, and I enjoy gospel and bluegrass. I enjoy the big-band sounds of the Dorsey Brothers and Sinatra. And I tried to dabble in all those other things. I'm limited in some ways, but I'm trying to watch it and not get beyond my limits."

This quote is fascinating for several reasons. For one thing, Nelson undervalues his own singing because he makes the common error of mistaking the quality of one's genetic instrument and the skill with which one uses it. It's true that Jones, Haggard, Roy Orbison, Ray Price, and Lefty Frizzell had fabulous vocal instruments, but no country singer this side of Hank Williams and Elvis Presley did more with phrasing, dynamics, and feeling than Nelson.

More importantly, perhaps, this quote puts the lie to Nelson's frequent assertions that he didn't believe in musical categories. Not only does he recognize them, but he can tick off their names in the middle of an interview. The implication is that there are different genres of music, each with its own history, vocabulary, instrumentation, and style that one must learn and respect to perform it effectively. You have to know the rules before you can break them.

If you consider Nelson's recordings, as we have in this book, you can hear how much he respects the history and vocabulary of each genre he tackles. He likes nothing more than to go back decades and revive a foundational song in country, gospel, blues, trad-jazz, Western swing, or the American Songbook and put his slight twist on it. He's not acting as if categories don't exist—he's acting as if he won't be limited to just one of them.

Nelson was able to master the five genres mentioned above, which is several more than most musicians can legitimately claim. Nelson tried several others—most notably reggae, Celtic-Appalachian folk, and indie rock—but he never quite got the hang of them. Many others—hard rock, hip-hop, classical, and so on—he never even tried. He knew what he liked, and he knew what he could do. He refused to be restrained by the industry's boundaries—and he refused to be pushed beyond his own boundaries.

There's an oft-forgotten term for the kind of multi-genre performer Nelson evolved into. In the late nineteenth and early twentieth centuries, a "songster" was a wandering musician who had to master multiple styles of music because such a performer had to entertain very different kinds of audiences. It was difficult to support oneself by playing only blues, only spirituals, only vaudeville, only nursery rhymes, or only sentimental ballads; one had to do it all. A few of these songsters—Leadbelly, Mance Lipscomb, Emmet Miller, Bob Wills, Jimmie Rodgers, Bert Williams, and John Hurt—passed into legend.

Willie and Ray Charles sing a duet while sharing a piano bench.
Opposite: A photo of Ray Charles is projected on the back wall of New York City's Apollo Theatre while Willie pays tribute to him on June 19, 2004.

After World War II, performers were as likely to become songsters for artistic as for economic reasons. Songster is a descriptor that might be applied to such figures as Elvis Presley, Fats Domino, Mose Allison, Arthur Alexander, and Jerry Lee Lewis. But no one represented the songster ethos in modern times more convincingly than Willie Nelson and Ray Charles.

The two men grew up poor in small Southern towns in the '30s and '40s—Nelson in Abbott, Texas, and Charles in Greenville, Florida. In those places at that time, the races were legally separated but always in close proximity—and the radio dial could cross both geographic and racial borders quite easily. It was easy for both young kids to hear Louis Armstrong and Frank Sinatra, Ernest Tubb and T-Bone Walker. Both youngsters grew up singing and playing gospel music in church, country and blues on the street corner, and swing at dances.

In those years, Nelson and Charles learned not only how to master the requirements of each genre but also how to love each genre. And that combination of skill and affection enabled them to move from style to style without turning it all into an indistinguishable mishmash. Each kind of music retained its distinctive character, but each was infused by each man's powerful personality.

And that songster background provided the tools to pursuing each man's lifelong mission. Charles was preaching that the ecstatic release of romance and sex was not so different from the release of religious belief, that the freewheeling improvisation of a jazz soloist in a nightclub was not so different from that of a soloist in a church choir. Loss of love could be as devastating as loss of faith, and reconciliation could be as thrilling as redemption.

Nelson was preaching that any loss in our lives—loss of parents, loss of money, loss of status, loss of friends—could best be viewed through the prism of songs about troubled love and shattered love. He was preaching that no matter how crushing the defeat, one can face up to it, process it, and emerge with one's dignity intact, ready to go on with life. He could sing this sermon as a country ballad, a blues lament, or a swing tune—and each might emphasize a different aspect of the same lesson.

There was a reason that Nelson is most often called a country singer. With its East Texas drawl, his voice sounds country. With their working-class laments about troubled romance and country kids lost in the big city, his songs sound country.

But the undercurrents in his music, the jazz chords, the swing rhythms, the blues harmonies, and the gospel yearning make it a different kind of country—as if Ray Charles or George Gershwin had grown up in Abbott. There was a fatalism in the lyrics—a recognition that happy endings can't be counted on—that stripped away the sentimentality of those other songs. There was a new sophistication and realism in Nelson's country songs.

After all, Gram Parsons and Waylon Jennings didn't invent nonconformism in country music any more than Sly Stone and George Clinton invented it in R&B. The rebelliousness was there all along. In fact, the history of the American music business can be told as the struggle of an industry trying to counter its artists' eccentricity by drawing a line between the acceptable and the unacceptable. Nelson has been on the wrong side of that boundary more than once in his career, but that says more about the line than it does about him.

Though Nelson and Charles never made an album together, they recorded a number of terrific duets and became good friends. And you can't understand twentieth-century American music without grasping how Nelson and Charles became songsters and then musical preachers.

They proved that their homeland's music reflects the Latin motto on the Great Seal of the United States: *E pluribus unum* (out of many, one). Our music is constantly creating a unified culture out of many sources—out of many ethnicities, religions, regions, and classes. The nation needs those sources to remain many—not a bland, homogenized whole—and it needs songsters—every year and everywhere—to alchemize those ingredients into America.

Appendix

Below are two lists of all the albums that received a box and a grade in this book. I combined all the studio and live albums into one list, because I believe the concert recordings deserve as much respect (and as much criticism) as studio sessions. I've also included several albums (e.g., *Sugar Moon* and *Willie Sings Hank Williams*) that went unreleased until they were included in a much later box set plus a handful of albums credited to an artist such as Hank Cochran or Jackie King, where Nelson made a major contribution. All albums are ranked in order of quality.

The second list ranks the compilations by slightly different criteria: not by the quality of the music alone but by how much they add to the preexisting albums—both in rarities and in clarifying information. Both lists are limited to American releases.

The 152 albums on these lists do not include every album Willie Nelson ever released. I tried to include every title that made a commercial or artistic impact. I excluded the many budget compilations released by RCA, Columbia, United Artists, and fly-by-night labels as well as some of the gospel and Don Cherry albums that seemed like needless duplication. Anything released after April 2025 is too late for our deadlines.

Everything graded an A is a must-have recording to my mind. Everything graded a B is well worth owning. Everything graded a C is for fanatics and completists (like me) only. Everything graded a D or F should be handled only with a hazmat suit.

THE BEST WILLIE NELSON STAND-ALONE ALBUMS IN ORDER:

1. Willie Nelson: *Phases and Stages*
(Atlantic, 1974) Grade: A+
2. Willie Nelson: *Tougher than Leather*
(Columbia, 1983) Grade: A+
3. Willie Nelson: *Willie Nelson Sings Kristofferson*
(Columbia, 1979) Grade: A+
4.Willie Nelson: *Stardust*
(Columbia, 1978) Grade: A+
5. Willie Nelson: *Spirit*
(Island, 1995) Grade: A+
6. Willie Nelson: *You Don't Know Me: The Songs of Cindy Walker*
(Lost Highway, 2006) Grade: A+
7. Willie Nelson: *Live at the US Festival*
(Shout Factory, 2012) Grade: A+
8. Willie Nelson: *Last Man Standing*
(Legacy, 2018) Grade: A+
9. Willie Nelson: *Me and Paul*
(Columbia, 1985) Grade: A
10. Willie Nelson: *Willie and Family Live*
(Columbia, 1978) Grade: A
11. Willie Nelson: *Live at the Texas Opry House, 1974* (Rhino, 2022) Grade: A
12. Willie Nelson: *Live Country Music Concert*
(aka *Willie Nelson Live*)
(RCA, 1966) Grade: A
13. Willie Nelson: *Always on My Mind*
(Columbia, 1982) Grade: A
14. Waylon Jennings, Kris Kristofferson, Willie Nelson, and Billy Joe Shaver: *Honky Tonk Heroes*
(Free Falls, 2000) Grade: A
15. Willie Nelson: *Teatro* (Island, 1998) Grade: A
16. Willie Nelson: *God's Problem Child*
(Legacy, 2017) Grade: A-
17. Willie Nelson: *Last Leaf on the Tree*
(Legacy, 2024) Grade: A-
18. Willie Nelson: *Yesterday's Wine*
(RCA, 1971) Grade: A-
19. Willie Nelson: *Somewhere over the Rainbow*
(Columbia, 1981) Grade: A-
20. Willie Nelson: *Red Headed Stranger*
(Columbia, 1975) Grade: A-
21. Willie Nelson and Merle Haggard:
Pancho & Lefty
(Epic, 1983) Grade: A-
22. Willie Nelson: *The Hungry Years*
(Sony, 1991) Grade: A-
23. Willie Nelson: *Sugar Moon*
(Rhino, 1993) Grade: A-
24. Willie Nelson: *Just One Love*
(Justice, 1995) Grade: A-
25. Willie Nelson: *Shotgun Willie*
(Atlantic, 1973) Grade: A-
26. Willie Nelson and Waylon Jennings:
Waylon & Willie
(RCA, 1978) Grade: A-
27. Willie Nelson and Ray Price: *San Antonio Rose*
(Columbia, 1980) Grade: A-
28. Willie Nelson and Roger Miller: *Old Friends*
(Columbia, 1982) Grade: A-
29. Willie Nelson: *Moonlight Becomes You*
(Justice, 1994) Grade: A-
30. Willie Nelson & Kris Kristofferson:
Music from Songwriter
(Columbia, 1984) Grade: A-
31. Willie Nelson: *The Troublemaker*
(Columbia, 1976) Grade: A-

32. Willie Nelson: *Live at Billy Bob's Texas* (Smith Music, 2004) Grade: A-
33. Willie Nelson: *Me and the Drummer* (Luck, 2000) Grade: A-
34. Willie Nelson and Webb Pierce: *In the Jailhouse Now* (Columbia, 1982) Grade: A-
35. Willie Nelson: *Live from Austin TX* (New West, 2006) Grade: A-
36. Willie Nelson: *Band of Brothers* (Legacy, 2014) Grade: A-
37. Willie Nelson: *A Beautiful Time* (Legacy, 2022) Grade: A-
38. Willie Nelson: *First Rose of Spring* (Legacy, 2020) Grade: A-
39. The Highwaymen: *The Road Goes on Forever* (Liberty, 1995) Grade: A-
40. Willie Nelson: *Family Bible* (Songbird, 1980) Grade: A-
41. Willie Nelson and Asleep at the Wheel: *Willie and the Wheel* (Bismeaux, 2009) Grade: A-
42. Willie Nelson and Ray Price: *Run That by Me One More Time* (Lost Highway, 2003) Grade: A-
43. Willie Nelson and Sister Bobbie: *December Day: Willie's Stash, Vol. 1* (Legacy, 2014) Grade: A-
44. Willie Nelson: *Pretty Paper* (Columbia, 1979) Grade: A-
45. Willie Nelson: *. . . And Then I Wrote* (Liberty, 1962) Grade: B+
46. Willie Nelson: *Across the Borderline* (Columbia, 1993) Grade: B+
47. Willie Nelson: *Who'll Buy My Memories?: The IRS Tapes* (Sony, 1991) Grade: B+
48. Willie Nelson: *Country Favorites Willie Nelson Style* (RCA, 1966) Grade: B+
49. Willie Nelson: *Night and Day* (Free Falls, 1999) Grade: B+
50. Willie Nelson: *The Promiseland* (Columbia, 1986) Grade: B+
51. Willie Nelson and Wynton Marsalis: *Two Men with the Blues* (Blue Note, 2008) Grade: B+
52. Willie Nelson: *Angel Eyes* (Columbia, 1984) Grade: B+
53. Willie Nelson: *The Words Don't Fit the Picture* (RCA, 1972) Grade: B+
54. Willie Nelson: *I Don't Know a Thing About Love* (Legacy, 2023) Grade: B+
55. Willie Nelson: *The Border* (Legacy, 2024) Grade: B+
56. Willie Nelson: *Oh What a Beautiful World* (Legacy, 2025) Grade: B+
57. Willie Nelson: *Ride Me Back Home* (Legacy, 2019) Grade: B+
58. Hank Cochran: *Make the World Go Away* (Elektra, 1980) Grade: B+
59. Willie Nelson: *The Willie Way* (RCA, 1972) Grade: B+
60. Willie Nelson: *My Way* (Legacy, 2018) Grade: B+
61. Willie Nelson with Merle Haggard: *Django and Jimmie* (Legacy, 2015) Grade: B+
62. Willie Nelson: *Summertime: Willie Nelson Sings Gershwin* (Legacy, 2016) Grade: B+
63. Various Artists: *Songs for Tsunami Relief: Austin to South Asia* (Texas Roadhouse, 2005) Grade: B+
64. Willie Nelson: *To All the Girls . . .* (Legacy, 2013) Grade: B+
65. Willie Nelson: *Songbird* (Lost Highway, 2006) Grade: B+
66. Willie Nelson: *Moment of Forever* (Lost Highway, 2008) Grade: B+
67. Willie Nelson: *Live at Budokan* (Legacy, 2022) Grade: B+
68. Willie Nelson: *Remember Me, Vol. 1* (R&J, 2011) Grade: B+
69. Willie Nelson: *Bluegrass* (Legacy, 2023) Grade: B+
70. Willie Nelson: *That's Life* (Legacy, 2021) Grade: B+
71. Willie Nelson and Merle Haggard: *Seashores of Old Mexico* (Epic, 1987) Grade: B+
72. Willie Nelson with Special Guest Curtis Potter: *Six Hours at Pedernales* (Step One, 1994) Grade: B+
73. Willie and Bobbie Nelson: *I'd Rather Have Jesus* (Arrival, 1986) Grade: B+
74. Willie Nelson: *Let's Face the Music and Dance* (Legacy, 2013) Grade: B+
75. Willie Nelson: *For the Good Times: A Tribute to Ray Price* (Legacy, 2016) Grade: B+
76. Willie Nelson: *The Sound in Your Mind* (Columbia, 1976) Grade: B
77. Willie Nelson: *Country Willie: His Own Songs* (RCA, 1965) Grade: B
78. Willie Nelson: *To Lefty from Willie* (Columbia, 1977) Grade: B
79. Willie Nelson: *Make Way for Willie Nelson* (RCA, 1967) Grade: B

80. Jackie King with Willie Nelson: *The Gypsy*
(Indigo Moon, 2001) Grade: B
81. Willie Nelson: *Country Music*
(Rounder, 2010) Grade: B
82. Willie Nelson, Merle Haggard and Ray Price:
Last of the Breed
(Lost Highway, 2007) Grade: B
83. Willie Nelson and Family: *Honeysuckle Rose*
(Columbia, 1980) Grade: B
84. Willie Nelson and Leon Russell:
One for the Road
(Columbia, 1979) Grade: B
85. Willie Nelson: *Heroes*
(Legacy, 2012) Grade: B
86. Willie Nelson: *Island in the Sea*
(Columbia, 1987) Grade: B
87. Willie Nelson: *Willie Sings Hank Williams*
(Rhino, 1993) Grade: B
88. Willie Nelson: *Born for Trouble*
(Columbia, 1990) Grade: B
89. Willie Nelson with Lukas Nelson and Micah Nelson: *Willie and the Boys: Willie's Stash, Vol. 2*
(Legacy, 2017) Grade: B
90. Various Artists: *Long Story Short: Willie Nelson 90 at the Hollywood Bowl*
(Legacy, 2023) Grade: B
91. Various Artists: *Willie Nelson: American Outlaw*
(Blackbird, 2020) Grade: B
92. Willie Nelson and Johnny Cash:
VH1 Storytellers: Johnny Cash & Willie Nelson
(American, 1998) Grade: B
93. Various Artists: *Outlaw Country Live from Austin TX*
(New West, 2006) Grade: B
94. Paul Buskirk featuring Willie Nelson:
Nacogdoches Waltz
(Justice, 1993) Grade: B
95. Willie Nelson: *Milk Cow Blues*
(Island, 2000) Grade: B
96. Willie Nelson: *Both Sides Now*
(RCA, 1970) Grade: B-
97. Willie Nelson: *Good Times*
(RCA, 1968) Grade: B-
98. Willie Nelson, Wynton Marsalis, and Norah Jones: *Here We Go Again: Celebrating the Genius of Ray Charles*
(Blue Note, 2011) Grade: B-
99. Willie Nelson: *A Horse Called Music*
(Columbia, 1989) Grade: B-
100. Willie Nelson: *Without a Song*
(Columbia, 1983) Grade: B-
101. Willie & Bobbie Nelson: *How Great Thou Art*
(aka *Just as I Am: 18 Hymns and Gospel Favorites*)
(Finer Arts, 1996) Grade: B-
102. Willie Nelson: *It Always Will Be*
(Lost Highway, 2004) Grade: B-
103. Willie Nelson and Bobbie Nelson:
Hill Country Christmas
(Finer Arts, 1997) Grade: B-
104. Willie Nelson and Waylon Jennings:
Clean Shirt (Epic, 1991) Grade: B-
105. Willie Nelson: *City of New Orleans*
(Columbia, 1984) Grade: C+
106. Willie Nelson: *The Untitled Third Liberty Album*
(Liberty, 1994) Grade: C+
107. Willie Nelson: *American Classic*
(Blue Note, 2009) Grade: C+
108. Willie Nelson: *Willie Nelson & Family*
(RCA, 1971) Grade: C+
109. Willie Nelson: *Live and Kickin'*
(Lost Highway, 2003) Grade: C+
110. Willie Nelson and Faron Young: *Funny How Time Slips Away*
(Columbia, 1985) Grade: C+
111. Willie Nelson: *The Willie Nelson Family*
(Legacy, 2021) Grade: C+
112. Willie Nelson and Waylon Jennings:
Take It to the Limit (Columbia, 1983) Grade: C
113. Willie Nelson: *The Electric Horseman*
(Columbia, 1979) Grade: C
114. Willie Nelson and Hank Snow:
Brand on My Heart
(Columbia, 1985) Grade: C
115. Willie Nelson: *Here's Willie Nelson*
(Liberty, 1963) Grade: C-
116. Willie Nelson: *Healing Hands of Time*
(Liberty, 1994) Grade: C-
117. Willie Nelson: *What a Wonderful World*
(Columbia, 1988) Grade: C-
118. Willie Nelson: *The Great Divide*
(Lost Highway, 2002) Grade: C-
119. Willie Nelson & Friends: *Stars & Guitars*
(Lost Highway, 2002) Grade: C-
120. Willie Nelson and Waylon Jennings: *WWII*
(RCA, 1982) Grade: C-
121. Willie Nelson: *Rainbow Connection*
(Island, 2001) Grade: C-
122. Waylon Jennings, Willie Nelson, Johnny Cash, and Kris Kristofferson: *Highwayman*
(Columbia, 1985) Grade: C-
123. Willie Nelson: *Texas in My Soul*
(RCA, 1968) Grade: D
124. Willie Nelson: *Partners*
(Columbia, 1986) Grade: D

125. Willie Nelson: *Outlaws and Angels*
(Lost Highway, 2004) Grade: D
126. The Highwaymen: *Highwayman 2*
(Columbia, 1990) Grade: D
127. Willie Nelson: *"The Party's Over" and Other Great Willie Nelson Songs*
(RCA, 1967) Grade: D
128. Willie Nelson: *My Own Peculiar Way*
(RCA, 1969) Grade: D
129. Willie Nelson: *Laying My Burdens Down*
(RCA, 1970) Grade: D
130. Willie Nelson: *Countryman*
(Lost Highway, 2005) Grade: F
131. Willie Nelson & Danny Davis with the Nashville Brass: *Willie Nelson & Danny Davis with the Nashville Brass*
(RCA, 1980) Grade: F
132. Willie Nelson and Don Cherry: *Augusta*
(Sundown, 1995) Grade: F

THE BEST WILLIE NELSON COMPILATION ALBUMS IN ORDER:

1. Willie Nelson: *Willie Nelson: The Complete Atlantic Sessions*
(Atlantic/Rhino, 2006) Grade: A+
2. Willie Nelson: *Willie Nelson: A Classic & Unreleased Collection*
(Rhino, 1993) Grade: A+
3. Willie Nelson: *One Hell of a Ride*
(Columbia/Legacy, 2008) Grade: A-
4. Willie Nelson: *Revolutions of Time . . . the Journey: 1975–1993*
(Columbia, 1995) Grade: B+
5. Willie Nelson, Waylon Jennings, Tompall Glaser, and Jessi Colter: *Wanted! The Outlaws*
(RCA, 1976) Grade: B+
6. Willie Nelson: *The Early Years: The Complete Liberty Recordings Plus More*
(Liberty, 1994) Grade: B+
7. Willie Nelson: *Things to Remember: The Pamper Demos*
(Real Gone, 2018) Grade: B+
8. Willie Nelson: *Naked Willie*
(RCA/Legacy, 1970) Grade: B+
9. Willie Nelson: *Nite Life: Greatest Hits & Rare Tracks (1959–1971)*
(Rhino, 1989) Grade: B+
10. Willie Nelson: *The Essential Willie Nelson*
(Legacy, 2003) Grade: B+
11. Willie Nelson: *Greatest Hits (& Some That Will Be)*
(Columbia, 1981) Grade: B+
12. Willie Nelson: *The Essential Willie Nelson*
(RCA, 1995) Grade: B+
13. Willie Nelson: *Crazy: The Demo Sessions*
(Sugar Hill, 2003) Grade: B
14. Willie Nelson: *Half Nelson*
(Columbia, 1985) Grade: B
15. Willie Nelson: *Lost Highway*
(Lost Highway, 2009) Grade: B
16. Willie Nelson: *Face of a Fighter*
(Lone Star, 1978) Grade: B-
17. Willie Nelson, Kris Kristofferson, Dolly Parton, and Brenda Lee: *The Winning Hand*
(Monument, 1982) Grade: B-
18. Willie Nelson: *Songs*
(Lost Highway, 2005) Grade: B-
19. Willie Nelson: *The Early Years*
(Scotti Bros., 2020) Grade: C+
20. Willie Nelson, George Jones, and Merle Haggard: *Walking the Line*
(Epic, 1987) Grade: C

Index

F

G

H

I

J

K

L

M

N

O

P

Bibliography

BOOKS

Allen, Bob. *Waylon & Willie.* Quick Fox, New York, 1979.

Duncan, Dayton, and Ken Burns. *Country Music: An Illustrated History*, Knopf, New York, 2019.

Nelson, Willie, with David Ritz. *It's a Long Story: My Life*. Little, Brown and Company, New York, 2015.

Nelson, Willie, with David Ritz and Mickey Raphael. *Energy Follows Thought: The Stories Behind My Songs*. William Morrow, New York, 2023.

Nelson, Willie, with Bud Shrake. *Willie: An Autobiography*. Simon and Schuster, New York, 1988.

Patoski, Joe Nick. *Willie Nelson: An Epic Life.* Little, Brown and Company, New York, 2008.

ARTICLES

Bordowitz, Hank. "Willie Nelson: Expecting the Unexpected," *Gallery*, March 2001.

Breskin, David. "Willie Nelson," *Musician*, July 1982.

DeYoung, Bill. "Willie Nelson: Funny How Time Slips Away." *Goldmine*, January 6, 1995.

Doyle, Patrick. "All Roads Lead to Willie." *Rolling Stone*, September 2, 2014.

Filippo, Chet. "Holy Man of the Honky Tonks." *Rolling Stone*, July 13, 1978.

Fyfe, Andy. "Road Warrior." *Mojo*, October 2013.

George-Warren, Holly. "Willie Nelson: Our Patron Saint of the Road." *Texas Music*, Spring 2003.

Grigoriadis, Vanessa. "Willie on the Soft Path." *Rolling Stone,* January 8, 2009.

Gross, Terry. *Fresh Air* radio transcript. National Public Radio, July 16, 1996.

Gross, Terry. *Fresh Air* radio transcript. National Public Radio, May 25, 2006.

Hall, Michael. "Funny How Time Slips Away." *GRAMMY Magazine,* 1994.

Hermes, Will. "Willie Nelson Salutes Another (Hidden) Legend." *New York Times,* March 12, 2006.

McLellan, Dennis. "Cindy Walker, 87; Wrote Hundreds of Songs Recorded by an Array of Artists." *Los Angeles Times,* March 29, 2006.

Mueller, Andrew. "Willie Nelson for President?" *Uncut,* July 2010.

Palmer, Robert. "The Pop Life; Willie Nelson Likes to Keep on the Move." *New York Times*, December 5, 1980.

Patoski, Joe Nick. "Outlaw Music." *Hustler*, November 1978.

Patoski, Joe Nick. "Willie Nelson and 'Whatever Happened to Peace on Earth?'" *No Depression*, September–October 2004.

Patterson, Rob. "A Great Spirit Enjoys an Uncloudy Day." *New Country*, 1996.

Reinert, Al. "King of Country." *New York Times*, March 26, 1978.

Rosenbaum, Ron. "The Ballad of Willie Nelson," *Vanity Fair*, November 1991.

Scheer, Bob. "It's a Long Story." *Scheer Intelligence* radio transcript, January 20, 2017.

Standish, David. "Saint Willie," *Playboy*, April 1981.

Steakley, Clay. "Willie Nelson: Gentleman Outlaw." *Performing Songwriter*, March/April 2002.

Von Drehle, David. "Willie Nelson's American Journey." *Washington Post*, December 6, 1998.

Ward, Chris. "Five Minutes with Willie Nelson." *Performing Songwriter*, 2009.

Acknowledgments

The author acknowledges the following for their help with this book:

First, my editor Dennis Pernu, who approached me with the idea for this book, was open to my alterations and shepherded the project to its successful conclusion. Thanks as well to his partners at Quarto Publishing.

Second, to the following periodicals who published some of the material in this book in an earlier form: *Texas Music*, *Washington Post*, *Nashville Scene*, *Country Music*, *New Country*, *Request*, *Baltimore City Paper*, *Baltimore Sun*, *Musician*, and *Columbia Flier*.

Third, to all the writers in the bibliography who paved the way. And to Nelson's publicist, Elaine Shock, who was always helpful.

And, finally, to my wife, Elizabeth Cusick, who read my early drafts and accommodated my work schedule so I could meet my deadline.

Photo Credits

B = bottom, L = left, M = middle, R = right, T = top

Alamy Stock Photos: 17 (Glasshouse Images), 19T (Archive PL), 19B (Pictorial Press), 20 (Archive PL), 25TR (Archive PL), 35 (Pictorial Press), 37 (Pictorial Press), 39TR (Pictorial Press), 40BR (Pictorial Press), 71 (Keith Adamek), 73BL (Shelley Dennis), 74 (Keith Adamek), 76TR (Pictorial Press), 81 (CSU Archives/Everett Collection), 88MR (Pictorial Press), 91 (PictureLux), 92BL (Archive PL), 98BR (Pictorial Press), 101 (© Globe Photos/ZUMA Wire), 104 (Dennis Brack), 110TR (Media Punch), 112 (Bob Daemmrich), 117BR (A7A Collection), 118BL (Pictorial Press), 126 (Impress (United Archives (GmbH), 128MR (Fiona Hanson), 147TR (Pictorial Press), 148TR (John Atashian), 158B (Billy Suratt/Apex MediaWire), 165TR (Allstar Picture Library Ltd), 169TR (David Atlas/Media Punch), 176 (Pictorial Press), 177TL (mcd/GTCRFOTO), 188BR (Edd Westmacott), 192M (White House Photo), 195TL (Archive PL), 201BL (PictureLux). **Associated Press:** 18 (Harry Cabluck), 77 (Associated Press), 116MR (Mel Evans), 119B (Willens), 127TL (Associated Press), 134-135 (Tsugufumi Matsumoto), 139M (Ron Frehm), 141 (Associated Press), 144T (Wyatt Counts), 155TL (Kaspar Wenstrup), 175B (Ron Wolfson/Media Punch), 185TR (Jeffrey Phelps), 190BR (Amy Sussman), 189BR (Hans Pennink), 205BL (Andy Kropa), 206TR (Al Wagner/Invision), 209TL (Associated Press). **Avalon:** Endpapers (Chris Casella), 13 (Chris Casella), 66BL (Andrew Kent), 95 (Michael Putland), 161 (Mitch Gerber), 171 (Dennis Van Tine). **Bridgeman Images:** 86 (© Alan Messer. All rights reserved 2025), 152M (REUTERS/Joe Traver), 158T (REUTERS/Jill Connelly), 181BL (© Alan Messer. All rights reserved 2025). **Getty Images:** 2 (Michael Ochs Archives), 24 (Michael Ochs Archives), 26TL (GAB Archive/Redferns), 29BL (Richard Weize/Michael Ochs Archives), 30 (Richard Weize/Michael Ochs Archives), 31 (Richard Weize/Michael Ochs Archives), 33 (Richard Weize/Michael Ochs Archives), 38 (Richard Weize/Michael Ochs Archives), 42 (Richard Weize/Michael Ochs Archives), 43BL (Michael Ochs Archives), 44TR (Michael Ochs Archives), 48TL (Michael Ochs Archives), 48TR (David Gahr/The Estate of David Gahr), 49B (Paul Harris), 59 (Paul Natkin), 60 (David Gahr/The Estate of David Gahr), 63TR (Bettmann), 66ML (David Gahr/The Estate of David Gahr), 67BR (Bettmann), 69BL (Tom Hill/Michael Ochs Archives), 79B (Tom Hill/Michael Ochs Archives), 82 (Richard McCaffrey/Michael Ochs Archives), 83TL (Historic Collection), 83TR (*Star Tribune*), 94BL (GAB Archive/Redferns), 99 (Paul Harris), 103 (Michael Putland/Hulton Archive), 105 (Al Clayton Photography, LLC), 107 (CBS Photo Archive), 109 (Jay Dickman/Corbis Entertainment), 120 (Mark Junge), 125B (Beth Gwinn/Michael Ochs Archives), 133TL (Gary Miller), 137 (Frans Schellekens/Redferns), 143BR (M. Caulfield/WireImage for NBC Universal Photo Department), 1543B (Lisa Lake/Michael Ochs Archives), 163 (Tim Mosenfelder), 167 (Robert Daemmrich Photography, Inc.), 170TL (M. Caulfield/WireImage for NBC Universal Photo Department), 172BL (Peter Pakvis/Redferns), 180 (M. Tram/FilmMagic), 182MR (Gary Miller/FilmMagic), 183BL (CBS Photo Archive), 187 (Gary Miller), 194T (Kris Connor), 195BR (Michael Ochs Archives), 197T (Gary Miller), 203B (Gary Miller), 204 (Rich Fury), 207BR (Mike Pont). **PhotoFest:** 8-9 (Lost Highway Records), 72BL (Photofest), 154BR (Photofest), 172TR (NBC), 212 (Photofest), 213 (NBC).

Frank White Photo Agency: 7 (Jay Good), 78TL (Jay Good).

Dedicated to my longtime songwriting partner Billy Kemp.

Quarto.com

First Published in 2025 by Motorbooks, an imprint of The Quarto Group,
100 Cummings Center, Suite 265-D, Beverly, MA 01915, USA.
T (978) 282-9590 F (978) 283-2742

29 28 27 26 25 1 2 3 4 5

ISBN: 978-0-7603-9584-4

Digital edition published in 2025
eISBN: 978-0-7603-9585-1

Library of Congress Cataloging-in-Publication Data

Names: Himes, Geoffrey, author.
Title: Willie Nelson : all the albums / Geoffrey Himes.
Description: Beverly, MA : Motorbooks, 2025. | Includes bibliographical references and index.
Summary: "Willie Nelson: All the Albums is a sprawling career retrospective of an American treasure, viewed through his 100-plus solo and collaborative albums"-- Provided by publisher.
Identifiers: LCCN 2025008840 | ISBN 9780760395844 (hardcover) | ISBN 9780760395851 (ebook)
Subjects: LCSH: Nelson, Willie, 1933---Discography. | Nelson, Willie, 1933---Criticism and interpretation. Country music--History and criticism. | LCGFT: Discographies.
Classification: LCC ML156.7.N47 H56 2025 | DDC
016.782421642092--dc23/eng/20250304
LC record available at https://lccn.loc.gov/2025008840

Design: Justin Page @justinpagedesignco
Cover Image: Gary Miller/Getty Images

Printed in China